PUBLIC PERSONNEL ADMINISTRATION

Fifth Edition

Public Personnel Administration

FIFTH EDITION

N. Joseph Cayer
School of Public Affairs
Arizona State University, Emeritus

Meghna Sabharwal
School of Economic, Political and Policy Sciences
University of Texas at Dallas

Birkdale Publishers
San Diego

Editor: Sidney Shiroma
Cover Design: Erika Shiroma
Copy Editor: Leonard Rosenbaum

ISBN 978-0-9724419-8-8

Birkdale Publishers, Inc.
P.O. Box 270261
San Diego CA 92198-0261

www.BirkdalePublishers.com

To
Matt
and
My loving husband, Nikhil

Contents

Preface

Since the publication of the fourth edition of *Public Personnel Administration* in 2004, American society and government have undergone many changes. To better explain and interpret these changes, Meghna Sabharwal, assistant professor at the University of Texas at Dallas, has signed on as coauthor to the fifth edition of *Public Personnel Administration*. She brings a fresh perspective, and her contribution to the fifth edition is enormous.

Though many aspects of theory and practice have changed, the basic themes and values of the field have remained consistent. This edition explores the themes and practices in light of changing environmental pressures and personnel practices. For example, the sustained pressures on government to reduce costs while increasing services have had major implications for the practice of personnel administration. Similarly, social equity issues and the responsiveness of government to these issues affect the specifics of personnel management. Ethical issues arose in each of the federal administrations since the publication of the last edition and continue to influence the image and expectations Americans have of public agencies and employees. Most recently, continuing efforts to stop terrorism have had a direct impact on public employees and agencies.

The fifth edition more fully explores legal aspects of public personnel administration, and controversies over affirmative action, sexual harassment, the costs of health care and pensions as well as collective bargaining. Also addressed are the implications of changing technology, controversies over sexual orientation and employment, privacy, and violence in the workplace. These and other issues lead government to constantly reform its approach to personnel administration. Readers will find an examination of changing policies and laws, as well as judicial decisions that affect the actions and decisions of public personnel managers.

Clearly, public personnel administrators and all managers face constantly changing pressures and concerns. This book presents public personnel management in the context of changing times and forces. Among the most significant factors facing public agencies is the changing demographic composition of American society. Readers of this book should come to recognize that public personnel administration is a dynamic field of endeavor that is crucial to effective government.

As with earlier editions, the fifth edition contains end-of-chapter mini-cases and exercises that provide opportunities for students to experience and apply what they learn. The mini-cases are based on actual occurrences. Each chapter also lists the websites of organizations and government agencies that could be helpful to students interested in further exploring topics covered in the chapter.

The fifth edition of this book has benefited greatly from the comments and suggestions of many people who read the first four editions. Students who have challenged some of the ideas presented in earlier editions have been particularly important in stimulating us to think about the issues. Thank you to our students at the University of Maine, Texas Tech University, Arizona State University, and the University of Texas at Dallas and to others who have written or talked to us and helped sharpen and clarify our approach to the field. Colleagues who have offered suggestions are too numerous to identify, but we would like to thank them for their questions, suggestions, and identification of new materials and ideas.

In preparing the manuscript, Matt Young did an incredible job of word processing parts of the manuscript. We thank our employers, Arizona State University and the University of Texas at Dallas, as well as our former teachers and our loved ones without whom we would not have accomplished this project. Meghna is especially thankful to her assistant, Imane Hijal-Moghrabi, whose help with other projects allowed her to focus on this book. Special thanks to her spouse, whose understanding and support was essential as she worked on the book. To all, a heartfelt thank you!

To Sidney Shiroma of Birkdale Publishers who demonstrated great patience and careful guidance, you have our grateful thanks. His efforts improved the work greatly.

Without the help of these talented people, the fifth edition would not be a reality. Nonetheless, any shortcomings are entirely ours.

N. Joseph Cayer   Meghna Sabharwal
Mesa, Arizona   Dallas, Texas

Public Personnel Administration

Fifth Edition

PeAchl Reaction

1

The Environment of Public Personnel Administration

Personnel administration (also called human resources management and human capital management) encompasses all activities related to people in organizations. It entails the use of human resources to accomplish an organization's objectives as efficiently and effectively as possible. Because successful management of people is the key to an organization's effective operation, good personnel management is essential to good administration. In turn, good personnel administration requires both technical and interpersonal skills. Personnel managers must know how to recruit, select, evaluate, promote, train, discipline, and dismiss employees. They must be adept at motivating, counseling, and bargaining with workers. In addition, personnel managers classify positions, develop compensation plans, measure productivity, and handle grievances and complaints. In short, personnel management involves all aspects of managing an organization's human resources, and public personnel administration refers to that function in government.

Personnel administration is also a universal management activity. Every supervisor is, in effect, a personnel manager. Whereas personnel offices develop and monitor personnel policies, supervisors are responsible for carrying them out. Supervisors are the critical links in the personnel process because they deal with employees daily. The organization's effectiveness, in turn, hinges, in part, on how well supervisors perform their personnel functions.

Those who perform personnel activities in the public sector do so in a political environment as stakeholders compete for favorable treatment or consideration from public bureaucracies. Therefore, bureaucrats have a stake in the process and engage in politics to maintain their status. The reactions to secret service agents engaging in inappropriate behavior in Colombia just prior to a summit attended by President Obama in 2012 illustrate the case. Congressional leaders quickly began hearings on the incident citing security concerns. But at the same time, they were also attempting to score political points with constituents and embarrass administration officials. In response, the Secret Service moved to institute new policies to prevent such incidents in the future. The actual agents involved also took steps to protect themselves against legal action. Another good example of the political environment of public personnel administration was the dramatic shift in policy toward public sector unions and collective bargaining after the 2010 elections in which many conservative governors and legislatures were elected and immediately began a process to curb the bargaining rights of public employees. Those efforts led to protracted political fights over the issue.

Political considerations include policy issues that are addressed by public personnel administration. The following are some important recurring issues:

1. How collective bargaining and the merit concept can coexist

2. Whether the public service should be used to solve social problems, for example, by being the employer of last resort, taking the lead in affirmative action, stimulating the economy, or satisfying the demands of myriad special interests with convincing claims

3. How to reconcile continued demands for a higher level of services with demands for lower taxes and smaller budgets

4. How to maintain a politically responsive bureaucracy without endangering the concept of merit

5. How to hire and retain the best talent.

More generally, the public service is an issue itself. Political candidates often promise to reduce the size of the public bureaucracy as part of their campaign platform. Public expectations, calling for reducing the size of government while maintaining the same level of services through greater efficiency and accountability, adds to the difficulty of personnel management in the public sector. In examining personnel management in government, this book analyzes the specific personnel responsibilities of supervisors and personnel offices. In particular, it evaluates the effects each of these elements has on government's responsiveness and accountability and the ways in which alternative approaches affect the delivery of services.

The Field of Public Personnel Administration

Public personnel administration has been accused of not having a sense of identity, being too narrow in scope, and lacking a theoretical foundation (Klinger & Nalbandian, 1978; Milward, 1978; Rosenbloom, 1973). These problems have resulted in large part from a slavish attachment to principles that seemed appropriate to developing civil service systems in an attempt to replace the abuses of the spoils system of the nineteenth century. In a zealous effort to remove partisanship from the personnel process, administrators focused almost exclusively on techniques such as testing and selection methods that could be applied to personnel activities. Lost in the shuffle was a concern with serving the purposes of management generally. As a result, the rest of management came to perceive personnel administration as a nonpolitical, technical service rather than as management per se. Nineteenth-century reform established a foundation of moral fervor among personnelists who labeled politics as evil and devotion to "neutral" principles of personnel management (as defined by personnelists) as good. As Wallace Sayre noted, public personnel management became a "triumph of technique over purpose" (1948). Public personnel management lost touch with its environment and became isolated. It assumed a policing role in which it seemed more interested in telling management what it could not do than in finding positive ways to assist management. It is little wonder that the personnel office became regarded with scorn (Morse, 1976; Mosher, 1982; Thompson, 1975).

Modern personnel managers realize that public personnel management is very closely connected with the environment in which it operates. For public personnel administrators, that environment is characterized first and foremost by politics. Whereas the reformers eschewed politics, contemporary personnelists recognize the political nature of the field and criticize traditionalists for ignoring the relevance of political concerns.

The environment of public personnel managers also includes many other forces. Employer and employee values affect the personnel system. These values affect the types of personnel policies developed, the decision-making rules, and the results of processes. Conflicts over values to be represented are resolved through politics (Lowi, 1967; Newland, 1967; Rich, 1982; Rosenbloom, 1981), and the error of many personnel reformers has been equating politics with partisan politics. By focusing on partisan politics, the reformers forgot that decisions were being made by compromising the differing values and interests of those participating in personnel decisions, a basic form of politics (Thompson, 1983).

Changes in society also affect public personnel management. As will be noted throughout the book, factors such as the civil rights movement, the women's movement, affirmative action and diversity efforts, cutback management and privatization of public services, and ever-changing technology all affect personnel management. The terrorist attacks of September 11, 2001, as well as subsequent threats, have had many effects on the public service. The culmination of these environmental changes results in changes in the way the public service functions. Paul Light suggests that we have seen the end of government-centered public service and the beginning of a multicentered public service (1999). By this, he means that government managers no longer can decide how to approach the public service from only their perspective. If government is to compete for employees, it must compete for talent and recognize that the diversity of the workforce requires focusing on what potential employees want from their jobs. Decent pay and security are no longer the only things potential employees seek. They now expect flexibility, interesting work, and the opportunity for professional growth and personal fulfillment.

Changes in management approaches have also had a significant impact on the organization of the personnel function. It is now recognized that managing human resources is a partnership between the personnel or human resources department and department managers and supervisors.

Today, civil service and merit concepts prevail in public personnel management. Nonetheless, many challenges to both concepts regularly occur. Numerous states have experimented with removal of civil service protections to use "at will" employment, in which employees can be easily terminated (Condrey, 2002; Gossett, 2002; Nigro & Kellough, 2000; Rau, 2012; West, 2002). Public sector labor unions enjoyed tremendous growth during the 1960s and 1970s. Although civil service systems have been under attack in some states since the 1980s, the public sector remained a major growth area for union membership until dramatic political changes in 2010 brought into office elected officials hostile to unions and bargaining. As a result, many public sector unions saw declines in their membership by 2012. In comparison, private sector unions have been on the decline for decades. Taking measures to curtail union activity is one way politicians have attempted to exert control over public sector personnel management. As the rest of the book demonstrates, the fortunes of management, employees, elected public officials, citizens, and the bureaucracies themselves are affected by the changing manner in which personnel are managed.

Although traditional personnelists exhorted public personnel administrators to apply neutral principles, the presence of competing values makes such an approach impractical. Value judgments must be used to implement differing selection systems, affirmative action, performance evaluation, and all other elements of personnel systems. Someone will gain and someone will lose with each decision made. For example, how should an agency respond to a cut in its budget? Are the newly hired let go? Are older employees urged to retire early? Are those hired under affirmative action programs protected? Are all departments required to contribute equally to the reduction? Are private vendors to be used for service delivery? All these and many other concerns affect the final decision, and each involves a value judgment. Decisions regarding competing value judgments are political decisions, so a modern personnel administrator is a participant in the political process.

Public vs. Private Sector Personnel Administration

Public and private sector personnel administration have much in common. For instance, the technical processes used for selecting, interviewing, evaluating, and training employees can be the same in both public and private organizations. However, the administration of personnel in the public sector differs from that in the private sector in four important ways:

1. Public employees operate in a different legal environment, especially concerning discipline and termination.
2. Lines of authority are less clear in the public sector.
3. Labor–management relations have followed different paths.
4. The political environment affects public personnel to a greater extent than it does in the private sector.

We shall examine these differences briefly; readers should keep in mind, however, that the differences are blurred by public and private sector interaction and the constant changes in society. In the past, people tended to have one career, and, often stayed with the same organization for their entire career. Today, people are likely to have several careers and are likely to move from organization to organization, including moving back and forth between public and private employers. Invariably, people bring with them their social and professional baggage, which affects the way things are done in each sector.

Legal Environment

Many laws, such as the Americans with Disabilities Act, Family and Medical Leave Act, Equal Pay Act, apply to both the public and private sector. Public employees, however, usually are governed by numerous legal limitations on their activities. For example, legislation or executive orders require employees to refrain from even the appearance of a conflict of interest; that is, that their official actions serve their self-interests, economically or otherwise, or that they favor family or friends. Public personnel administrators and supervisors must monitor their employees' activities to make sure that they have no conflicts of interest so that the integrity of the agency is not called into question, thus undermining public support.

Government employees often are prohibited from engaging in political activities. At the national level, the Hatch Act of 1939 prohibited most partisan political participation by federal employees until 1993, when the act was amended. State and local governments have their own rules, which sometimes prohibit participation even in nonpartisan elections. These restrictions are aimed at making the delivery of services nonpartisan and protecting employees and citizens from abuses typical of the spoils system.

After many years of relaxing regulations on personal appearance, dress, and residency, some government agencies have been reinstituting such rules. For example, police officers typically are prohibited from growing beards or long hair, and employees may be required to live in the jurisdiction in which they are employed. Employees may also be prohibited from smoking, even off duty. Although employees have challenged such restrictions in the courts, the courts have been inclined to side with the employer (*Kelly v. Johnson*, 1976; *McCarthy v. Philadelphia Civil Service Commission*, 1976).

The federal system has implications for the public sector that do not affect private employment to the same extent. The national government sets policy for its employees, and each state sets policy for its personnel system, including local government systems. Although some national government policies apply to all employment, public and private, each state has much discretion in how it operates. Thus, public personnel management in the United States does not have one universal public system. This differs from many other nations, such as France and Korea, in which all public employment is governed under one national policy. National policy concerning private sector employers covers all private employers within the guidelines established in the policy.

A stricter standard of behavior is generally expected of public employees than of workers in the private sector. Because citizens pay the taxes that pay government salaries, managers and personnel administrators are sensitive to the image public employees project, and their concerns have encouraged administrators to curtail behavior that could create a negative public reaction. When public displeasure is aroused by employees who are intoxicated in public, have unorthodox lifestyles, or promote controversial causes, elected political leaders often put pressure on managers to do something about the "problem." Although private employers may attempt to affect or influence the conduct of their employees after hours, they are much less likely to be concerned with behavior outside of work.

Although public employees can experience more legal restrictions than their private sector counterparts, they also enjoy more protections. In particular, public employees are protected by the U.S. Constitution, including the Bill of Rights. As a result, they are entitled to procedural due process in disciplinary actions. For example, public employees are entitled to a predetermination hearing when an employer wants to fire them. In the private sector, employees do not enjoy the same protection unless the employer decides to give it to them. As will be discussed later in the book, some states have changed their policies to offer jobs to new employees on the condition that they waive this protection.

Lines of Authority

The lines of authority for public employers tend to be more diffuse and much less clear than are those for employers in private enterprise. Although the public agency organization chart can suggest a clear line of authority, it does not show all outside pressures brought to bear on public employees. Theoretically, public employees must respond to the "public interest" and various representatives of the public and interested parties. As David Rosenbloom observed, the constitutional principle of separation of powers fragments political power and creates multiple command points for public employees (1982). Agency employees may be asked to do different things by the chief executive, an influential member of the legislature, a clientele group, and a consumer group. Such multiple command posts often make it difficult for public employees to decide exactly what they should do in a given situation.

Public employees are often not sure which authority to accord more attention. Should they respond to their clientele, their superiors, their legislators, or their interpretation of the public interest? The case of Bertrand Berube illustrates this difficulty. Berube was fired by the General Services Administration (GSA) in 1983 after revealing problems of neglect and deterioration in federal buildings in Washington, DC. Ironically, the firing came from the same administration that had awarded him a $7500 bonus for similar conduct in 1981 publicizing problems in the GSA under the previous administration (McAllister, 1988). What is in the public interest is never completely clear. Each participant in the political process can have a different interpretation. Thus, a public employee's action can precipitate a negative reaction from someone in a position to act against that employee. Finally, not only the employee but also the personnel system as a whole must respond to the confusion produced by these multiple commands. The response of both normally takes the form of new personnel rules and regulations, codes of conduct, and the like. However, some of these restrictions severely limit the ability of administrators to adapt to changing circumstances and organizational needs.

Labor–Management Relations

Unlike in the private sector, in the public sector, the power balance in labor–management relations has traditionally favored management. There have been exceptions in both sectors. Some governments such as those in New York City and Milwaukee, Wisconsin, have long histories of public sector union activities, and many corporations, especially in the Sun Belt, are fervently antiunion. However, in general, the public sector only gradually shared personnel decisions with employees through the bargaining process. The implications for public personnel, which will be discussed in Chapter 8, have been and will continue to be manifold.

Political Environment and Scrutiny

Perhaps the most significant factor unique to public personnel administration is that citizens and their representatives closely watch the public service. Because taxpayers foot the bill for government, they are entitled to know what is being done with their money. Since the late 1960s, freedom of information and open meeting statutes have also become common across the country. Thus, the activities of most agencies have become subject to public examination, and personnel management must accommodate such scrutiny. Although personnel actions involving individual employees are exempt from these "sunshine" laws, personnel policies are not. The elements of the political environment important to public personnel management include the executive, legislative, and judicial bodies; the media, interest groups, and political parties; and the general public.

Executive, legislative, and judicial bodies.

The U.S. Constitution established the separation of executive, legislative, and judicial powers. In theory, public employees are under the direction of the executive branch although employees of the legislature and judiciary report directly to those branches. In reality, the chief executive has limited authority over the public bureaucracy. Because civil service regulations protect most public employees, the chief executive has little power to change the conditions of their employment or control their activities. In addition, because chief executives usually are elected for a fixed and relatively short term, the permanent bureaucracy generally finds it relatively easy to resist direct pressure. Chief executives usually control the appointment of upper-level officials in departments and hope to influence public employees through them. However, the number of appointments is usually small in proportion to the total bureaucracy. In 2002, conflict over President George W. Bush's desire to have more appointment and removal authority over employees in the Homeland Security Department led to a delay in moving legislation creating the department through Congress.

The president has direct appointment authority for approximately 4,500 positions in the civilian bureaucracy of about 2.7 million (U.S. Office of Personnel Management, nd.; and nd,a). Many of these appointments including the appointment of judges and officers of regulatory agencies require Senate confirmation. However, once confirmed, they are independent of the president thus severely limiting the president's ability to direct the bureaucracy through appointment. The legislative body and the judiciary limit that authority even more through the confirmation power and review of attempts to discipline employees, respectively. States and their local governments follow similar patterns.

Through the budget process, the executive and legislative bodies have a great impact on the personnel system. Because the chief executive is responsible in most governments for developing budget recommendations, agencies must be aware of the administration's desires. The agencies work hard to ensure adequate funds for their personnel needs because a loss of funds normally means a reduction in the number of an agency's employees. Once the chief executive makes recommendations to the legislative body, the agency's attention turns to legislative politics. In the legislature, it is often possible to increase agency budgets by mobilizing clientele and publicizing the good work by agency personnel thus demonstrating the agency's value to the legislative body. Of course, agencies often get caught up in a struggle between the executive and legislative branches. At the national level, for example, conflicts over the budget often lead to a temporary layoff and delay of paychecks for federal employees at the end of a fiscal year. Ordinarily, Congress then passes an emergency resolution authorizing the agencies to continue operating until a budget finally is adopted. Nonetheless, planning is difficult when the agency does not know whether it will have a budget for the next year. Such politics at the local level was demonstrated in July 2012 when a conflict between the Scranton, Pennsylvania mayor and council over the budget led the mayor to reduce pay to minimum wage for city employees, including fire and police, claiming there were no funds to pay their regular salaries. The courts also became involved as employees successfully petitioned the court to require the mayor to pay the regular salaries.

The basic policy concerning public personnel generally is determined through executive and legislative efforts. The Civil Service Reform Act (CSRA) of 1978 serves as the basic foundation of the national government's civil service. Most state and local governments have adopted similar systems. CSRA was the result of trade-offs between the president and Congress. Many interests—employees, managers, veteran's groups, political parties, unions, civil rights groups, and women's groups—participated in the process leading to the adoption of CSRA. President Jimmy Carter initiated the process with his proposal for reform, but many of his suggestions were modified in the political jockeying that determined the final outcome. The law states the broad policy, but its operational meaning results from the actions of the Office of Personnel Management (OPM), Merit Systems Protection Board (MSPB), and Federal Labor Relations Authority (FLRA). Of course, the judicial branch participates by court decisions on litigation concerning the act's provisions and the agencies' implementation of them.

Public employers and employees must also pay attention to the politicization of their actions. Any missteps by public employees or their agencies can be exploited by people in political office if doing so will work to their advantage. Thus, public managers and employees are under much pressure that does not apply to any great extent to private sector employees.

The Media

It is difficult to imagine a force in the political environment with greater potential for influencing public personnel administration than the communications media. Because of constitutional guarantees of freedom of press and speech, the media can keep the public well informed about the public service and its activities and problems. Indeed, the public and political actors depend on the media for much of their information. Even though the media often focuses on the negative aspects of the public service, it frequently is responsible for improvements. Many problems in the public service are spotlighted and scrutinized by the media whereas the private sector rarely undergoes such close examination of its staff or personnel policies and practices. The media cannot, however ensure that agency personnel continue to perform effectively. They are unlikely, for example, to expose unenthusiastic performance of duties, an important form of evaluation of the public service. Critics also note that the media may distort the reality of public service performance by focusing on the negative.

Interest Groups

Many interest groups also exert pressure on public personnel operations. Among these are clientele groups, minority and women's groups, public interest groups, professional associations, civic groups, taxpayer associations, and public employee associations and unions. Although interest groups generally are most concerned about issues other than personnel management, they recognize that having some influence over the people who make decisions will affect an agency's response to their concerns.

Most groups tend to concentrate on relatively narrow issues of self-interest. Thus, clientele, minority, women's, professional, and public employee groups are likely to seek policies that ensure that the agency will give their particular welfare as much consideration as possible. Public interest and civic groups such as civil service leagues, good government associations, the League of Women Voters, taxpayer reform associations, and the Center for the Study of Responsive Law take a more general approach. They pursue policies beneficial to the "public interest" and usually promote personnel systems that reduce the potential for partisan political influence. These groups also tend to favor policies that require public employees to disclose personal financial interest and control conflict of interest situations.

Political Parties

Political parties and politicians have always had an interest in public personnel operations. Politicians often view patronage as a means of exerting control over and ensuring the responsiveness of public employees. They also see that getting action by a public agency on an issue that is important to their constituents helps in getting reelected. Furthermore, politicians often find public bureaucrats to be easy targets for political rhetoric and thus exploit public service problems and inadequacies for political purposes. In fact, public personnel reform in 1883 and 1978 came about partly because politicians used corruption and inefficiency as issues; therefore, personal political gain is not always the overriding concern behind such appeals. Too often, however, criticism of the public service does little to improve it and serves merely to denigrate it.

Campaigns regularly use references to the "incompetent" or "oversized" public bureaucracy. Indeed, today most candidates for public office promise to reduce taxes and cite reducing the bureaucracy as one way to do so. The promise has obvious implications for personnel management and it is not surprising that once elected, the office holders often face distrust from government employees. The 2010 and 2012 elections included many candidates critical of the Obama health care reform saying that they did not want Washington bureaucrats making medical decisions thus using public servants as scapegoats in their campaigns.

Among personnel policies attracting attention in recent years have been affirmative action and nondiscrimination, and public sector bargaining and pensions. Affirmative action became so controversial that many states, including California and Washington, have outlawed it. Public employers have had to find other ways to insure diversity. After the 2010 elections, several states passed laws limiting or restricting unions and bargaining by public employees. Facing severe budget crises, many elected officials addressed rising pension costs for public employees by reducing the benefits or requiring higher contributions to the systems by employees themselves (Bunnell, 2012). All of these issues arise in election campaigns for Congress, state legislatures, and city councils. Many candidates attain office by campaigning on the issues.

The political parties traditionally depended on government jobs as a way of building party strength, but the pervasive adoption of merit systems greatly diminished this source of support. States such as Louisiana, Indiana, Illinois, and New Jersey, however, demonstrate that patronage is still alive and well in some state bureaucracies (Friedman, 1994; Hamilton, 2002). Some local governments also still indulge in political favoritism. However, court decisions and a public less attached to political parties, has led to a decline in partisan politics.

The General Public

In a democracy, the public service is supposed to serve the interest of the general public. The problem lies in defining what the "public interest" is. Responsiveness to the public and its wishes (which are difficult to determine), is one aspect of serving the public. Some people believe that responsible public service does not veer from the system's long range goals even when they sometimes run counter to the public's short-term wishes (Rourke, 1984). What is important to the administration of public personnel is not that the public expects responsiveness but that many political leaders exploit this expectation by promising attractive but impractical short-term solutions to problems. Other individuals and groups, particularly public interest groups, direct their attention to long-range objectives, and public administrators, including personnel administrators, are caught in the middle.

The public's view of bureaucracy is determined by society's general value system. People's assumptions about the work ethic, self-reliance, and individualism color their responses to the public service, especially as society weighs the effects that government programs and employees have on those values. A common impression is that the public service is composed of indolent employees with secure jobs who have too much power over people's lives and who consume tax money with little beneficial effect. These views, along with the idea that the bureaucracy is oversized and uncontrollable, sometimes make it difficult for the public service to recruit employees.

Relentless attacks on the bureaucracy certainly have an impact on the perception that people have of the public service. Even more damaging, however, are the ethical and behavioral lapses of public officials. Although most scandals involve elected officials and their political appointees rather than career public servants, the public does not make much distinction between the two. Thus, trust in the efficacy and integrity of the public service generally suffers. The Watergate scandal during the Nixon Administration, which was covered extensively on television, brought public misbehavior to people's living rooms. Every administration since has had some embarrassing scandal leading to Congressional hearings thus ensuring that the public stays aware of the misdeeds of elected and politically appointed officials. The state and local levels have not fared any better. It is not surprising that citizens are cynical. Add to that the ineptitude of some states in conducting elections and cynicism increases. Career public employees are tainted by these situations, most of which they cannot control.

Summary

Public personnel management resides in a complex environment and is part of a larger governmental system. Because the system in the United States contains a variety of interests competing for position and power, the personnel system becomes entwined in the political process. The various political actors and forces outlined in this chapter obviously have different interests in the personnel system. The personnel function cannot be viewed as a neutral instrument of management; instead, it is at the center of the decision-making process and can easily become a pawn in the struggle for political power and influence. Although all actors, such as the president and members of Congress, insist that they want only the most efficient and responsive public service possible, they could actually be concerned primarily with maintaining or improving their political positions. Thus, expressions of outrage from either side regarding personnel actions often are calculated more for political advantage than for improving personnel practices. Similarly, other participants in the political environment have conflicting interests, which can lead to compromise and accommodation in public personnel management.

This chapter has identified the role of public personnel management in the governmental process and has introduced the major forces that affect public personnel management and the issues that are of concern to personnel managers. The remaining chapters elaborate on these topics. Chapters 2 and 3 focus on political considerations in the development of public personnel systems. Chapter 2 traces the evolution of public personnel management, and chapter 3 examines some of the enduring political forces that shape the way the management of personnel is organized in government.

Chapters 4, 5, and 6, evaluate the tools and techniques used in managing personnel, and chapters 7, 8, and 9 consider some challenges faced by contemporary personnel managers. Finally, chapter 10 discusses continuing challenges.

Exercises

1. Access the Web site of the personnel/human resources office of a municipality, tribal government, county, or school district. Review the mission and organization of the office. Then interview the director of the office to determine how the office functions. Also ask if there has been an instance in which the behavior of an employee or employees has caused public criticism or embarrassment to the government. Ask how the office reacted and why.

> Once you have gathered the information, explain what you think are the basic values represented by the office. Assess whether the values reflected in the mission statement of the office appear to be the ones reflected in the director's explanation of the office's function.

2. Dina Peroni is the principal of Theo Crane High School. Over the weekend, one of her best teachers, Clarissa Teel, was arrested on a charge of driving under the influence (DUI). The incident was reported widely in the media. There was immediate reaction by parents of students at the school. Some want Teel fired immediately while others thought she should be retained as she is one of the best teachers there.

> If you were Peroni, what would you do on Monday morning? What would you do in the long run? Explain your reasoning.

3. Kevin Spells is an animal control officer for the city of Maryville. He has worked for the city for ten years and has won many awards for his work. He also has received exemplary performance evaluations and he was voted the employee of the year for the city last year. Spells' supervisor learned that Spells was arrested for staging cock fights on his property. Cock fighting is illegal in the state. Because of Spells' position with the city, many residents and elected officials are demanding that he be fired.

> As his supervisor, what is your recommendation to the city manager? Explain the reasons for your recommendation.

4. Kelly Davis was excited to be on local radio to talk about her role as a child advocate in the state's Office of Child Protection. She has worked for the office for seven years in various capacities, and she is very passionate about her job and agency. The interview went well with Davis explaining what the office does and how she helps children. The interview turned to funding for the office, and Davis noted that funding had decreased dramatically over the past two years. She said that there needed to be a change in the legislature if the office was going to be able to perform its function adequately. She criticized the Republican governor and legislature for slashing funding and suggested that voters should put Democrats in charge as they were more supportive of her office's mission.

When Davis got to her office after the interview, she had a message to see her supervisor, John Tepper, right away. Tepper told her that she was fired and said that he was tired of her going on her crusades and embarrassing the office. He noted that he had already heard from the governor and several Republican legislators who were outraged by her comments. They all demanded that Davis be fired.

> You are the personnel department liaison to the Office of Child Protection. Davis complained to you. What do you tell Davis? What do you tell Tepper? What information do you need before you deal with either of them? Explain your advice to them.

Selected Websites

Directorate for Public Governance and Territorial Development of the OECD. Organization for Economic Cooperation and Development directorate that helps countries adapt governance structures and policies to changing society.

http://www.oecd.org/department/0,3355,en_2649_33735_1_1_1_1_1,00.html

International Personnel Management Association for Human Resources (IPMA-HR). Membership organization of people employed and interested in public personnel administration. Publishes extensively on public personnel/human resources management.

www.ipma-hr.org

National Association of State Personnel Executives (NASPE). Membership organization of the state personnel directors/executives. Publishes a newsletter and reports.

www.naspe.net

National Congress of American Indians (NCAI). Organization of tribal governments that serves as a forum for policy development and provides governmental services among tribes. Website includes tribal directory.

www.ncai.org

Office of Personnel Management (OPM). Executive branch agency with responsibility for the personnel function in the national government. Works with federal departments/agencies in implementing personnel policy.

www.opm.gov

Partnership for Public Service. Nonpartisan organization to restore public confidence and prestige to the federal public service.

www.ourpublicservice.org

Section on Personnel and Labor Relations (SPALR). Section of the American Society for Public Administration that publishes the journal, *Review of Public Personnel Administration*; also serves its membership by sponsoring conference panels and networking.

www.aspanet.org

Society for Human Resource Management (SHRM). Membership organization for those interested in and employed in personnel/human resources management with an emphasis on the private sector.

www.shrm.org

University of Oklahoma Law Center—Native American Resources. Organization that conducts and disseminates research on tribal government issues including personnel matters; has links to tribal nation home pages.

www.law.ou.edu/indian

References

Bunnell, B. (2012, June 29). Marin Voice: Public pensions—San Jose and San Diego voters have spoken. *Marin Independent Journal*. Retrieved from http://www.marinij.com/opinion/ci_20967680/marin-voice-public-pensions-san-jose-and-san.

Condrey, S. E. (2002). Reinventing state civil service systems: The Georgia experience. *Review of Public Personnel Administration, 22*(Summer), 114–124.

Friedman, A. (2002). *Patronage: An American tradition*. Chicago: Nelson-Hall, 1994.

Gossett, C. W. (2002). Civil service reform: The case of Georgia. *Review of Public Personnel Administration, 22*(Summer), 94–113.

Hamilton, D. K. (2002). Is patronage dead? *Review of Public Personnel Administration 22*(Spring), 3–26.

Kelly v. Johnson, 425 U.S. 238 (1976).

Klingner D. & Nalbandian, J. (1978). Personnel management by whose objectives? *Public Administration Review, 38*(July–August), 366–372.

Light, P. C. (1999). *The new public service*. Washington, DC: Brookings Institution Press.

Lowi, T. J. (1967). Machine politics—old and new. *The Public Interest, 9*(Fall), 83–92.

McAllister, B. (1988, July 20). GSA told to reinstate official who cited perils at buildings. *Washington Post*, p. A1.

McCarthy v. Philadelphia Civil Service Commission, 424 U.S. 645 (1976).

Milward, H. B. (1978). Politics, personnel and public policy. *Public Administration Review, 38*, 391–396.

Morse, M. (1976). We've come a long way. *Public Personnel Management, 5*, 218–221.

Mosher, F. C. (1982). *Democracy and the public service* (2nd ed.). New York: Oxford University Press.

Newland, C. A. (1967). Public personnel administration: Legalistic reforms vs. effectiveness, efficiency, and economy. *Public Administration Review, 36*, 529–537.

Nigro, L. G. & Kellough, J. D. (2000). Civil service reform in Georgia. *Review of Public Personnel Administration, 20*, 41–54.

Rau, A. B. (2012, May 11). Brewer signs bill to revise state's personnel system. *The Arizona Republic*, pp. B3 & B11.

Rich, W. C. (1982). *The Politics of urban policy: Reformers, politicians and bureaucrats*. Port Washington, NY: Kennikat Press, 1982.

Rosenbloom, D. H. (1973). Public personnel administration and politics: Toward a new public personnel administration. *Midwest Review of Public Administration, 7*, 98–110.

Rosenbloom, D. H. (1982). Public policy in a political environment: A symposium. *Policy Studies Journal, 11*, 245–254.

Rosenbloom, D. H. (1981). The sources of continuing conflict between the constitution and public personnel management. *Review of Public Personnel Administration, 2*, 3–18.

Rourke, F. E. (1984). *Bureaucracy, politics, and public policy* (3rd ed.). Boston: Little Brown.

Thompson, F. J. (1983). The politics of public personnel administration. In S.W. Hays & R.C. Kearney (Eds.), *Public personnel administration: Problems and prospects* (3rd ed.) (pp. 3–16). Englewood Cliffs, NJ: Prentice Hall.

Thompson, F. J. (1975). *Personnel policy in the city*. Berkeley and Los Angeles: University of California Press.

U.S. Office of Personnel Management. (n.d.). *Facts & figures*. Plum Book. http://www.opm.gov/ses/facts_and_figures/plumbook.asp.

U.S. Office of Personnel Management. (n.d.). *Federal employment statistics historical tables: Total government employment since 1962*. http://www.opm.gov/feddata/HistoricalTables/TotalGovernmentSince 1962.asp.

2

Evolution of the Public Personnel System

All governments face the problem of determining how to staff and maintain a public service that is consistent with society's political values and goals, competent, loyal to management, and responsive to the public. There has been constant conflict among these competing criteria for the establishment and operation of a personnel system, and there have been numerous dramatic changes in the public service in accommodating ever-changing political, social, and economic realities.

As noted earlier, this book's major premise is that public personnel administration can best be understood in terms of its relationship to political values and processes. Therefore, the brief historical overview of the public service presented in this chapter emphasizes the influence of political values on public personnel operation. There was the period of early development, 1789 to 1829; the period in which spoils predominated, 1829 to 1883; the period in which the merit system developed and dominated, 1883 to 1978; and finally, the period of contemporary reform, 1978 to present. During each of these time spans there were significant events that can be used as milestones in the development of public personnel administration in the United States, but the periods suggested here break at the times when major new perspectives on the public service emerged. The last sections of this chapter evaluate the legacies of reforms by examining legislative–executive conflicts, professionals as inheritors of the system, and spoils versus merit.

The Early Roots

President George Washington is usually credited with developing a competent public service. Because there was no established bureaucracy when he assumed the presidency, Washington was in the unique position of being able to build a public service from scratch. Although political considerations are usually not attributed to Washington in his personnel actions, he did make numerous concessions to political reality (Kaufman, 1965; Mosher, 1982; Van Riper, 1958). However, he was not as politically partisan as many of his successors were.

One of the realities with which Washington had to contend was the fact that political power in the nation's early years was held almost exclusively by an aristocracy of large landowners. Although Washington established fitness and ability as requirements for appointment to public service, fitness usually meant social status or prestige rather than technical competence (White, 1948). Washington was free to use such a criterion because the tasks of the public bureaucracy were not highly specialized as they were later when our social and political systems became more complex. The important point is that Washington chose public servants from politically powerful sectors of society.

Washington was influenced by other political considerations as well. He had the enormous task of integrating a new nation of previously independent-minded states, and to do this he had to plan and act carefully. A requirement for public service employment under Washington was support of the new federal political system. Although supporting the political system does not seem radical today, it was a controversial issue at the time because many people hoped the new system would fail. Thus, oddly enough, a political position with which many citizens strongly disagreed was a requirement for holding a public job.

There were also regional considerations. President Washington wanted to ensure that local programs would be administered by members of each community and that all regions of the country would be represented in the upper echelons of the public service. He thus hoped to gain nationwide support for and identification with the new political system.

Another political move by the new president was to defer to the wishes of Congress on many appointments. Recognizing that members of Congress could greatly affect his administration's success, Washington conferred with them, even though he was not legally required to do so in most instances. Indeed, presidents still consider congressional wishes in their appointments. Another group to whom Washington accorded special attention consisted of army officers from the Revolutionary War. They were often hired in preference to others, although Washington was careful to limit the number of such appointments. Preferential treatment of veterans, now common in national as well as state and local merit systems, derives in part from Washington's policies.

The fact that Washington's decisions often were politically motivated should not come as a surprise. In a democratic system, it is expected that public officials will respond to political pressure. As Van Riper (1958) noted, it is fortunate that these political considerations were consistent with the development of a highly competent public service (p. 27) because many of these political accommodations left enduring marks on the staffing of public bureaucracies. Regional representation, partisan political support, loyalty, preference for veterans, and consultation with members of Congress have been and often still are significant concerns when filling public service positions.

Washington's immediate successors made a few changes in their criteria for staffing the public service. Partisan concerns became more important under John Adams, but Thomas Jefferson made the most significant break with Washington's practices. Representing a new party in power, Jefferson wanted to reward his Republican followers with appointments. The long years of Federalist control, however, had resulted in the entrenchment of Federalists in public service positions. Therefore, to obtain a bureaucracy more to his liking, Jefferson removed many government employees, justifying this policy by claiming a need for a balance of partisan viewpoints (White, 1961). He believed that because the people had elected him president, they should have like-minded public servants to help him carry out his policies, a view that all modern presidents have also articulated. Political party affiliation was not Jefferson's only criterion; he also evaluated potential employees on their ability and fitness using the same standards as Washington. By bowing to party pressure in appointments, Jefferson was the real father of the spoils system. Yet he diligently resisted debasing the public service by making it strictly partisan.

Although partisan politics became more important during Jefferson's presidency, the character of the public service remained unchanged. Despite his Republican philosophy, Jefferson had to contend with a politically powerful elite. Jefferson's successors followed much the same tradition. Consequently, the aristocracy retained its hold on public service positions through the administration of John Quincy Adams. Tests of loyalty, regional considerations, preference for veterans, and consultation with Congress remained factors in public service staffing.

Jacksonian Democracy

With a dramatic shift in the center of political power came an equally dramatic change in the public bureaucracy. The results of the election of 1828 reflected the political frustrations that had been building in the populace. From 1800 to 1829, the U.S. political system became more democratic because new groups in society gained the opportunity to participate in politics. The addition of eleven states to the Union—nine in the West—brought a new flavor to politics and elections. Previously, only landowners and the aristocracy had the vote, but electoral reforms in the early nineteenth century and the admission of new states in which the common man ruled broadened electoral participation. The Western states led in extending suffrage, but by 1829 the right to vote was almost universally enjoyed by white males. The egalitarianism of the frontier influenced national politics by changing the power relationship between the upper and lower classes in favor of the latter.

The extension of suffrage resulted from political considerations. With more voters, the parties could increase their ranks and thus saw the advantage of extending the right to vote. As the common man participated in the choice of elected political leaders, he also expected some of the fruits of politics, so it is not surprising that resentment toward the aristocracy's monopoly on public service positions developed. Astute political leaders could not ignore the expectations of their new constituents. Recognizing that political patronage could be used to build up their parties, politicians made the spoils system a standard feature of public service staffing in state and local governments.

The triumph of the common man extended to the national level with the election of Andrew Jackson in 1828. His inauguration celebrations are often cited as examples of the dramatic changes in the locus of political power. Social critics of the day were aghast at the antics and crudeness of Jackson's followers, many of whom descended on Washington, DC in search of government employment (Fish, 1963; Hoogenboom, 1961).

The expectations of Jackson's followers were high, and the genteel elements of Washington politics anticipated disaster. As it turned out, the expectations of both groups were exaggerated. Jackson was interested not only in realigning the public service's political makeup but also in reducing government activity and hence the size of the bureaucracy. Consequently, the hordes of office seekers found that Jackson meant to cut back on government jobs. However, and most important for our consideration, Jackson followed Jefferson's lead in insisting that the bureaucracy reflect the results of the election; accordingly, he removed many people from office and replaced them with his own followers.

Although Jackson did not turn out a significantly higher proportion of employees from the public service than Jefferson had, he is more closely identified with the spoils system because he was more openly partisan and proud of it. He saw his administration as one that revolutionized the U.S. political system. His administration broke the aristocracy's political power over both elective and appointive positions. The revolutionary character of Jackson's approach lay in the fact that the public service was democratized in response to the democratization of the electoral system.

The shift in political power caused intense criticism of Jackson's public personnel policies. However, despite his feeling that government's work was so simple that anyone could do it (which was much more accurate then than it is today), Jackson insisted on competence and the judicious use of patronage. He would have been as uncomfortable as any of his predecessors to see the extent to which many of his successors used and abused patronage.

Weakening of Spoils

After Jackson's administration, the alternation of political party control of the presidency led to a revolving door for public servants, with the door turning every four years. Even though there were many carryovers from one administration to another, public servants were usually assigned to different positions by the new administration. Even the election of a new president of the same party (which occurred when James Buchanan succeeded fellow Democrat Franklin Pierce), did not ensure the retention of the same public servants. Buchanan represented a different faction of the party and was pressured into changing the bureaucracy to reflect that fact.

The election of Lincoln in 1860 represents both the high point and the onset of the demise of the spoils system. Lincoln used the system to a greater extent than any other president had. Mobilizing the Union for the Civil War required a loyal public service, and Lincoln believed that the only way to create one was to use patronage (Fish, 1963, p. 213). Lincoln's sweep of people from office, the most extensive in U.S. history, was warranted by the political considerations of the time. His concern was to consolidate the Republican Party, which had been in disarray, and to conduct a controversial war. As the Union started to come apart, officeholders from the South were removed and those loyal to the Union were put in their places.

Despite his wide use of the spoils system, Lincoln also must be credited with initiating its gradual decline. After his election to a second term, he was pressured to make a clean sweep of his appointees because his supporters had become accustomed to having a completely new team every four years. Lincoln's refusal to oblige gave hope to critics of the spoils system and led to an examination of the system that produced significant change in the next two decades. President Andrew Johnson, faced with internal political problems of his own, found it necessary to replace many of Lincoln's loyalists. However, the spoils system was marked for destruction, and in less than twenty years it was dealt a blow from which it never recovered. In the years between Lincoln's administration and 1883, political forces gradually chipped away at the patronage system. Much like the growth of democratic political participation from 1800 to 1829, the growth of discontent with the spoils system from 1865 to 1883 led to a revolution in the staffing of the U.S. government bureaucracy.

The Civil War greatly increased the power of the executive branch vis-à-vis Congress, and the end of the war brought an opportunity for Congress to attempt to regain some of its influence. With Andrew Johnson in office and plagued by internal party struggles, the stage was set. The area of greatest struggle and the immediate issue in the impeachment proceedings against Johnson was control over government personnel. The difficulties Johnson had with Congress and his party led him to drop many of Lincoln's supporters in favor of his own. Predictably, this action only heightened congressional opposition to him.

The Tenure of Office Act of 1867 symbolized Congress' attempt to gain control over patronage. This act limited the president's removal power by requiring Senate approval in cases involving the removal of officers who had been appointed with Senate confirmation. Defiance of Congress and the Tenure of Office Act led to Johnson's impeachment by the House of Representatives; the Senate acquitted him by only one vote. The power to appoint and remove was the immediate issue over which this momentous confrontation developed, but the political issues were much broader. For students of public personnel management, however, it is a significant occasion because it signaled a movement away from presidential control over patronage and personnel policy issues. Congress subsequently consolidated its power over the general policy during the next decade and a half. Eventually, congressional interest led to the establishment of the merit system, although Congress's major interest at that point was in controlling the spoils (Hoogenboom, 1961).

President Andrew Johnson's lack of control and the weak administrations of Ulysses S. Grant and Rutherford B. Hayes produced even greater congressional interest in and control over the personnel process. At the same time, efforts at reform were being made. During Grant's administration, Congress passed the Civil Service Act of 1871, although its proponents had to attach it as a rider to an appropriations bill to get it passed (Fish, 1963, p. 213). Surprisingly, President Grant supported civil service reform and had actually proposed legislation similar to that which was passed in 1871. More importantly, and to the surprise of many Republicans in Congress, he tried to institute a merit system. In effect, the Act of 1871 reestablished presidential control over the personnel process by giving the president the authority to establish rules and regulations for employees in the public service and appoint advisers to help draw up and administer the rules and regulations. Grant did just that by appointing a seven-member civil service commission and issuing executive orders for a limited use of merit concepts.

However, political realities did not permit Grant's experiment with reform to endure. Congress was not willing to give up the control it had obtained. Fearing a loss of power through the loss of patronage, Congress refused to fund the system after 1873, so it could no longer operate, although some commissioners continued to work without compensation. Despite its short tenure, Grant's commission had lasting effects; its recommendations formed much of the basis of public personnel thought reflected in the 1883 reforms (Murphy, 1942).

Although the experiment had to be abandoned, it whetted the appetites of reformers, and the issue would not die. The ensuing scandals of the Grant administration helped make civil service reform a more vital political issue. Another supporter of merit, Rutherford B. Hayes, became the president in 1877 and made some tentative moves toward reform. However, the controversy surrounding his election left him politically weak, and he was unable to accomplish much. What he did to institute reform in some departments appeared to be more than offset by his lack of effort in other departments. Furthermore, Hayes's inconsistency in implementing executive orders against assessment (requiring employees to contribute a percentage of their salaries to their political parties) and partisan activity leads one to question the sincerity of his commitment to reform (Hoogenboom, 1961, pp. 143–178).

Nonetheless, the issue of reform was attracting an ever-widening group of supporters. During the late 1870s and early 1880s, various associations favoring civil service reform organized and became more vocal. They attempted to pressure political leaders, but more important, they tried to educate the public about the evils of spoils. They portrayed the spoils system as one that undermines the work ethic and feeds the avarice of the bad citizen. Somehow the people still did not become intensely interested in the issue, although some public concern was manifested by the election of presidents committed to reform. However, with the aid of an increasingly interested press, the reformers made their mark on the public and politicians alike (Hoogenboom, 1964; Nelson, 1964, pp. 1–3)

The assassination of James A. Garfield became a dramatic symbol of the evils of the spoils system. Garfields's assassin, Charles Guiteau, had unsuccessfully sought patronage employment. His actions gave the reformers the impetus they needed, and the fact that Garfield supported reform only added to their sense of urgency.

Another political factor favoring reform was the Supreme Court's decision in *Ex Parte Curtis* in 1882 (106 U.S., 1882) Congress had passed a law in 1876 that prohibited the assessment of government workers. This practice involves a "contribution," or kickback, of a portion of an employee's salary to his or her political party organization or another benefactor. Obviously, when the patronage system operates, assessment could be easily enforced; an employee who refuses to "contribute" could be removed from his or her position. In any case, assessment became a scandal when Newton Curtis, a Treasury Department employee and treasurer of the New York Republican Party, was brought to trial for violating the 1870 law. The Supreme Court upheld his conviction and the law, and reform efforts benefited from that decision.

In addition, the congressional elections of 1882 led the Republicans to reflect upon the political consequences of reform. Republican fortunes slipped badly in the elections, and a continuation of that trend would have meant the loss of the White House in 1884, the loss of power to appoint public servants, and possible large-scale purges of Republican officeholders. Congressional Republicans thus saw the wisdom of supporting reform.

As a result of these political forces and the persistent efforts of reformers, the Pendleton Civil Service Act (named after the Ohio senator who was the driving force behind it) became law on January 16, 1883. This act created a personnel system that was based on the merit concept and required the formulation of rules and regulations by which all personnel activities would be conducted. It had taken a long time and the assassination of a president, but Congress finally acted. The character of the public service had undergone another revolution.

However, passage of the Pendleton Act did not bring an end to the spoils system, nor did it mean that reform became a dead issue. Only about ten percent of the public servants were covered by the act and hired based on merit. To implement the system, the president was authorized to appoint a bipartisan civil service commission. Among many other features, the basic elements of the civil service included competitive examinations, lateral entry (entry at any level), neutrality, and the prohibition of assessments of civil servants by politicians. Apparently some supporters of reform expected the public service to become the domain of the aristocracy once again (Hoogenboom, 1958–59, 1961), but this did not happen, partly because of the act's provisions and partly because of its gradual application. The increased attention to educational criteria for employment, though, gave an advantage to the upper socioeconomic groups.

By passing the Pendleton Act, Congress attempted to exert control over the personnel system of the federal government. Because the Constitution gives executive authority to the president, the constitutionality of congressional control was questioned. Consequently, Congress made the legislation permissive, meaning that the president could provide for the establishment of the merit system but was not directed to do so. Certainly the political squabbles between the president and Congress had an impact, but the realities of the constitutional provisions had to be accommodated.

Each of the act's major provisions had political implications. The first, authorizing rather than mandating presidential action on the matter, has been discussed in terms of the conflict between the president and Congress. Open competitive exams and lateral entry can be seen as adherence to the democratic tradition of equality. The reformers were actually interested in adopting the British system, requiring entry at the bottom and promotion from within. However, because the egalitarian tradition of the United States was inconsistent with that provision, the open system was adopted. Some suggest that the Democrats put the Republicans on the defensive and forced them to adopt the open system for fear of being branded as undemocratic by the press and the public (Hoogenboom, 1961; Van Riper, 1958). Certainly this is true, although the Democrats were not entirely altruistic. They were concerned about being able to balance the public service in their favor if they won the presidency in 1884, as they did. It would be difficult to reward Democratic partisans if the current Republican president chose all high-level public servants. By contrast, with lateral entry, any vacancies at higher levels could be given to Democrats within the limits of the competitive system.

Apportionment of the positions in Washington offices among the states meant that the constituents of each member of Congress had a realistic chance to obtain employment. The South also was concerned about its inadequate representation in public service positions. In addition, apportionment helped further integrate the nation by ensuring participation by people from all parts of the country.

Both political parties realized the importance of the provisions regarding extending or reducing the extent of the merit system's coverage. Congress could hardly direct that all public employees be covered, given the constitutional question discussed earlier, so the extent of coverage was to be determined by the president. Because of the potential for abuse of this power, especially by a lame duck, the president was also authorized to roll back the coverage (or remove positions from civil service protection)—a power that has been used infrequently. President William McKinley exercised this power in his first term, precipitating a bitter reaction, and others thus have been reluctant to try it. In contrast, presidents frequently have extended the coverage (called blanketing-in), particularly at the end of their terms—so that approximately 90 percent of federal government civilian employees are now under some sort of merit system.

It is clear that political considerations affected the decisions to reform the public service in 1883 and have been factors ever since in the system's evolution. David Rosenbloom has suggested that the 1883 reform was political because its intent was to rescue government from the professional politicians (Rosenbloom, 1982). The conflicting values of professional politicians and advocates of strict merit continue to influence the debate on how to make government personnel more responsive to the public interest.

Changing Concerns of the Merit System

Although the Civil Service System seemed to have a fairly broad grant of power under the Civil Service Act, it really exercised little power, devoting most of its early years to screening applicants. Considering the political climate in which it was born, it is little wonder that presidents and the commission moved cautiously. Remember that Congress created the new system more because of public sentiment and reformers' pressure than because it was committed to reform. Gradually, however, the commission gained prestige and influence and became the major force in public personnel policies. When Theodore Roosevelt became president in 1901, the civil service system had a friend in its chief executive. A former commissioner of civil service, Roosevelt did much to improve the service's image and increase its coverage. From that day on, with minor exceptions, the commission's position remained strong.

During the late nineteenth and early twentieth centuries, many changes in society and politics brought adaptive changes to the civil service system. In 1883, the jobs of public servants were still primarily clerkships, but the Industrial Revolution brought technological change, and the post–Civil War era was characterized by a period of intensive economic development. Technological advances and their consequences imposed new demands on the political system and resulted in an ever-larger public service. Jobs became more specialized, and with this development came the need for yet another specialty, the personnel administrator.

The new system faced constantly changing political forces. Workers' movements resulting in union organization had an early impact on the public service; the National Association of Letter Carriers, for instance, was organized in 1889. Concern for employees' welfare became another important consideration. As a result, there have been a gradual development and extension of benefit packages available in the United States.

As noted earlier, the spoils system first took hold at the national level but quickly spread to state and local jurisdictions. When the federal government instituted reforms, however, most state and local governments were slow to follow its lead (Aronson, 1979). In 1883, New York adopted the first civil service law, but only one other state, Massachusetts, enacted such a law before the turn of the century. In 1884, Albany, New York, became the first city to create a civil service system. Several other cities and one county (Cook County, Illinois) followed suit during the 1880s and 1890s. Coverage usually only applied to clerical workers and the uniformed services of police officers and firefighters.

With the muckrakers' attention focused on corruption in municipal government in the early years of the twentieth century, the pressure for reform increased. The exposure of patronage abuse in state governments had the same effect. Many state and municipal governments therefore developed civil service systems beginning in 1900 and continuing through the 1920s. Although limited in scope, these reforms did herald an era of major change in state and local personnel practices. The Great Depression of 1929, however, brought a halt to most reform efforts. State and local governments reduced their funding of such programs as they attempted to cope with other, more pressing problems relating to their citizens' well-being.

During the 1930s, the national government was consolidating its reform effort, and the U.S. Civil Service Commission gradually centralized its authority. Established to protect the neutrality of the federal government service, the commission performed the major personnel functions and monitored agencies' activities to ensure that they abided by the new civil service rules and regulations.

At the same time, the Depression brought changes in the federal government service, just as it did in state and local governments. President Franklin Roosevelt, in his efforts to create programs to deal with the economic crisis, believed that the already established bureaucracy was not flexible and adaptable enough to act quickly and that speedy action was required if people were to receive the help they needed to avoid total disaster. Convinced that the existing agencies were not up to the task, Roosevelt persuaded Congress to create many agencies outside the civil service such as the Works Progress Administration (WPA), Civilian Conservation Corps (CCC), and Tennessee Valley Authority (TVA). Although most of the employees of those agencies eventually were "blanketed in" (given civil service coverage by executive order), they represented a loss of control by the Civil Service Commission.

Roosevelt also directed individual departments and agencies to create their own personnel units. These units eventually performed the majority of personnel functions for their agencies. The Second World War was another factor leading to the decentralization of personnel functions. Because the Civil Service Commission was unable to keep up with demands made by the new and rapidly growing agencies created for the war efforts, these departments enjoyed relative independence.

Although there were efforts to reestablish the commission's authority, decentralization characterized the personnel function after the war. Individual departments became increasingly responsible for implementing personnel policies. The role of the

Civil Service Commission also changed, becoming that of a policy maker, a provider of technical and support services, and a monitor of personnel activities. These changes in its role remain today, even though the old commission was abolished and a new organization was created in its place.

Other changes in personnel activities also occurred during this period. During the 1930s and 1940s, the federal government began to impose limits on state- and local-level personnel practices. For example, the Social Security Act of 1935 created programs in which federal funding assisted state governments and required such programs to be efficiently administered, but it had no provisions for enforcing such a vague prescription. In 1940 the act was amended to permit specific federal personnel requirements in state and local programs utilizing federal monies under the Social Security Act. Over the years, Congress has provided for similar regulations requiring merit systems be put in place in the personnel practices of other programs. Currently, a uniform set of merit principle guidelines exists for federally funded projects.

Another 1940 provision, and amendment to the 1939 Hatch Act, prohibited most political activities by employees of state and local government programs funded by federal monies. These provisions were repealed in 1974, but most states have their own statutes restricting partisan political activities; therefore, the federal repeal has not resulted in much change for most state and local employees.

During the 1930s and 1940s, there was a slow but steady growth in the number of states and municipalities adopting civil service systems. During the 1950s, however, the pace quickened, and (partly because of the federal government's grant-in-aid restrictions on personnel) all states adopted some form of merit requirement for their personnel systems. Still, all states did not cover every employee in one system. Although civil service protections were removed in Georgia and Florida in the 1990s, merit was still supposed to be the basis for personnel decisions. Some states such as Texas still have several different systems covering employees in particular departments and programs. Typically, public safety personnel are in separate systems as are public college and university employees. Municipalities tend to operate under merit systems, and counties (the last bastion of patronage) increasingly do so as well.

The federal government public service continued to change from the 1930s to 1950s. The Hatch Act of 1939 gave legislative force to the Civil Service Commission's prohibition on political activity, and the Ramspeck Act of 1940 prohibited discrimination in the personnel process. Preference was given to veterans in the Veteran's Preference Act of 1944, and the Government Employees Training Act of 1958 focused attention on the need for employees' continued personal growth.

In the 1960s and 1970s, personnel systems were challenged by developments in collective bargaining, antidiscrimination, and equal employment opportunity policies. In the 1980s and 1990s, performance and accountability became major issues. These issues continue as concerns for personnel systems in the twenty-first century.

Civil Service Reform Act of 1978 and Beyond

Ever since the Pendleton Civil Service Act was passed, advocates have pushed for its reform. Although many changes have been made over the years, there was no comprehensive reform of the civil service until the enactment of the Civil Service Reform Act of 1978. Fulfilling an election campaign promise to reform government to improve its efficiency, President Jimmy Carter pushed strongly for adoption of the reform. Along with the act, Congress approved two reorganizations of the Civil Service Commission and shifted some of its responsibilities to the Equal Employment Opportunity Commission (U.S. Civil Service Commission, 1978). These reforms took effect in January 1979.

This 1978 legislation divided the activities of the Civil Service Commission (CSC) between the new Office of Personnel Management (OPM) and the Merit Systems Protection Board (MSPB). The Federal Labor Relations Authority (FLRA) was also created to monitor policies regarding federal employee labor–management relations. This division of responsibilities reflects the objection of employee organizations and others, to one organization having policy-making, implementation, and reviewing authority. Employees often viewed the CSC as representing management and did not feel comfortable approaching it with complaints or requests to review personnel actions.

The director and deputy director of OPM, appointed by the president, have responsibility for general personnel policy development for federal employees as well as for examinations, personnel investigations, evaluation of personnel programs, and training and development. OPM also offers technical assistance to departments and administers retirement and benefit programs for federal employees.

The independent MSPB was designed to protect federal employees against unfair personnel actions and other abuses. It must also ensure that the merit system is protected and that it makes annual reports to Congress on merit system operations. Federal employees are able to appeal personnel actions to the MSPB, which has the authority to institute actions to correct abuses. An important feature of the reform is that the special counsel established within the MSPB has the power to investigate the activities of agencies and officials. The special counsel can also ask the MSPB to take action against those who violate merit system laws.

The FLRA monitors federal collective bargaining activities such as the establishment of bargaining units and collective bargaining elections and works with departments and agencies on activities that involve labor–management relations. A general counsel in the FLRA investigates and prosecutes unfair labor practices. The Federal Service Impasses Panel is an independent agency that helps resolve negotiation impasses in the federal service.

Several features of the Civil Service Reform Act of 1978 deal with personnel policy issues. For example, OPM is authorized to delegate many of its functions to operating departments, thus continuing the post-1933 trend toward decentralizing personnel functions. The Senior Executive Service (SES) created by the act permits some high-level managers to be assigned as needed to maximize the use of their talents. These managers are also eligible for substantial pay increase for meritorious service. Indeed, merit also became the basis for pay increases for other managers in the federal service.

The 1978 legislation also streamlined the processing for dealing with incompetent employees. In addition, whistleblowers—that is, employees who expose illegal activities or mismanagement in their agencies—are supposed to be protected against reprisals by their supervisors. One of the act's most important features is that it put into law some policies that previously had existed only by executive order or through Civil Service Commission policy. One provision spells out and protects public employees' collective bargaining rights. Another provision lists specific merit principles and prohibited practices.

The Reform Act of 1978 was intended to improve the federal personnel system in general and the performance of public employees in particular. Many state and local governments were considering reform at the same time, and many others acted after the federal government passed this legislation. Federal law thus became a model for state and local governments (Cayer, 1995; Chi, 1998; Kellough & Nigro, 2010; Saltzstein, 2003).

Numerous political issues (of which popular disenchantment with government and the willingness of a president to push for such legislation were among the most important) combined to bring about the reform efforts (Knudsen, Jakus, & Metz, 1979) Problems created by the Nixon administration's attempt to politicize the public service and changes in congressional leadership were influential in making Congress more receptive to reform. The appointment of a prestigious task force to study the civil service system and make recommendations for change gave the effort additional credibility. Similar forces at the state and local levels, along with fiscal retrenchment, led to efforts to improve their public services.

Passage of the Civil Service Reform Act of 1978 did not end efforts for change or lead to a system that satisfied everyone. As rapid change continues in our society, calls for change arise at all levels of government. Distinguished task forces and commissions have studied the public services and called for changes. In 1989 the National Commission on the Public Service (Volcker Commission) recommended far-reaching changes at every level of government to improve the effectiveness of the public service (National Commission on the Public Service, 1989). The recommendations stimulated much discussion among personnel professionals and public policy makers.

In 1993, two additional reports were issued, again calling for significant changes. The Commission on the State and Local Public Service (Winter Commission) covered numerous public policy issues with an emphasis on improving state and local government performance (National Commission on the State and local Public Service, 1992). Also in 1993, the National Performance Review (chaired by Vice President Al Gore) submitted its report to the president (National Performance Review, 1993). The National Performance Review based its recommendations on the theme of reinventing government. Many other less visible studies and reports have focused on the fact that no reform ever completely fixes the system and the fact that constant effort is needed to adapt personnel systems to the ever-changing demands of the environment.

The political environment since the mid-1990s has resulted in new pressures for changes to personnel policies. Tax cut policies at all levels of government have put pressure on all public employers to find ways to reduce government spending and thus reduce the size of the workforce. Strong political reactions to affirmative action and set-aside programs in which minority-and female-owned firms must be included in projects funded with federal monies also resulted in numerous lawsuits and policy changes. Continued pressures for evaluation of public programs also focus on performance of public employees and their agencies.

The George W. Bush administration embraced many of the ideas associated with reduced government size and spending, and greater evaluation and accountability. The President's Management Agenda (PMA) outlined the basic principles of his administration. For human resources management, the basic values of PMA were a "citizen-centered, results-oriented, and market-based" civil service (Breul & Kamensky, 2008; Bush, 2001). In practical application, the Bush administration focused on reducing the size of the public bureaucracy by having public agencies compete with the private sector to deliver services (competitive sourcing), a score card system to evaluate progress toward results for all agencies, and eliminating civil service protection for many employees, especially in those agencies moved into the newly created Department of Homeland Security. The Bush efforts also targeted employee unions by eliminating their bargaining rights, again particularly in the Department of Homeland Security.

President Barack Obama has not announced any big initiative regarding human resources management reform for his administration but has begun a number of initiatives that reflect his administration's approach to the public service (Balutis, 2009–10; Kettl, 2009–10). His administration seems more concerned with ideas from public employees than with reforming from some top down agenda. He encourages agency managers to adopt a more collaborative approach and is much more supportive of union participation in decision making than was his predecessor. He also called for more transparency in decision making and actions by government agencies. Consistent with Bush though differing in his approach to assessment, Obama also focuses on performance. His administration also focuses on work-life balance and the Results Only Work Environment (ROWE) to attract and retain the best and brightest to the public service. Under Obama, OPM also started the End-to-End (E2E) hiring initiative which strives to make the hiring process more applicant friendly. Unlike his predecessor, Obama is less enamored of privatization and outsourcing.

Many issues addressed by various reform efforts continue to provide challenges to public personnel management. Among the most prominent are the conflict between legislatures and executives over control of the bureaucracy, the role of professionals, and spoils versus merit (Ingraham, Romzek & Associates, 1994; Lane & Wolf, 1990; Light, 1999; McDowell & Leavitt, 2011). In 2002, The Brookings Institution announced the creation of a second National Commission on the Public Service also chaired by Volcker. Its report in 2003 recommended comprehensive reform in the federal service. Issues addressed include recruitment, performance improvement, pay competitiveness, outsourcing, streamlining presidential appointments, leadership, and restoring trust in government (National Commission on the Public Service, 2003). These types of recommendations are recurring themes in government.

Legislative–Executive Conflicts

Legislators and elected executives constantly strive to control many aspects of the personnel function. Executives traditionally view government personnel as an instrument through which their policy perspectives can be translated into governmental action. In reality, most elected political executives complain that civil service personnel impede their efforts to deliver on campaign promises supposedly desired by the voters. Newly elected presidents, governors, and mayors customarily deplore the bureaucracy's lack of response to their policy directives. Thus, executives often view the merit system as decreasing their ability to control policy and the spoils system as augmenting that ability (Mansfield, 1965).

Legislative bodies also wish to control policy. They see influence over the personnel system as one way to do this or at least to weaken the executive's ability to exercise such power. The close relationship of legislative committees to administrative agencies serves to ensure legislative influence over agency personnel. In addition, wedges often are driven between lower-level officials and their superiors by committees that insist on hearing employees' personal views in opposition to official policy (Somers, 1965).

Lower-level bureaucrats are often protected by legislative committees or influential members of the legislative body. The State Department, for example, tried for years to change passport regulations, but Frances Knight, the director of the Passport Office, took a cautious approach toward easing the restrictions. Furthermore, even a hint at replacing her invariably met with opposition from conservative supporters in Congress who viewed her as a protector of U.S. security. Although Knight did institute some changes, she was able to withstand pressure to change passport regulations for most of the Cold War era and beyond because congressional support insulated from her nominal superiors. J. Edgar Hoover, longtime director of the Federal Bureau of Investigation (FBI), also received such protection. The same situation existed for former FBI Director Louis Free, who was able to withstand accountability to the Clinton administration because he was a favorite of powerful members of Congress. Only after the September 11, 2001, terrorist bombings of the World Trade Center and the Pentagon did FBI mismanagement and ineptitude under Free's watch surface.

As noted in our discussion of the Civil Service Act of 1883, legislative and executive conflict over which should control the public service resulted in compromises in the establishment of the civil service system. A similar conflict arose in the consideration of the Civil Service Reform Act of 1978. President Jimmy Carter definitely was interested in exerting more control over the personnel function and wanted OPM to answer to the president. Congress, of course, was wary and built in some safeguards against too much presidential control. Thus, the creation of the MSPB was one way of allaying some fears of Congress.

The issue of control was highlighted again in 2002 as President George W. Bush and Congress disagreed on civil service coverage for employees in the proposed Homeland Security Department. The president wanted Homeland Security to be exempted from the civil service and labor protections afforded to employees in the federal government in opposition to many in Congress who wanted to maintain the protections that exist. The president primarily supported his position with the argument that he needed the authority to ensure that the department would be responsive to the need for quick action in an emergency. After the elections of 2002, the president quickly prevailed. The differing concerns of executives and legislators will continue to be a source of conflict as public personnel systems evolve.

Professionals: Inheritors of the System

President Jackson characterized the work of the government as being simple enough for any citizen to perform, which was not far from the truth because at that time, most government work consisted of simple clerical tasks. Today, however, even clerical work requires complex skills and training. More to the point, modern governmental activities call for a high degree of expertise in practically every field of endeavor. The challenge of creating a personnel system capable of managing a highly skilled and diverse work force is great. As the public service has become more specialized, it has had to deal with the professionalization of personnel activities.

Professionalization occurs with the development of specialized bodies of knowledge and standards for applying that expertise. Modern society has produced many new professions and professional associations that strive for the best possible performance of the specialty. These associations enable professionals to meet with and learn from fellow specialists and keep up with recent developments in the field. Professional groups also develop codes of ethics or codes of conduct. The professionalization of public personnel thus has the potential to benefit the public service by both disseminating knowledge and establishing standards. However, there are costs as well.

Professionalism normally is characterized by (1) decision making on the basis of criteria that are universal rather than dependent on the particular situation, (2) specialization, (3) neutrality, (4) success as measured by performance, (5) elimination of self-interest from the decision-making process, and (6) self-control of professional activities (Blau & Scott, 1962). The first five of these characteristics are beneficial to the public service and are consistent with most of its features. The last, self-control of professional activities, is dramatically opposed to the principle that public personnel should be accountable to the public and its elected representatives.

Frederick Mosher suggested that professionals have assumed control over the public agencies in which they work, have developed an elite core within each agency to exercise that control, have dominated many personnel policies, and have provided protection for members of the profession (1982). Let us look at the consequences of that control.

As professionals became more numerous in public agencies, their efforts often turned from striving for the best performance to striving for power (Schuman, 1976). Thus, the emphasis is often on gaining policy control through domination of an agency. Professional groups tend to establish their territorial jurisdiction in agencies and draw up operating procedures and approaches that are based on expertise (Seidman, 1986). For example, biologists could compete for control with engineers in an environmental agency; there are problems in permitting each group's professional organization to have control. In such circumstances, an elite group, the professional organization (not accountable to the general public) is in control, so questions about the relationship of the public service to the rest of the political system arise.

In public education, for instance, teachers' associations have been successful in establishing the criteria by which personnel decisions are made and persuading school districts and state education agencies to accept them. Many current criticisms of the quality of public education are directed at the professional associations that have so much influence over the system. Many critics believe that the professional education establishment seems more concerned about its own welfare than about the welfare of students. Of course, the associations reply that they support their criteria and standards precisely because these elements lead to the best education of students.

Personnel systems are affected to the extent that professional associations dominate various personnel policies as they gain effective control over agency activities. A professional association can influence recruitment or selection in agency employment by dominating the process of establishing qualifications for applicants. Thus, the recognition or certification of programs and projects as meeting professional standards normally requires, in part, an agency's hiring of personnel with recognized professional training, certification, or experience. Such efforts restrict the flexibility and weaken the authority of personnel agencies and administrators.

Professional associations also emphasize a profession's status and autonomy. Professionals tend to respond to the pressure of the professional organization and their professional peers rather than to the agency's authority structure. The effect can be to undermine the agency's hierarchical lines of authority. In many ways, professional associations become protective shields for their members and theoretically ward off formal and legal control (Goerl, 1975; Schuman, 1976).

Related to the issue of control is employees' loyalty to their agencies. As people become more professionalized, they become less loyal to their employers and more loyal to professional associations and standards (Blau & Scott, 1962, pp. 64–67). Such employees often view the employing organizations as instruments for advancement as they move from one organization to another. In such cases, employees could also pursue their personal interests at the expense of the public and the public service. Nonetheless, their professional development is encouraged because it also brings the latest expertise to the agency. Intense specialization also often produces a narrow view on the part of individual employees. They become so preoccupied with their particular fields of interest that the organization's work can suffer from a lack of coordination and interchange among different specialties. Such circumstances make personnel activities, particularly effective supervision, more challenging.

With its emphasis on performance and merit, professionalization is antithetical to spoils and patronage and thus helps further insulate the personnel system from partisan politics. Similarly, professionalization conflicts with the preferential treatment of individuals on bases other than merit. For example, policies that give preference to veterans can be inconsistent with basic professional standards.

On balance, professionalization of the public service has improved performance of public employees. Governments increase professionalization of their employees through training and development programs. Such programs expose employees to the best practices and equip them with the skills to use the most up-to-date technology, thus contributing to the quality of the public service. Personnel administrators have their own professional associations and thus see firsthand some effects of professionalization.

Spoils versus Merit

Another issue that affects the personnel function is the conflict between spoils and merit as bases for personnel actions. The main distinction between the systems is that the spoils approach emphasizes loyalty whereas the merit concept stresses competence or expertise. However, each system needs both attributes to be effective.

Because the abuses of the spoils system led to political corruption, that system is viewed negatively and there is little appreciation for its positive contributions. Yet the spoils system was largely responsible for democratizing the public service. By breaking the aristocracy's hold on government jobs, the system brought people from all walks of life and all areas of the nation into the public service. It provided a mechanism for integrating and unifying the political system. The epitome of this functional role was Lincoln's use of patronage during the Civil War when partisan appointments were instrumental in gaining support for a controversial cause.

The spoils system also helped build and unify political parties in the United States. Voters were attracted by the prospect of patronage rewards, and party finances were strengthened by employee assessments. In addition, with the buildup of party machines, the spoils system aided in the political socialization of various ethnic groups in large cities and provided many of the social services now performed by governmental agencies.

Jacksonian democracy's focus on egalitarianism somehow became obscured in the quest for patronage positions, and in an ironic twist, egalitarianism also became on important issue in the reform movement's arguments. The abuse of the spoils system pointed out some of its costs. The constantly changing bureaucracy led to gross inefficiencies, incompetence, and even chaos and insecurity for public employees. In addition, the president and members of Congress found themselves constantly at odds over appointments, meaning that government was often at a standstill. More important, the president squandered much time and energy worrying about whom to appoint to what position. Office seekers arrived in never-ending streams, and whether or not jobs were available, the president wasted valuable time dealing with these individuals. The quality of social services provided by political machines was undermined by corruption and partiality of the political and administrative processes.

The spoils system inevitably led to favoritism and inequity in the treatment of the public, so the reformers tried to neutralize and democratize the public service. The civil service system was heralded as the savior of our political order, and it created a neutral public service that chooses and relates to employees on the basis of competence and ability to perform. The merit system also was supposed to foster egalitarianism in that everyone—not just those who happened to support political leaders—could compete for government jobs.

Reformers were concerned with bringing morality back to the public service. The merit system would free public servants from the control of evil politicians and machines and permit the bureaucracy to focus on serving the public. The merit system led to vast changes in bureaucracy and aided in reviving the prestige of the public service. Ultimately, however, the merit system revealed problems.

One of the unintended consequences of the merit system is that it weakens a supervisor's authority. The merit system increases employees' independence because supervisors no longer completely control the selection and removal process thereby giving employees greater job security. This fact frequently leads to exaggerated criticism of merit systems, but it is worth considering. A related criticism is that under a merit system, bureaucracy is insufficiently responsive to the people because their representatives have less control when they must consider factors other than loyalty in making appointments. Of course, others argue that the bureaucracy is more responsive because it is more competent and better able to serve the "real" needs of the people.

A major criticism of the merit system is that it has strayed from the egalitarian concept, just as the spoils system did. The examination process obviously eliminates some people from consideration and it is seen as a positive instrument for selecting the most qualified employees, but questions about the appropriateness of the exams have been raised. Do they measure the qualities required for successful performance? Similarly, questions are raised about the appropriateness of the credentials required for positions. These issues are central to a merit system and are the cause of many conflicts.

It is an extreme oversimplification to characterize the distinction between spoils and merit as the difference between evil and good, but many people unfortunately do just that. In reality, each system is a product of particular political and social forces. Neither can provide an effective bureaucracy without some cost. Although all levels of government have moved to a neutral bureaucracy, patronage is still important. The use of patronage had adapted to changing conditions and demands, just as the merit system has adapted (Sorauf, 1960). Some argue that the merit system has created a politics of its own that seeks support for its programs, agency autonomy, professional association interests, and clientele interests (Kaufman, 1965). These interests and groups play the game of politics and insist that the spoils be theirs rather than the political party's. However, regardless of how the system is perceived, it is certain to change in response to demands and pressures in the political environment.

Summary

The conflict between spoils and merit principles has been an enduring issue in the public service. Merit systems were developed originally to rid public personnel of political patronage. Consequently, the primary emphasis of merit systems has been on policing personnel actions. Traditionally, most personnel departments spend much of their time making sure that others comply with personnel policies, rules, and regulations. Although there has been much change, such policing still is prominent in the activities of personnel administrators, particularly at the state and local levels.

The role of personnel administration has changed. Currently, the most common model teams central personnel agencies with line department managers so that departments can comply with personnel policies and regulations and improve the quality of public service. Central personnel agencies offer technical assistance, training programs, and expert advice on legal compliance requirements and labor–management relations. Through such activities, personnel administrators can reduce the tension between themselves and department managers so that they can work together to accomplish the governments' objectives. Cooperation seems more evident as the central personnel agency has focused on policy development, review, and technical assistance, and individual agencies have been performing more day-to-day personnel functions. The Civil Service reform Act of 1978 and its progeny at the state and local levels have accentuated this trend. The remainder of this book considers this trend and other challenges facing the public personnel function.

Exercises

1. Interview the director of a department in city, county, state, or tribal government. In your interview, ask about the director's perceptions of how much the central personnel office of the government focuses on monitoring, customer service, and leading and educating departments about personnel issues. Also ask what the department manager would like to see changed about the central personnel office's function.

> Based on the interview, write your assessment of whether the central personnel office takes a traditional or a strategic approach to personnel administration.

2. Copper County is newly established after citizens decided to secede from Sliver County because they felt that they were being ignored by county government. The new Copper County is primarily rural but has a population of approximately 300,000. The newly elected county board of supervisors is attempting to establish the new structure for the county and wants to start with the Human Resources Department and Budgeting Department to help establish the rest of the agencies. You are hired as a human resources management expert to help design the new Human Resources Department.

What values would you emphasize as the most important for the Board to use as it proceeds? What type of structure would you recommend? Provide justification for your recommendations.

3. Jessica May was just elected mayor of the City of Colwell. She ran a very aggressive campaign on reducing spending and cutting taxes. She was particularly critical of public employees, calling them leeches who did not understand what it was to really work for a living. The city of 750,000 has a civil service system with due process protections for public employees meaning that they cannot be dismissed except for cause. As May took office, she realized that she would have to depend on these career public employees to achieve her goals for the city. So she hired you as a consultant to help gain the trust and cooperation of the public servants.

What would you recommend she do and how?

4. Find a state that has reformed its personnel system in the recent past.

Examine what exactly was changed. Did the changes improve the functioning of the system? Also identify any potential unintended consequences of the reform.

Selected Websites

Brookings Institution. A think tank focusing on government and public policy issues, especially at the federal level. Many of its publications focus on the public service.

www.brookings.org

International Public Management Association for Human Resources (IPMA-HR). Membership organization for people working in human resources management at all levels of government. Publishes journals and reports on various human resources management issues.

www.ipma-hr.org

National Academy of Public Administration (NAPA). Organization comparable to the National Academy of Sciences for public administration that conducts and publishes research on various public administration issues including human resource management, with a focus on the federal public service.

www.napawash.org

National Association of State Personnel Executives (NASPE). Membership organization of state human resources directors that provides support to state governments regarding personnel issues and publishes reports on various human resources issues.

www.naspe.net

U.S. Congressional Budget Office (CBO). Entity that analyzes and publishes reports on many government issues including human resource management.

www.cbo.gov

U.S. Government Accountability Office. Office that publishes reports on agencies and programs at the request of congressional committees and members, many of which deal with personnel issues. Issues a monthly list of reports.

www.gao.gov

U.S. Merit Systems Protection Board (MSPB). Organization that serves as an appeals board for federal employees who appeal personnel actions. Publishes an annual report on its activities and special reports on managing the federal workplace.

www.mspb.gov

U.S. Office of Management and Budget (OMB). Executive branch agency that analyses use of resources by federal agencies, including utilization of personnel.

www.omb.gov

U.S. Office of Personnel Management (OPM). Body that oversees the federal government personnel function and publishes materials to help agencies implement policies. Also publishes many analyses of public personnel and labor relations issues.

www.opm.gov

References

Aronson, A.H. (1979). State and local personnel administration. In F.J. Thompson (Ed.), *Classics of public personnel policy* (pp. 102–111). Oak Park, IL: Moore.

Balutis, A. P. (2009-2010). The Obama management agenda: Five steps toward transformation. *The Public Manager, 38*, 43–47.

Blau, P. M. & Scott, W. R. (1962). *Formal organizations: A comparative approach.* San Francisco: Chandler.

Breul, J. D. & Kamensky, J. M. (2008). Federal government reform: Lessons from Clinton's "Reinventing government" and Bush's "Management agenda" initiatives. *Public Administration Review, 68*, 1009–1026.

Bush, G. W. (2001). *A blueprint for new beginnings.* Washington, DC: Government Printing Office.

Cayer, N. J. (1995). Merit reform in the states. In S. Hays & R. Kearney (Eds.), *Public personnel administration: Problems and prospects* (3d ed.) (pp. 291–305). Englewood Cliffs, NJ: Prentice-Hall.

Chi, K. S. (1998). State civil service systems. In S.E. Condrey, (Ed.), *Handbook of human resource management in government* (pp. 35–55). San Francisco: Jossey-Bass.

Ex parte Curtis 106 U.S. 371 (1882).

Fish, C. R. (1963). *The civil service and the patronage.* New York: Russell & Russell, 1963.

Goerl, G. F. (1975). Cybernetics, professionalization, and knowledge management: An exercise in assumptive theory. *Public Administration Review, 35*, 581–588

Hoogenboom, A. (1961). *Outlawing the spoils: A history of the civil service reform movement 1865-1883.* Urbana IL: University of Illinois Press.

Hoogenboom, A. (1958-59). The Pendleton Act and the civil service. *American Historical Review, 64,* 301–318.

Hoogenboom, A. (1964). *Spoilsmen and reformers.* Chicago: Rand McNally.

Ingraham, P. W., Romzek, B. S. & Associates. (1994). *New paradigms for government: Issues for the changing public service.* San Francisco: Jossey-Bass.

Kaufman, H. (1965). The growth of the federal personnel service. In W. Sayre (Ed.), *The federal government service: Its character, prestige, and problems* (2nd ed.) (pp. 7–69). Englewood Cliffs, N.J.: Prentice-Hall.

Kellough, J. E. & Nigro, L. G. (2010). Civil service reform in the United States: Patterns and trends. In S. E. Condrey (Ed.), *Handbook of human resource management in government* (pp.73–97). San Francisco: Jossey-Bass.

Knudsen, S., Jakus, L., & Metz, M. (1979). The Civil Service Reform Act of 1978. *Public Personnel Management, 8,* 170–181.

Kettl, D. F. (2009–2010). Obama's stealth revolution: Quietly reshaping the way government works. *The Public Manager, 38,* 39–42.

Lane, L. M. & Wolf, J. (1990). *The human resource crisis in the public sector.* New York: Quorum Books.

Light, P. C. (1999). *The new public service.* Washington, DC: Brookings Institution Press.

Mansfield, H. C. (1965). Political parties, patronage, and the federal government service. In W. Sayre (Ed.), *The federal government service: Its character, prestige, and problems* (2nd ed.) (pp. 70–113). Englewood Cliffs, NJ: Prentice-Hall.

McDowell, A. M. & Leavitt, W. M. (2011). Human resources issues in local government: Yesterday's headlines remain today's hot topics. *Public Personnel Management, 40,* 239–250.

Mosher, F.C. (1982). *Democracy and the public service* (2nd ed.). New York: Oxford University Press.

Murphy, L.V. (1942). The first federal civil service commission: 1871-1875. *Public Personnel Review, 3*(January, July, October), 29–39, 218–231, and 299–323.

National Commission on the Public Service. (1989). *Leadership for the Public Service.* Washington, DC: National Commission on the Public Service.

National Commission on the State and Local Public Service (1992). *Hard truths / tough choices: An agenda for state and local reform.* Albany, NY: Rockefeller Institute of Government.

National Performance Review. (1993). *From red tape to results: Creating a government that works better and costs less.* Washington, DC: U.S. Government Printing Office.

Nelson, C. J. (1964). The press and civil service reform. *Civil Service Journal, 13*(April–June), 1–3.

Rosenbloom, D. H. (1982). Politics and public personnel administration: The legacy of 1883. In D.H.Rosenbloom (Ed.), *Centenary issues of the Pendleton Act of 1883: The problematic legacy of civil service reform.* New York: Marcel Dekker.

Saltzstein, A. (2003). Personnel management in the local government setting. In S. Hays and R. Kearney (Eds.), *Public personnel administration: Problems and prospects* (4th ed.) (pp.46–61). Upper Saddle River, NJ: Prentice-Hall.

Sayre, W. S. (Ed.). (1965). *The federal government service: Its character, prestige, and problems* (2nd ed.). Englewood Cliffs, NJ: Prentice-Hall.

Schuman, D. (1976). *Bureaucracies, organization, and administration: A political primer.* New York: Macmillan.

Seidman, S. (1986). *Politics, position, and power: The dynamics of federal organization.* New York: Oxford University Press.

Somers, H. M. (1965). The president, congress, and the federal government service. In W. Sayre (Ed.), *The federal government service: Its character, prestige, and problems* (2nd ed.) (pp. 70–113). Englewood Cliffs, NJ: Prentice-Hall.

Sorauf, F. J. (1960).The silent revolution in patronage. *Public Administration Review, 20,* 28–30.

U.S. Civil Service Commission. (1978). *Introducing the Civil Service Reform Act.* Washington, DC: U.S. Government Printing Office.

Van Riper, P. P. (1958). *History of the United States civil service.* New York: Harper and Row.

White, L. D. (1948). *The Federalists: A study in administrative history.* New York: Macmillan.

White, L. D. (1951). *The Jeffersonians: A study in administrative history 1801–1829.* New York. Macmillan.

3

Personnel System Design

Although everyone in an organization, especially the managers and supervisors, has personnel responsibilities, certain individuals or units have the primary function of developing and implementing personnel policies. The personnel function can rest with the chief executive officer or a personnel office ranging from a few people to a large complex bureaucracy. This chapter analyzes the various bases on which personnel activities can be organized and the alternatives for structuring the personnel function. First the chapter explores the function of the personnel office.

Personnel Office Roles

Personnel offices are often seen as negative policing agencies that make sure that operating departments obey rigid rules and procedures (Campbell, 1978; Nalbandian, 1981; Staats, 1976). As a result, many department managers view personnel units with suspicion and hostility rather than as a source of support and assistance. This attitude, though, is changing. The personnel office is supposed to be a service office for the rest of the organization. It performs what normally is referred to as a *staff function* as it helps line departments deliver their services to the public by supporting the departments in staffing and managing their workforce. Today personnel offices are expected to perform policing and monitoring roles and to provide service to line departments. Personnel offices are also expected to take a leadership role in formulating personnel policies for the entire agency (Ban, 2002; Pynes, 2008).

The personnel office's main service traditionally has been the recruitment of employees. The operating department notified personnel of its need for persons to fill vacancies. The personnel office then advertised and screened applicants and administered the appropriate exams to certify candidates for selection. Along with these duties, the personnel office updated position classification and compensation systems. Its audit and review functions meant policing departmental activities and often finding problems that had to be corrected. Any review of activities from outside the departments tended to produce anxiety and suspicion, and personnel offices created both, partly because they often emphasized abiding by "good" rules and regulations while ignoring the need to be flexible and to get things done, which is important to department managers (Coggburn, 2000; Kellough & Selden, 2003; Morse, 1976; Nigro & Kellough, 2008).

However, the role of personnel offices has changed and expanded greatly over time. Personnel offices are now expected to support all aspects of management. Public sector jurisdictions recognized the need to make personnel part of general management and emulated the private sector by integrating personnel into the overall management function. The ever-present fiscal constraints since the late 1970s have prodded public managers to include personnel administration in decisions involving the largest resource expenditure, the employees (human resources). The 1978 Civil Service Reform Act was predicated in large part on President Carter's promise to revamp management at all levels of the federal government. State and local government reforms were and continue to be motivated by similar concerns. The reforms brought the personnel management function into a strategic role, integrated with management to support operating departments in addition to monitoring their personnel activities

Because of the evolution in views of the personnel function, many more activities have become the province of the personnel office. Now it must deal with issues such as equity and discrimination, labor–management relations, retention and development of good employees, training, accommodating employees with disabilities and family leave. Reform efforts since 1978 have decentralized many personnel functions, leading to conflicts over the proper role of the central personnel agency and departmental personnel offices. In addition, concerns over the political responsiveness of public servants have created new issues. Especially important is the maintenance of effective services in times of fiscal restraint, which could mean borrowing practices from the private sector and contracting out services. The reinventing government and quality management movements have also focused attention on the role and processes of personnel management. As a result, personnel offices increasingly are playing strategic roles in overall management.

Types of Personnel Systems

Public personnel systems may vary based on the size and type of jurisdiction as well as the values important to the jurisdiction. For very small jurisdictions, the personnel function can be combined with other functions. For example, in villages, towns, or townships, the manager of the jurisdiction can perform all management functions including personnel. As the size of the jurisdiction increases, personnel can be the responsibility of a manager who also has budgeting and finance or other responsibilities. As size continues to increase, personnel specialists are often employed, and in large jurisdictions, full-fledged personnel (or human resources) staff are common. Very large jurisdictions have separate divisions or departments dealing with different aspects of personnel administration. Thus, among the various divisions there could be a human resources department, a labor relations department, and an equal opportunity employment office, among others.

The way personnel management functions also depends on the dominant values of the governmental jurisdiction. Most personnel systems in the United States value merit and competence; thus, merit principles are at the core of the systems. Nonetheless, other values are also important and can affect the way the organization functions. Fairness and equity are strong values of the U.S. political system and they are reflected in governmental personnel systems. Government agencies that have to deal with strong unions could have a separate organization to handle the collective bargaining. The civil rights and women's movements have had a significant impact on most public personnel systems as reflected in the creation of programs and organizational units to deal with issues of equality and nondiscrimination.

Historically, public bureaucracies have been conceptualized variously as guardian, caste, patronage/spoils, merit, welfare, affirmative action, and labor–management dominated (Klinger, 2003; Marx, 1957). Each of these approaches supports different societal values and illustrates how the personnel function can be organized to serve the values.

The **guardian bureaucracy** is based on a predetermined selection process in which the guardians protect the good and right. Plato's *Republic* presents an example of the guardian approach to bureaucracy. The rulers' bureaucracy maintains the system, which reflects the good society. However, determining who is born to rule is not easy. The **caste bureaucracy**, by contrast, offers a simpler method of choosing the members of the bureaucracy. People are born into a social caste, and only those in the higher caste can rule. Thus, the system normally reflects society's structure. Traditionally societies and monarchies reflect these values.

Although the **patronage, or spoils system** of personnel management in the United States stems from the model associated with Jacksonian democracy, its underpinning values were part of administration from the beginning of our nation. All systems use it to some extent. In this system, a political leader or another patron rewards supporters by giving them jobs. Although merit can be taken into account, the primary consideration is whether the potential employee has worked or will work for the interests of those in power. Loyalty is the overriding value in this system. As explained in Chapter 2, many employees in the U.S. public service still are selected on the basis of patronage. Cabinet members and other high level officials are chosen through patronage as are members of regulatory and other independent agencies as well as the judiciary in many jurisdictions. The spoils system still operates in many state and local governments (Hamilton, 2002).

Merit personnel systems are predominant in the United States, at least in theory. Under the merit system, personnel decisions are based on specified standards, qualifications, and performance. Although most civil service systems are justified as being merit systems, merit and civil service systems are not synonymous. The major premises of the Weberian theory of bureaucracy (developed by the nineteenth-century German sociologist Max Weber) form the bases of merit personnel systems. This system is characterized by career service employees with fixed salaries, specified selection and training procedures, rules and regulations for all program activities, and evaluation of performance as parts of the personnel function.

Welfare and affirmative action personnel systems are founded, in part, on the idea that government employment is the answer to social problems. In the welfare-based approach, government serves as the employer of last resort for people who would not otherwise have jobs, lack skills, or are among the hard-core unemployed. The public service training employment programs such as the Job Training Partnership Act (JTPA) and Americorps are examples of such a system.

Similarly, **affirmative action personnel systems** are based on accomplishing a social purpose. Equal employment and affirmative action policies require that personnel policies consider people who had previously experienced discrimination. Affirmative action implies some preference for target groups, just as veterans' preference accords advantages to those with military service. Systems based on preferential treatment require that a person's membership in a specified group be taken into account in the employment decision. Other preferential considerations could involve citizenship and residency.

Labor–management–dominated systems are those in which personnel activities reflect values negotiated by labor and management. The labor agreement or contract can specify criteria for selection of employees, promotion, and discipline. The agreement also establishes procedures for conducting many of the personnel functions, particularly discipline and employee appeal procedures.

All of the values and systems discussed above except guardian and caste are part of most U.S. public personnel systems. Thus, it is unusual to find a system that reflects only one of the approaches. Each governmental unit determines which values or systems to put into practice. Merit and spoils dominate the discussion in this book because they are the two most commonly found in U.S. public personnel administration.

Organizing Personnel Activities

The structure of the personnel system in every jurisdiction is based on a legal framework. In many cases, the state constitution or local government charter spells out the major requirements for personnel operation such as the creation of a civil service commission or the appointment of a personnel or human resources director. There are usually provisions which state that the public service must be based on merit and provide for policy-making and implementation organizations. In the absence of or in addition to constitutional or charter provisions, laws or ordinances establish the system's legal foundation. Executive officers and civil service commissioners or the like may also issue rules and regulations that affect the personnel system structure. Normally, the constitutional or charter provision grants authority to the legislative body that then authorizes the personnel or civil service commission to issue rules and regulations.

Three key organizational questions must be considered in establishing a personnel system:

1. Is an independent personnel board or commission desirable? If so, what are its powers and functions?
2. Will a central personnel office carry out the personnel activities, or should each department perform its own personnel activities?
3. Should the final personnel authority rest with the chief executive, the legislature, or an independent personnel board or commission?

The answers to these questions depend on the needs of the jurisdiction. Naturally, the needs of a very small unit of government will not be the same as those of one with a large employee force. Similarly, jurisdictions with partisan political elections have expectations different from those of jurisdictions with nonpartisan elections. Each Jurisdiction must determine what works best.

A bipartisan or nonpartisan civil service commission or personnel board is the model that dominated public personnel administration at all levels of government in the United States after the adoption of such a system at the national level in 1883. Such agencies generally are responsible for personnel policy development and implementation. Furthermore, the civil service commission often serves as the appeals board of last resort for employees who claim to have been mistreated by their supervisors and managers. Although the commission commonly has overall responsibility for personnel functions, it cannot carry on day-to-day activities. Instead, an executive director is usually employed for that purpose. However, some systems, (e.g., New York State) designate a chairperson or president who is responsible for implementing personnel policies.

The main alternative to the independent commission is creating a central personnel office directly responsible to the chief executive and thus closely connected to the administration's management. The Civil Service Reform Act of 1978 created such an arrangement at the national level, with the Office of Personnel Management reporting to the president. Many state and local governments instituted similar reforms both before and after the national government did. This arrangement permits the personnel function to be a strategic player in the management of the organization. When a personnel office reports to the chief executive and supervises personnel administration, an appeals board normally is created to review employee appeals. The Merit Systems Protection Board at the national level serves this function. In some cases, a personnel board provides advisory services to the chief executive or legislative body and recommends personnel rules and regulations. New York City, Chicago, and Mesa, Arizona, use this approach, which is common in state and local government.

Another aspect of personnel organization pertains to whether the function is centralized in one department of personnel or decentralized among the agencies in the jurisdiction. Most systems combine both approaches. In a few places, such as Texas, individual departments still have a great deal of autonomy over most of their personnel activities.

The reform movement stimulated by the 1883 Civil Service Act led to the creation of central personnel offices in most large jurisdictions. After World War II, however, the trend was toward decentralizing implementation functions. Legislation such as the 1978 Civil Service Reform Act institutionalized this decentralization at the national level. Although central personnel agencies (for example, Office of Personnel Management) were created to make policy, develop programs, ensure compliance with policy, and provide technical assistance, operating departments have the day-to-day personnel responsibilities.

Centralizing the personnel function has many advantages. It provides for uniformity in dealing with personnel activities and permits a high degree of specialization in the technical aspects of these activities. Economies of scale also result when recruiting, examining, and the like are performed for a jurisdiction as a whole. Moreover, uniformity of policy and procedures helps management maintain consistency across departments when negotiating with unions. This is important because employee morale and productivity could suffer if individuals compare their position with others in the organization and feel unfairly treated.

There also are disadvantages to giving a central office all personnel responsibilities (Coggburn, 2000) Critics point out that centralized personnel offices tend to be out of touch with and unresponsive to the needs of the operating agencies. Indeed, many managers view the central personnel office as an outside force, not a support service. The personnel office also tends to deal with problems in a generic way, not from the perspective of the operating department and its needs. It is often difficult for it to adapt decisions to the particular situation of each department.

Under a decentralized system, each department has its own personnel officer and staff. The personnel policies and activities are likely to reflect the particular circumstances of the department or unit and are likely to vary across the jurisdiction. When each department is permitted to adapt policies and actions to its own needs, the personnel function tends to be integrated with the management of the department. The principal problems of the departmental personnel office model are the lack of uniformity among departments, the cost of duplicating activities in numerous agencies, fewer opportunities for specialization, and the absence of objectivity in handling personnel problems.

In most large jurisdictions, the extremes represented by the centralized and decentralized systems are ameliorated by combining the approaches. The central office has certain responsibilities, and officials in each department are responsible for daily personnel activities. Thus, the central office can focus on policy development, specialized expertise, monitoring, and review, and the departmental office can concentrate on carrying out the policy in the relevant setting. The departmental office can ask the central office specialist for help when it is needed. Central personnel offices are now likely to have liaisons to individual departments and to actually station a personnel staff member in large departments. With such an arrangement, the operating departments are more likely to see personnel policy as supportive of their activities.

The quality management and reinventing government movements of the 1980s and 1990s stimulated reforms in many personnel activities at all levels of government. The movements resulted in efforts to empower employees, an increase in labor–management cooperation, a shift in focus from inputs to results, and personnel becoming better aligned with their organization's mission. At the national level, these movements have also led to a reduction in the size of the federal workforce. Florida and Georgia went so far as to abolish their civil service systems. Clearly, reform strikes a chord with many critics of government performance, and the popular themes of reinvention and accountability provide a strong foundation for reform efforts.

As mentioned earlier, the 2010 election brought to office many governors and legislators who focused on reforming their state personnel systems in order to make public employees more accountable to elected leaders. As a result, states such as Wisconsin, Ohio, and Arizona passed legislation reforming their personnel systems. Reforms such as eliminating civil service protection for employees and thus making them at-will employees were popular. Eliminating collective bargaining was also a popular reform. However, the 2012 election slowed some of the efforts at reform as unions became very active in helping elect officials sympathetic to their cause.

As personnel policies have evolved, many new agencies have developed to deal with specialized human resources management functions. As noted, labor–management relations activities led to the creation of a separate agency, the Federal Labor Relations Authority, to manage labor relations at the national level. Similar organizations, usually called *public employee relations boards*, exist at the state and local levels (e.g., in Maine, Minnesota, and Los Angeles). Similarly, equal employment opportunity and affirmative action produced agencies in most jurisdictions to administer these policies. Training and development are the other functions often found in separately created units. Although these activities can take place outside the personnel office, they are still personnel functions and will be examined later in this book.

Career Systems

Different types of systems operate within the varied personnel structures. Political appointees and career civil servants represent two different systems that interact within the organization. Typically, political appointees oversee the career service employees. During the early part of every administration, the top-level political appointees promise major shake-ups in the career bureaucracy, but usually there is little change. Career bureaucrats provide the information and support needed for the programs desired by the agency or department head appointed by the elected chief executive. In most departments, the top administrator cannot risk the opposition of career civil servants. Accommodations are made, and the administrator usually follows the career servant's recommendations. When this does not happen, career servants often lobby for their positions before sympathetic legislative committees (Golden, 2000; Reed, 1978)

A political executive's career pattern differs from that of a career service executive in that the former's tenure in a position depends on the election cycle. If a new party wins the presidency, governorship, or mayoralty, for example, the political appointees normally change. Even if a party or administration is reelected, changes in emphasis and thus changes in personnel are likely. Loyalty to the current administration and its policy positions are also obligatory for political executives, and dismissal for disagreement is common.

Even more difficult for political executives is the fact that they could have the confidence of the chief executive but become a liability because of political considerations. For example, Securities and Exchange Commission Chair Harvey Pitt became an embarrassment to President George W. Bush. Although the president claimed Pitt had his full support (even as Pitt seemed to be allowing the financial industry to influence his decisions and to be withholding important information from other commission members) the president dumped him after the 2002 elections. Pitt was generating too much controversy. Of course, top political executives usually have no difficulty finding alternative work and fade into the background for a while only to reappear in a new administration. The George W. Bush administration brought back a number of high-level appointees from the previous Bush and Reagan administrations, including William

Ruckelshaus and Donald Rumsfeld. Barack Obama did the same thing, keeping Robert Gates, as Secretary of Defense from the previous administration. Even people discredited in one administration can show up later in another.

Career civil servants, of course, have protected tenure, so accordingly, they continue from one administration to the next. Within that career system, however, are what are referred to as *open* and *closed career systems*. Closed career systems are those in which high-level positions are filled entirely through promotion from below. To become a high-level official within the organization, a person must begin at the bottom and advance up through the hierarchical ladder. The military, FBI, Foreign Service, police and fire departments and British civil service use such a system. The military is the strictest; with some exceptions, the others usually require experience at a lower level of the organization in order to attain a higher rank.

An *open system* means that positions are filled through competition from both inside and outside the organization. Sometimes called *lateral entry,* the open system allows employees to enter an organization at any level. Open systems are supposed to make an organization more dynamic by bringing in people with fresh ideas and approaches, thus eliminating the stagnation often created by the culture and socialization processes within the organization. However, in practice, most systems that are technically open—as in the case of most government jurisdictions—usually lean toward the closed system approach. Employees and employee organizations often prefer closed systems. Consequently, many collective bargaining agreements call for promotion on the basis of seniority, which is a closed system approach. High-level managers often are more comfortable with a closed system because it allows them to deal with known quantities in selecting staff. People from below can be chosen according to how well they get along in the organization, whereas someone from outside the organization is an unknown quantity.

Closed systems also usually include an up-or-out feature. *Up-or-out*, or *selection-out*, refers to the situation in which a person is either (1) expected to qualify for promotion within a certain period of time or (2) must achieve a particular performance level. If the promotion or performance level is not attained, the person is asked to resign or is dismissed. The military and foreign service use this process, and academic departments in most colleges and universities employ a less-strict version Another version of the up-or-out system in the federal service is called the Senior Executive Service (SES) which requires achievement of a particular performance level in order to remain in the service.

The Senior Executive Service represents another type of personnel system. Although the national government's SES, formalized in law by the Civil Service Reform Act of 1978, is the most visible, several states actually preceded the national government in experimenting with this concept. The basic purpose of the SES is to permit flexibility in using the talents of high ranking administrators. The following are the objectives of such programs:

1. Offer managers opportunities to use talented administrators where they can contribute the most
2. Offer talented administrators opportunities to broaden their perspectives through wider experiences
3. Improve communication across organizational units
4. Improve the image of public service and thus make recruitment and retention of competent administrators easier
5. Improve administrators' performance by rewarding them for outstanding performance

The success of SES is debatable. Evaluative studies differ in their conclusions concerning its effectiveness.

Another way of structuring the personnel system is choosing between *rank-in-person* or *rank-in-job*. Rank-in-person means that the individual is evaluated and ranked according to his or her personal qualifications and performance. Compensation and other benefits are based on the person's rank, regardless of the duties performed. Qualifications such as education and experience also help determine the rank. Military, police, and fire departments use rank-in-person systems as do academic faculties. Personnel at different ranks can perform similar activities, but they are paid differently because of their ranks. Thus, for example, an assistant professor and a full professor perform the same basic functions (i.e., teaching, research, and public service), but they receive very different levels of pay. Of course, performance expectations within each of these ranks are also different. The Senior Executive Service is a variation of the rank-in-person system.

The *rank-in-job system* means that the organization is structured around the work to be done and the basic structural unit is the position. Thus, position classification is a key aspect of rank-in-job systems. Jobs (positions) are arranged in a hierarchy, and compensation is based on where the job fits in the organization's hierarchy. Most public sector organizations are based on the rank-in-job concept. Thus, regardless of the education, experience, or seniority of the individual, the compensation for that individual is based on the position she or he holds.

The rank-in-job and the closed system often produce problems in dealing with good employees because the only way to advance in salary and prestige and acquire other badges of success is to move up through the hierarchy. People are thus rewarded for effective service by promotion to supervisory and managerial positions. These jobs, however, require different skills, and often those good at doing the organization's tasks are not good at managing or supervising others. As a result, some people suggest that a dual-track or multitrack career system would permit the rewarding of individuals for good technical performance and would provide for promotion within the managerial ranks for those with management skills. Dual and multitrack systems have not caught on to a great extent in the public service, but they represent a way to alleviate the problems created by the pressures for promotion common in our society as they allow people to focus on what they do best and get rewarded for that without having to become supervisors.

Since the 1970s, government increasingly has partnered with private sector organizations, both for profit and nonprofit, to deliver public services. The result is another twist on the organization of the public personnel function. Government agencies (sometimes their personnel office) have become managers and monitors of employee contracts. One part of managing the contracts has been monitoring aspects of their personnel activities. Government partnership agreements and contracts usually include provisions regarding personnel activities. Provisions commonly include equal employment policies and labor protections for those employed by the partner or contractor. In recent years, some jurisdictions have required a minimum level of benefits for employees of partners or contractors as well. These arrangements raise concerns that public employees are treated differently than employees of private-sector partners and contractors which can also affect employee morale. Moreover, personnel functions themselves can be outsourced (Coggburn, 2007, The Conference Board, nd)

Intergovernmental Personnel Issues

One of the most significant factors affecting the development of state and local government personnel systems has been the variety of federal government requirements imposed on jurisdictions receiving federal funds. Stemming from the Social Security Act of 1935 through the proliferation of categorical grant-in-aid programs during the 1950s, 1960s, and 1970s, state and local governments have been prodded to use merit principles for programs funded by federal monies. State and local officials often criticized federal government requirements as being onerous and costly, but the requirements also have been credited with improving many personnel systems across the country (Greene, 1982). At present, all states except Texas have statewide systems, most of which are direct results of the federal government's requirements although some agencies can be exempted. In 1981, the Reagan administration succeeded in ending many federal government personnel conditions associated with grants, but general requirements related to equal employment opportunity, nondiscrimination, and employee rights still exist or have been broadened through nonfunded federal mandates.

If left to the states and local governments, policies protecting equal employment opportunity, older workers, people with disabilities, and other groups would be difficult to ensure in all places. Thus, affected groups still look to the federal government for protection.

Summary

The personnel function requires that jurisdictions develop structures appropriate to their needs and resources. Systems vary according to the concerns and values important to the particular governmental jurisdiction. Thus, in organizing personnel activities, governments must consider whether they wish to base the system on merit, patronage, or a social purpose. Questions about who should have the authority for personnel activities also must be addressed. Generally, a jurisdiction must create a structure and develop policies that best keep the system responsive to the public while finding and using the best talent available. All of these concerns also depend on resource availability.

Exercises

1. The Town of New Hope was created after some residents of Hope felt that they were not being represented fairly and seceded from the city and incorporated their own town. The town council must develop the structure for its government and has turned to you for recommendations for its human resources function.

Of course, the system must be consistent with the state constitution and laws. The council also wants the system to be based on the merit system but wants it to be responsive to the council and citizens as well.

> Draft your recommendations to the town council. Include a basic personnel policy statement. Describe the system's structure. Justify your recommendations. Assume that the town has a weak mayor system.

2. Your county government still operates with an organization that was created in the late nineteenth century. There are five county supervisors each of whom represents a specific district or precinct in the county. They elect one of their own to be chair of the Board of Supervisors, but the chair has few powers. Each county supervisor has the authority to appoint employees who provide many services in their individual supervisory districts. As a result, some districts have large turnover because their supervisors rarely win reelection. In other districts, the staff remains the same because the same supervisors are returned to office regularly. In addition, several county officers (for example, county sheriff, county attorney, county assessor) are elected independently and have their own personnel rules and procedures for their offices.

The county voters have elected to create a task force on county reform and it has hired you to help with recommendations on personnel reform since you are a national expert on county personnel matters.

What issues would you want to consider in developing the recommendations? What are the political realities you would have to consider? What would be the basic outline of your recommendations? Provide a justification for them.

3. Jason Cosby was the city manager of Webley for six years when he was fired by the city council. Jason was not given a reason for his termination but surmised it was because three of the newly elected members of the five member council were concerned that he was too old and no longer seemed to think creatively. Jason decided to sue the city council to get his job back.

You are advising Jason about his options. What would you want to know about the situation before you recommended that he go forward with his suit? Do you think Jason is likely to have a case? Explain your rationale.

4. Interview someone in state government who serves at the pleasure of the governor. Then interview someone who is in the covered civil service. In your interviews, ask about the interviewees' sense of job security. Also ask about how the political appointee views those with civil service protection who work for him or her. Ask the civil servant how he/she views those who are political appointees.

What do your interviews tell you about the relationship between political appointees and civil servants? Do you think there should be both types of positions in the public service? Explain your response.

Selected Websites

International City/County Management Association (ICMA). Membership organization of local governments with council manager forms that publishes materials on best forms and practices in local government.

www.icma.org

National Academy of Public Administration (NAPA). Organization for public administration similar to the National Academy of Sciences that publishes reports on improving government including the public service.

www.napawash.org

National Association of State Personnel Executives (NASPE). Membership organization of state managers responsible for personnel administration. Publishes a newsletter and reports dealing with the structure and processes of personnel management. Focuses on innovative policies and practices.

www.naspe.net

National League of Cities (NLC). Membership organization of local governments that publishes materials on and assists local governments in providing quality services to their citizens including human resources issues.

www.nlc.org

Office of Personnel Management (OPM). Agency responsible for managing human resources for the national government. Publishes guides and information on personnel practices and organization.

www.opm.gov

References

Ban, C. (2002). The changing role of the personnel office. In C. Ban & N.M. Riccucci (Eds.), *Public personnel management: Current concerns, future challenges* (pp. 8–25). New York: Longman.

Campbell, A.K. (1978). Revitalizing the federal personnel system. *Public Personnel Management, 7,* 58–63.

Coggburn, J.D. (2000). Is deregulation the answer for public personnel management? Revisiting a familiar question. *Review of Public Personnel Administration, 20,* 4–8.

Coggburn, J.D. (2007). Outsourcing human resources: The case of the Texas Health and Human Services Commission. *Review of Public Personnel Administration, 27,* 315–335.

The Conference Board (n.d.). *HR outsourcing in government organizations: Emerging trends, early lessons.* New York: The Conference Board.

Golden, M.M. (2000). *What motivates bureaucrats? Politics and administration during the Reagan years.* New York: Columbia University Press.

Hamilton, D.K. (2002). Is patronage dead? The impact of antipatronage staffing systems. *Review of Public Personnel Administration, 22,* 3–26.

Kellough, J.E. & Selden, S.C. (2003). The reinvention of public personnel administration: An analysis of the diffusion of personnel management reforms in the states. *Public Administration Review, 63,* 165–176.

Klingner, D.E. (2003). Competing perspectives on public personnel administration. In S.W. Hays & R.C. Kearney (Eds.), *Public personnel administration: Problems and prospects* (4th ed.) (pp. 16–28). Upper Saddle River, N.J.: Prentice-Hall.

Marx, F.M. (1957). *The administrative state.* Chicago: University of Chicago Press.

Nalbandian, J. (1981). From compliance to consultation: The changing role of the public personnel administrator. *Review of Public Personnel Administration, 1,* 37–51.

Nigro, L.G. & Kellough, J.E. (2008). Personnel reform in the states: A look at progress fifteen years after the Winter Commission. *Public Administration Review, 68,* S50–S57.

Reed, L. (1978). The bureaucracy: The cleverest lobby of them all. *Washington Monthly, 10,* 49–54.

Staats, E.B. (1976). Personnel management: The starting place. *Public Personnel Management, 5,* 424–441.

4

Techniques of Personnel Administration

Various instruments, procedures, and techniques are used to carry out personnel functions. These activities represent the mainstream of traditional personnel management and remain important components of public personnel administration. Among the instruments of personnel management discussed in this chapter are human resource planning, position classification, compensation, and strategies for controlling compensation costs. Chapter 5 addresses recruitment, examinations, selection, promotion, performance evaluation, and discipline of employees.

Human Resources Planning

Planning has become a mainstay of public sector organizations and human resource systems are an integral part of the planning process. Strategic planning, which focuses on the way an organization relates to its environment and relates all activities to achieving the organizational mission, has emerged as a basic tool of government. Strategic planning requires an organization to identify its goals clearly and examine alternative means for achieving them. Then, after considering the internal and external environments, the organization chooses appropriate methods and establishes processes for accomplishing its goals. A major consideration must be, what resources, including human resources, are needed and what resources are available for the effort.

Human resources planning (also referred to as *human capital planning*) is critical for agencies to understand what their human resources needs are and how they can attain those resources (International Personnel Management Association, 2002; Jacobsen, 2010; Johnson & Brown, 2004; Perry, 1993). Agencies need to assess what types of employees they need to accomplish their goals and then assess their workforce to see how they fit those needs. Thus, it is necessary to know what future needs are likely to be and what the labor market will be like. Once human resources managers understand the changes that will affect them in the future, they need to do some action planning to guide them in overcoming future challenges. For example, if they find that they are going to need highly skilled information technology specialists and there is a shortage of them in their own workforce and in the labor market generally, they need to plan ways to overcome these shortages. The action plans may include ways to train their own workers to fill the need or they may plan to change their recruitment approach, adapt their compensation packages, or restructure their jobs to attract suitable employees. The objective of strategic planning and management is to identify future needs and to take action to fill those needs. Public human resources management traditionally did little long-range planning. Instead, it reacted to crises or just depended upon the labor market to meet its needs. The traditional view was that there was appropriate labor in the market to meet the needs of the public employer. With the rapid changes in technology and occasional labor shortages, human resources managers have had to become much more proactive.

With a large number of employees expected to retire from the public service in the near future, a major concern is how to replace those retirees without interrupting organizational activities. Some projections suggest that nearly 30% of federal government employees are eligible for retirement by 2016 and that many public employers will lose as much as 50% of their workforces to retirement by 2016 (Center for State & Local Government Excellence, 2009; U.S. Government Accountability Office, 2012). The aging of the workforce and early retirement incentives are making it difficult to keep positions filled. On the other side of the coin, cutbacks in the late 1970s, in the early 2000s, and again in 2010–2012 have created the need for the opposite type of planning. How do you plan your reductions-in-force? Do employers use reverse seniority, or do they use performance criteria? These are the kinds of questions that call for careful planning.

Faced with the need to determine the wisest use of human capital, personnel professionals and line managers have had to engage in continuous human resource planning. In the planning process, they consider forecasts of personnel needs in terms of both numbers and the knowledge and skills needed. In addition to personnel capacity, financial resources are critical. Depending on the availability of needed knowledge and skills in the labor market, planning for training and development is necessary. Planning for human resource development is also essential to ensure that the existing workforce remains up to date. In reality, human resource planning contributes to the effectiveness of all aspects of the personnel process. Without knowing the organization's personnel needs, managers cannot anticipate and plan for all the other decisions and processes associated with maintaining a competent and effective workforce.

Though the need for planning seems obvious, public managers often find it difficult to do. Of course, political and other considerations may constrain the amount of planning that can be done. Sudden shifts in political values or priorities can also destroy plans. During the 1960s and early 1970s, for example, government employment increased dramatically, especially at the state and local levels. As a result, it was expected that there would be continued growth and a need for more employees. Most jurisdictions therefore were unprepared for the radical change that came with the tax revolts and the passage of tax reduction and limitation laws inspired by Proposition 13 in California in 1978. With financial resources suddenly and drastically reduced, governments had to start planning how to reduce, rather than increase, payrolls. Similarly, the economic boom of the 1990s left state and local governments with surpluses, but by 2001 with the economy in distress, tax revenues dropped. Most state and local level jurisdictions faced increasing demands for social services but saw their revenues dwindle. Budget cuts led to cuts in human resources, and planning once again had to reverse directions to accommodate reductions-in-force yet maintain or increase service levels. The same phenomenon arose with the recession of 2007–2009 and the election of 2010 which resulted in the election of officials committed to cutting government at the same time that the economy slowed.

Workforce planning is usually not a priority for public managers when they have to face the daily demands of citizens and others interested in their activities. Indeed, planning of any kind in government is often difficult because of the lack of stability in the tenure of elected officials; when elected leaders change, so do many of the system's priorities. Thus, plans can quickly become obsolete. Government cutbacks have not produced significant evidence that planning is any greater a part of public personnel management now than it was before (Johnson, 1982; Johnson and Brown, 2004). Clearly, planning could be a significant aspect of all personnel management activities, but there are very few public managers who support much planning.

Position Classification

Position classification is a cornerstone of the traditional approach to personnel management and is still the basis on which most public personnel systems are built. In their efforts to make the system fair and just, civil service advocates need to be able to compare all the jobs in an organization. Position classification provides that mechanism and helps managers determine the pay level of any position in accordance with its relative importance. The process describes the duties and responsibilities of each position in the organization and groups the positions into classes in accordance with their similarities. The classification system's main objective is to permit management to make the most rational decisions about the relationship of duties and responsibilities to the other concerns of personnel administration. For instance, a fair compensation plan requires an understanding of the demands of each position, effective examination and recruiting require knowing what the agency is examining and recruiting for, and determining the qualifications necessary for performing a job requires understanding what the job entails. Position classification evolved as a convenient and useful tool and an extension of the Scientific Management School's focus on efficiency and economy. It offers a rational and efficient approach to organizing activities in a hierarchy.

Also contributing to the development of position classification was the growing public outcry over the spoils system which resulted in the creation of the Civil Service Commission in 1883. The commission was set up to establish a means of making personnel decisions on the basis of objective considerations rather than on personal and political factors. For the Civil Service Commission to reform the chaotic federal pay system of the late nineteenth and early twentieth centuries and establish practical examinations, it needed to have some idea of position duties and responsibilities. These factors led to pressure for reform. In democratic societies, equal pay for equal work is a readily accepted slogan, at least in the abstract. To apply the principle, positions must be evaluated and classified to establish a basis for comparison. Thus the movement toward comprehensive position classification arose from the desire for equality and was reinforced by the increasing complexity of technology and specialization. The fact that it also facilitated the managing of positions and people enhanced its appeal.

Position classification originated in the United States, and it is used more extensively in this country than in other nations. Partly as a response to good government movements and partly from concern for fairness and equity, the city of Chicago created position classification in 1909, and many state and local governments followed suit (Civil Service Assembly, 1941; Naff, 2002). The national government initiated position classification in the federal service with the passage of the Classification Act of 1923. The Civil Service Commission acquired responsibility for the process in 1932, and the Classification Act of 1949 authorized the delegation of responsibility for classification to operating departments and agencies. The commission (now the Office of Personnel Management) retained monitoring authority to ensure uniformity in the process.

Job Analysis

To develop the position classification system requires a job analysis. Job analysis is the process of collecting information about the tasks a job requires to be performed and the knowledge, skills, and abilities necessary to perform the tasks. The analysis identifies the exact activities of the job and the conditions under which the job is performed. It also identifies the qualifications necessary for successful performance.

Job analysis is conducted in various ways. The incumbent of the job may be asked to describe the duties and responsibilities of the job. The employee may be asked to fill out a questionnaire and/or to be interviewed by the job analyst. A variation on this process is to ask the employee to keep a diary of his or her activities over a two- or three-week period. Because employees are the most knowledgeable about their specific duties and responsibilities, their input is important. In this process, the incumbent employee has the opportunity to explain exactly what he or she does and how much time typically is spent on each activity. The employee is also asked to explain the level of independence and supervision involved in the job as well as interactions with other personnel, parts of the organization, or clientele. However, the employee may think that particular activities are unimportant or may exaggerate the importance of other activities. Thus, it is important to include the supervisor's views in the collection of information.

The same information may be collected from the incumbent's supervisor. The supervisor may review the employee's description of activities or may be asked to explain independently what the subordinate does and what levels of independence and supervision he or she has. Similarly, the supervisor is asked to explain how the position or job fits with the rest of the organization. Again, this information can be collected through a questionnaire or interview or both. The supervisor's perspective is important, but supervisors may not always be aware of some activities or the extent to which some activities dominate the job.

The job analyst may also observe the incumbent employee in performance of the duties. Direct observation is common in reclassification requests. Direct observation allows the analyst to see how the job actually is done and to gauge the relationship among the various tasks. It also has limitations, however, in that the employee may be affected by the presence of the analyst and perform differently. Additionally, no employee is likely to perform all the tasks of a job in a specified period of time. Some tasks come at particular times of the day, week, or year. Direct observation will miss some of them.

Job analysis may also involve collecting information from other organizations that perform the same functions and tasks. This is especially true in situations in which new agencies or departments are created. Reviewing how other jurisdictions and agencies perform the same tasks can be helpful in understanding a job.

Effective job analysis requires a combination of these approaches. By using all of them, the analyst can capitalize on the strengths of each and reduce the impact of the weaknesses of each. Relying on the various techniques for collecting the information lends balance to the data.

Position Description

From a job analysis, a position description is created. The position description is the basic building block of the position classification system. A position is described in terms of its duties, responsibilities, complexity, working conditions, and skills requirements called *job factors*. In traditional position classification systems—variously called *whole job ranking* and *grade description*—positions are described according to the degree to which each factor is present. The rankings of positions within the system are then determined on the basis of the differences among positions. The rankings may be made by a panel of classifiers or by a classification specialist in the personnel agency or operating department. Grades and classes are established in order to differentiate positions within similar groupings of positions. For example, word processers represent a class of positions and Word Processor I, Word Processor II, Word Processor III, and so on, represent grades within a class.

Another method of differentiating positions, the point-factor comparison system, relies on quantification. The same job factors may be used, but points are assigned to each factor in each job description. Then the points are weighted for each factor according to how dominant they are in the job, and then the points are added together. The total points represent the point-factor comparisons for each position. The points then are used to distinguish among positions within a class or throughout the organization. The point-factor comparison method is attractive to those who believe that position classification based on quantification reduces subjectivity. The problem is that subjectivity is only transferred. Now the subjectivity rests in the points assigned to each factor rather than in the decision about the relative place of the position in the organizational hierarchy. Nonetheless, using panels for rating factors helps validate the ranking system.

Whichever approach is used, the operating agency or department needs to be closely involved in the classification process,
as it knows its unit's tasks best. However, it is also necessary
to monitor the classification process to ensure that there are
no abuses, and especially to protect against overclassification
(Penner, 1983). Supervisors and managers gain status according
to the number and level of positions they supervise. Thus, they
have an incentive to upgrade the classification of their subordinates' positions to inflate the importance of the unit and their
own jobs. Another problem is that people often become locked
into a level of pay, and the only way to increase their pay is to
upgrade their positions. Although position classification is not
supposed to be used for this purpose, frustrated managers often
see no other way of rewarding good and loyal employees.

Regardless of the reasons for overclassification, the problem
requires remedial action. Central personnel offices generally
monitor the classification process. In most cases, the positions
may be reviewed at any time, but most audits are done in response to an agency or employee request. Most personnel systems also do a periodic review. The typical approach is to review
each agency's classification plan at regular intervals, but some
systems review occupation groups across all agencies. Reviewing a complete plan aids in comparing the different positions in
an agency, and reviewing similar positions across departments
helps standardize classes of positions. In the latter system, the
importance of any type of position may be exaggerated because
it is the focus of evaluation and the relationship to other positions is often neglected.

Monitoring position classification can put personnel administrators in a difficult situation. The internal political considerations of agency behavior and the concerns of individual employees make downgrading a position classification particularly
problematic (Naff, 2003; Schulkind, 1976). Monitors who attempt
to lower a classification are viewed as indifferent to the individual's welfare and as a threat to the agency manager's ability to
control his or her operation. Moreover, the employee union or association is likely to get involved as well. Given the alignment of
opposition to downgrading classifications, it is no surprise that
classification auditors tread lightly before taking such action.

The task of position classification comes under attack from many quarters and often represents the policing role personnel agencies are perceived to play. Managers of operating departments often see the classification process as one that inhibits them. Because traditional personnel offices tend to view classification as an end in itself rather than as an administrative means to support management, their efforts at classification are often met by resistance from departmental management. Similarly, the strategic planning process, with its focus on mission and goals, seems to be inconsistent with traditional position classification, which focuses on the position as the building block. The strategic planning process puts pressure on classification systems to be more flexible and to continually examine how the positions and classifications relate to the purpose for which the organization exists.

One attempt at dealing with the tendency of department managers to want to overclassify positions is the average grade approach. In such a system, all positions in an organization are assigned points according to their class, grade, and salary level (DeSanto, 1980). The sum of points for all positions in the organization then becomes a base for the organization. When an employee leaves a position, the points assigned to that position may be reallocated among other positions in the unit. Thus, for example, a Data Entry Operator I may be assigned three points, a Data Entry Operator II seven points, and a Data Entry Operator III ten points. If a Data Entry Operator III resigns, the unit will have ten points to redistribute. There are several possibilities for this redistribution. Depending on financial resources available, a new Data Entry Operator I and a new Data Entry Operator II may be hired. Or, the Data Entry Operator II may be promoted a grade, using three of the points, and then another II may be appointed to use the remaining seven points. Of course, the department manager will have other positions with other point values within the organization and may distribute the points among them. The advantage is that the manager has flexibility in recognizing employee contributions and using the points to reward them and realign positions in the organization to adapt to its changing needs.

The position classification system described above is known as the *rank-in-job* approach to organizing positions. An alternative is the *rank-in-person* approach, in which jobs are differentiated on the basis of incumbent employees. The rank-in-job system uses the individual employee's abilities, credentials, and experience as the basis for making personnel decisions, particularly on compensation. Personnel decisions in this system tend to be more subjective than are those in rank-in-job systems. Moreover, subordinates find it difficult to accept comparisons with other employees when they cannot see the whole picture. Criteria for making decisions are much less clear than they are in the position classification approach. In contemporary results oriented public administration, this system is viewed as holding managers more accountable because they have to provide justification for their personnel decisions based on outcomes. Employees do not always see it that way and they fear favoritism.

Rank-in-person systems appear to be most appropriate for professional personnel who are accustomed to being evaluated on the basis of their expertise, education, and other credentials. The military, police and fire departments, and academic departments typically use rank-in-person systems. The rank goes with the individual regardless of what particular tasks she or he is doing.

In reality, the position classification (rank-in-job) and rank-in person approaches tend to be combined. It is almost impossible to conceive of a position classification system in which the incumbent does not influence the classification. Some of the abuses of the system, such as overclassification, result from supervisors taking into consideration the needs and qualities of the incumbent in the position. Each employee brings different capabilities to the position, and each may expand or contract its scope of duties and responsibilities. The average grade approach is an example of intentionally mixing the systems.

Critiques of the traditional classification system abound (Ban, 1991; Cipola, 1999; National Academy of Public Administration, 1991; Risher, 2012; Thompson, 1976). The system is rigid, making it slow to adapt to the changing environment and changing personnel needs. Money is wasted on maintaining and monitoring the system, depriving managers of the flexibility to deploy those resources where they can be used most effectively for the organization.

Broadbanding is an alternative to the traditional classification system that combines similar jobs at various levels into broader groupings. The broader groupings are called *bands*. In some systems the groups are referred to as *job families*. Figure 4.1 on the next page, is an example from a recommendation by the National Academy of Public Administration (NAPA) resulting from its study of the national government classification system. NAPA recommended broadbanding the federal government's classification system of 459 occupational groupings into 22 categories in 10 occupational families (National Academy of Public Administration, 1991). The model shifts the focus from the work of the individuals to the work of the organization. The occupational families are grouped on the basis of similarities in "career progression, basic skills, recruitment, training, and performance management" (National Academy of Public Administration, 1991, p. 44). As Figure 4.1 indicates, the families are as follows: (1) Officer Services, (2) General Support, (3) Technical, (4) Administration, (5) Analysis, (6) Engineering, (7) Sciences, (8) Health, (9) Law enforcement, and (10) Other. Within the families, agencies could adapt to the uniqueness of particular occupations by developing more specific series. The figure also demonstrates another feature, the fact that the bands cover broader pay ranges than do typical position classes. The broadbanding approach permits agency managers more flexibility in assigning specific tasks and managing the financial resources of the agency assigned to personnel functions. NAPA has continued to recommend reform in the classification system at the national level, but so far with little effect (National Academy of Public Administration, 1995).

Though alternative approaches continue to be suggested, position classification is likely to retain its hold on most public personnel systems. Most bureaucracies are still organized according to the traditional hierarchy and position classification is a natural complement to that form of organization (French & Goodman, 2012; Whalen & Guy, 2008). Personnel administrators and department managers are likely to resist innovations that require less convenient criteria for making personnel decisions.

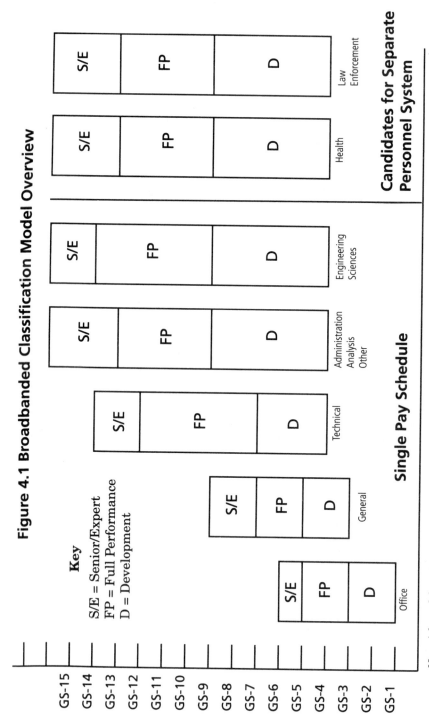

Figure 4.1 Broadbanded Classification Model Overview

Key

S/E = Senior/Expert
FP = Full Performance
D = Development

Note. Adapted from "Modernizing Federal Classification: An Opportunity for Excellence," (p. 45) by National Academy of Public Administration, 1991, Washington, DC.

Job Design

Job design is the process of deciding how to structure the job factors that are included in a particular job. It is closely related to position description, but is more than that. Position description merely explains what the position is. Job design is the actual creation of the content of the position. It is important to the discussion of classification because it can have an impact on the effectiveness of the whole system by keeping employees motivated and interested in their jobs. Narrowly defined positions often become repetitive, boring, and demotivating. Effective job design can eliminate such problems by making a job challenging and giving employees as much discretion as possible. Recognizing that behavioral concerns such as employee needs, motivation, and environment are as important to job performance as are assigned duties, contemporary human resource managers attempt to incorporate these concerns into job design.

Consider an office responsible for monitoring the receipt of sales tax monies. If one position deals only with receiving monies, another with recording receipts, a third with checking records, and a fourth with follow-up investigations, employees will likely become bored with their repetitive tasks. If, however, they are assigned to particular accounts and are responsible for all the activities associated with those accounts, they are likely to find their jobs more interesting and challenging.

Qualification Requirements

A direct result of the classification and job design processes is the development of qualification standards. These are the qualities an individual must possess in order to perform the duties and meet the responsibilities of a position. Because qualification standards are pertinent to the recruitment process, they will be discussed more fully in our treatment of that topic.

Compensation

Compensation is the financial reward individuals receive for
their work in an organization. It consists of direct salary and
wages (pay) and benefits such as vacation, sick leave, a retirement pension, and health insurance. Direct pay and benefits together constitute what is called *total compensation*. In the public
sector, compensation is always a major issue because taxpayers
want to make sure that their tax money is not wasted. Public
employee compensation represents a major expense to taxpayers and is an easy target when citizens become upset with government. Public managers are concerned with compensation because it affects their ability to recruit and retain employees and
to influence employee behavior in the organization through rewards. Employees are concerned for obvious reasons. Compensation, especially direct pay, becomes a sensitive issue if any group
perceives itself to be under-remunerated. Employee morale, in
particular, is affected when employees feel that their pay is not
equitable and appropriate.

As with all other features of the personnel system, a jurisdiction's basic policy normally establishes guidelines for compensation. For example, legislatures usually have the authority to
set compensation. However, because they always are pressed for
time and generally prefer not to get into the details of pay scales,
they usually delegate the authority to the executive branch
which relies on recommendations from the civil service board
or personnel agency. Thus, the executive branch commonly pro-
poses compensation plans and makes recommendations to the
legislative body for its final approval. Of course, in state and local governments that bargain over pay, compensation levels are
established through negotiation between management and employee representatives.

Political leaders and citizens tend to focus on the costs of public personnel. Because personnel costs typically make up three
quarters or more of government expenditures, it is easy to single
out the public bureaucrat as the culprit in government spending.
Given the image of the public bureaucracy, taxpayers are easily
swayed by politicians who rail against the bureaucracy. In the
past, public employees were perceived as underpaid compared
with their counterparts in the private sector. Now, however, many

public employees fare well relative to others, especially if benefits are included in the comparison. Although top managers in the public sector lag far behind their private sector counterparts, employees in the middle and lower levels often do better than do comparable employees in the private sector. However, there is great variation from jurisdiction to jurisdiction, with many trailing far behind the private sector and others paying their employees comparatively well. In the federal government, the Federal Salary Council consistently recommends large increases for federal employees based on its annual comparability studies, which reveal a significant gap between federal and private sector pay (Federal Salary Council, 2012; Yoder, 2012). The Federal Salary Council has recommended a pay increase of 34 percent for federal employees in 2013 (Federal Salary Council, 2012; Davidson, 2012). At the same time, many critics complain that public employees are overpaid (federal employees by as much as 30–40 percent) and the issue gains saliency in election rhetoric (Davidson, 2012; Lunney, 2012; Reilly, 2012; Yoder, 2012).

Compensation Plans

Compensation or pay plans follow classification plans. As jobs are designed and organized, they are priced or put in the compensation plan. Using the differences established by describing and ranking positions, the pay plan establishes a pay rate on the basis of the position's classification. Theoretically, the resulting compensation plan reflects the relative value of positions to the organization. As explained later in this chapter, that assumption is not necessarily well-founded.

The pay plan typically has several ranges and steps within ranges, as illustrated by Table 4.1. Positions are placed in a specified pay range or ranges. Specific placement depends on factors such as the skill levels required, education, and experience. Over time, with satisfactory performance, the employee moves up steps in the pay range. Differentials between ranges and between steps within ranges normally are fixed at some percentage such as 3.5, 5, or 10 percent. Table 4.1 shows the pay schedule for federal employees.

Table 4.1 2012 Federal General Salary Schedule Table in Annual Pay

Annual Rates by Grade and Step

Grade	Step 1	Step 2	Step 3	Step 4	Step 5	Step 6	Step 7	Step 8	Step 9	Step 10	WGI*
1	17803	18398	18990	19579	20171	20519	21104	21694	21717	22269	varies
2	20017	20493	21155	21717	21961	22607	23253	23899	24545	25191	varies
3	21840	22568	23296	24024	24752	25480	26208	26936	27664	28392	728
4	24518	25335	26152	26969	27786	28603	29420	30237	31054	31871	817
5	27431	28345	29259	30173	31087	32001	32915	33829	34743	35657	914
6	30577	31596	32615	33634	34653	35672	36691	37710	38729	39748	1019
7	33979	35112	36245	37378	38511	39644	40777	41910	43043	44176	1133
8	37631	38885	40139	41393	42647	43901	45155	46409	47663	48917	1254
9	41563	42948	44333	45718	47103	48488	49873	51258	52643	54028	1385
10	45771	47297	48823	50349	51875	53401	54927	56453	57979	59505	1526
11	50287	51963	53639	55315	56991	58667	60343	62019	63695	65371	1676
12	60274	62283	64292	66301	68310	70319	72328	74337	76346	78355	2009
13	71674	74063	76452	78841	81230	83619	86008	88397	90786	93175	2389
14	84697	87520	90343	93166	95989	98812	101635	104458	107281	110104	2823
15	99628	102949	106270	109591	112912	116233	119554	122875	126196	129517	3321

Note. GS rates frozen at 2010 levels. Effective January 2012. Adapted from U.S. Office of Personnel Management http://www.opm.gov/oca/12tables/html/gs.asp *WGI = Within-grade increase

Once employees reach the maximum pay for a position, many jurisdictions provide *longevity pay*, called *loyalty pay* in some places. Longevity pay is a reward for employees who stay in a position for many years. They are valued by the organization because of their experience. Longevity pay provides increases typically after five, ten, and fifteen years and more. In some instances, the employee receives a bonus every year based on longevity. Employees must maintain satisfactory performance to receive longevity pay. As public sector organizations have focused more on performance and results, longevity pay has decreased in popularity.

Most formal compensation plans tend to be inflexible, and they can lead to abuses. In particular, supervisors try to reclassify positions as a way to increase the pay of good employees who reach the top of their pay range and who have no other way of receiving increases. The problem is exacerbated by fiscal stress, which often precludes pay increases or leads only to very small increases. Of course, promotions also lead to movement into new pay ranges for individual employees.

To overcome problems associated with the inflexibility of pay plans that use the range and step system, some employers have experimented with pay banding (French & Goodman, 2012; National Academy of Public Administration, 2003; Selden & Ingraham, 2001; Selden & Kellough, 2003; Whalen & Guy, 2008). As Figure 4.1 indicates, NAPA recommends a system in which most positions span multiple pay grades. Managers would have discretion in placing people at different stages in the pay band. Combined with effective performance reviews, this system could be used to pay individuals on the basis of performance as well.

The International Public Management Association for Human Resources (IPMA-HR) conducted a study in 2012 of public sector pay and found that 29 percent of the respondents in their survey use some form of variable pay, down from 45 percent in 2007 (International Public Management Association for Human Resources, 2012). Thus, many jurisdictions are not slavishly adhering to formal compensation plans. Instead, they are using some form of variable pay such as pay-for-performance, skill-based pay, competency-based pay, or gain-sharing. These approaches are explained later in this chapter as we look at adjusting pay. Numerous factors go into setting pay levels including comparability, collective bargaining, equity, and performance.

Comparability Pay

As noted above, the pay for a particular position should be based in part on the value of that position to the organization. Realistically, however, the labor market and collective bargaining play significant roles. The labor market plays its role through what is called *comparability pay* as well as through union bargaining strength. *Comparability* refers to the pay similar positions command in the relevant labor market. To determine the level of pay in the market, comparability studies are conducted. The national government uses a formal system in which a nationwide survey is conducted to provide data for establishing appropriate pay rates in the General Schedule. Most levels of government use some form of comparability, but the sophistication of the systems varies greatly. Some conduct formal surveys, but commonly, Department of Labor data and review of pay plans in other jurisdictions serve as the basis for the initial setting of pay and for decisions about the level of pay increases.

In some cases, especially in the national government, comparability pay may reflect differences among regions. Different employees doing the same job in Eloy, Arizona, and Boston, Massachusetts, find that the same rate of pay has dramatically different buying power because of the differential in the cost of living in the two places. Therefore, with the Federal Employees Pay Comparability Act of 1990, the national government adopted locality pay, in which adjustments are made to compensate for the higher cost of living in some places. The Federal Salary Council studies pay comparability and establishes *locality pay* rates. Some larger states also may differentiate between large urban and rural areas.

Comparability also has the potential to bring more equity between the public and private sectors. The benefits for lower- and middle-level public employees in larger jurisdictions generally have been better than for those for their private sector counterparts; although, top-level managers in the private sector normally have many more benefits and perquisites than do comparable employees in the public sector. In the past, comparability studies excluded benefits from the comparability formula. By focusing only on direct salary and wages, public employees have generally improved their status relative to that of private sector employees, because whereas their salaries have become more comparable, they continue to have better benefits packages. However, these inequities have been disappearing, as governments now include benefits in their comparability studies. Some critics suggest that comparability pay leads to never-ending increases in compensation costs.

Collective Bargaining

In organizations where collective bargaining exists, pay is often determined by negotiations. The federal government and many other jurisdictions preclude compensation from the formal bargaining process although pay certainly is discussed. Collective bargaining is used to establish pay for approximately two-thirds of public employees, as described in Chapter 8. In the collective bargaining process, prevailing wages for similar positions clearly are important to the negotiators. Other factors, such as the cost of living and availability of skills in the labor market, also affect the negotiations, as does the relative political power of the parties to the negotiations.

Adjusting Pay

Adjustments to compensation are made on a regular basis. Employees usually expect annual raises, but there is no assurance that this will happen. In most jurisdictions, the legislative body makes the basic policy decision on adjustments, but the details are left to administrators. Raises are usually given-across-the board or based on merit and/or performance. Increasingly, raises are skill- or competency-based or are based on gainsharing or other factors (Iberman, 2010; Risher & Wilder, 2007; Shareef, 1994; Waters, 2006).

Merit pay (often called *performance pay* or *pay-for-performance*) achieved prominence in the public sector during the 1990s. Elected public officials tend to like the concept and often hail it in election campaigns as a way to make sure public employees are productive and accountable. Research on merit pay and pay-for performance indicates that the concept retains strong support among governmental jurisdictions but has consistently failed to live up to expectations (Alonso & Lewis, 2001; Cohen & Murnane, 1985; Ingraham, 1993; Kellough & Lu, 1993; Perry, 1986; Weibel, Rost, Katja, & Osterloh, 2010). The reasons for the failure are many, including a lack of adequate planning and design of systems, lack of money to make rewards significant, and difficulties in designing specific performance criteria with which to differentiate individuals. Pay-for-performance became prominent at a time when most governments were experiencing fiscal stress and were forced to streamline and cut workforces; thus, morale was fragile. As governments have continued to cut taxes and expenditures, the morale problems persist.

Although it is difficult to find people opposed to the concept of paying on the basis of merit or performance, there are serious reservations when it comes to who is to define merit, what criteria are used, and how the merit money is to be distributed. Employees, and especially their unions, are concerned that if management determines the criteria and decides who will receive merit pay, the abuse of discretion will lead to favoritism and inequity. Legitimate concerns often become politicized. Some jurisdictions' policies allow only half of the employees (or fewer) to receive merit increases. Thus, a unit with productive employees would be penalized, as only a portion of its employees could receive merit increases whereas, theoretically, less productive employees in an unproductive unit could qualify for such increases. Moreover, because merit money may not be available every year, good employees could become demoralized as they are not rewarded for good work on a consistent basis. Obviously, the problems and inconsistencies of merit pay result from policy particulars, not from the concept itself. However, the mechanisms for implementing merit pay have contributed to problems and resistance to it by employees.

Merit pay may come in the form of an adjustment to an individual's base pay or as a one-time bonus for high-level performance. When it is added to the base, it becomes a permanent reward for past performance, and it can be costly as the employee's pay is permanently increased. A one-time bonus is used by the national government and increasingly by state and local governments. The advantages of the one-time bonus are that the merit pay is attached to a specific performance, and for individuals to receive it again, they must continue to perform at a high level. Thus, if merit pay is supposed to be a motivator, the bonus or reward system would seem to be the type of system that most closely ties pay to performance.

Gainsharing is another form of performance-based pay, but it is group based. Thus, members of high-performing groups share in the rewards. They are rewarded for the increased productivity of the group or the savings produced by the group's activities. Although gainsharing is relatively rare in the public sector, it is used in San Diego, California; Baltimore County, Maryland; Charlotte, North Carolina; Virginia Beach, Virginia; Seattle, Washington; and the U.S. Postal Service.

Skill-based pay (also known as *competency pay*) is another alternative that has been adopted by some organizations in the public sector (French & Goodman, 2012; International Public Management Association for Human Resources, 2012; Shareef, 1994). In this system, pay increases are based on the level, breadth, and types of skills employees have. Thus, they are paid according to what they can do and not necessarily on the basis of what they actually do on a regular basis. For example, employees may receive a premium in their pay for being able to speak different languages or for a specific computer skill. Public school teachers may receive extra pay for being able to teach math or science. Garland, Texas, the Virginia Transportation Department, and the State of North Carolina have adopted skill-based pay for some of their programs. Many school districts use competency or skill-based pay systems. However, in times of tight resources and taxpayer scrutiny of government, it is a hard sell to get legislative bodies to adopt skill-based pay. Legislatures are more interested in paying according to what employees actually do, however difficult that is to measure.

Gender Equity in Pay

A persistent problem in compensation is inequity in pay between jobs dominated by men and those dominated by women. Since the 1980s, efforts have been made to reduce these inequities. Advocates for comparable worth, or equal pay for equal work, call attention to the role of gender in determining the value placed on different jobs, and they note that discriminatory criteria often are incorporated into job evaluation systems (Arvey, 1986; Johansen, 1984; Neuse, 1982). As a result, classes of positions dominated by women or minorities are usually valued at a lower pay rate than are those dominated by white males. From the time of the passage of the Equal Pay Act of 1963 until the early 1980s, the median salary of women hovered around 60 percent of the median salary of men. Although pressure has been brought to bear on personnel systems to rectify discriminatory practices through legislative efforts, litigation, and collective bargaining, the results have been modest. Today, on average, women earn approximately 82 percent of what men earn (Corbett & Hill, 2012; Institute of Women's Policy Research, 2012). Women have turned to the courts hoping that they would resolve the issue.

In 2007, the U.S. Supreme Court ruled against the pay discrimination claim by Lily Ledbetter who was employed by Goodyear Tire and Rubber since 1979 and discovered in 1998 that she was paid between $500 and $1500 less per month than men in similar situations. She claimed discrimination under the 1964 Civil Rights Act. The court ruled that she sued too late, as the law required a claim within 180 days of the discrimination even though she did not know of the discrimination until 1998 (*Ledbetter* v. *Goodyear Tire and Rubber Co, Inc.,* 2007). The decision became an issue in the 2008 presidential campaign and Barack Obama promised to push for legislation to remedy the situation. The first piece of legislation he signed as president was the Lily Ledbetter Fair Pay Act in 2009. Although the law did not help Ledbetter, it changed things for future female employees.

On the more complex issue of *comparable worth,* the U.S. Supreme Court ruled in 1981 that the courts could not mandate comparable worth but legislation could do so (*County of Washington v. Gunther,* 1981). Legislative bodies in some jurisdictions, such as Colorado Springs, Colorado, and the State of Minnesota have adopted comparable worth. In using the comparable worth criterion to establish pay, a jurisdiction needs to do a job analysis to determine the value of each type of position to the organization. Thus, the focus is not on equal pay for the same job, but equal pay for work of equal value. However, the job analysis process itself first needs to be reviewed in order to make sure all discriminatory criteria are purged.

Benefits

Employee benefits constitute an important part of the compensation of public employees. Benefits include those mandated by national or state law (Social Security, unemployment compensation, worker's compensation, family leave) and those that an employer may choose to provide, called *discretionary benefits* (vacation leave, dependent care, retirement pensions). These benefits are usually available to all the employees in an organization, and they represent a significant and growing cost to employers.

From 1929 to 2002, for example, benefits grew from representing 3 percent to representing more than 30 percent of total payroll for U.S. employers (U.S. Bureau of Labor Statistics, 2012).

The public sector historically has had a more generous employee benefits package than has the private sector, in part because it is easier politically to increase benefits than it is to increase pay (Cayer, 2010; Reddick, 2009). Especially with retirement benefits, decision makers can put off paying until people actually retire; therefore, the current policy makers do not have to take much political heat for improving a benefit. The better benefits packages in the public sector have often been justified as being important in recruiting and retaining good employees, especially as pay in the public sector is often not as high as it is in the private sector. In the aftermath of the 2010 elections, benefits costs became a major issue in state and local governments as efforts to cut spending took priority. Voters also had little sympathy for public employees as benefits plans in the private sector were cut or eliminated so governments took action to reduce benefits for public employees.

Mandated benefits are provided to all employees in the public and private sectors because the federal government requires them to do so. States may also have mandated benefits. Some of these federally mandated benefits arose from the New Deal legislation of the 1920s. Social Security (including Medicare), for example, is a mandatory benefit that provides pensions to those who retire. Originally, state and local governments were not required to include their employees in the Social Security system, but a 1981 law requires that employees hired or rehired after March 31, 1986 must be covered under Medicare. The law was changed in 1991 to require that all state and local government employees not covered by a public retirement system be included in Social Security. Every year, legislation is proposed in Congress to make Social Security mandatory for everyone including those with public pensions, but state and local officials have so far been successful in keeping it from passing.

Worker's compensation and unemployment compensation (part of the Social Security Act programs), are also mandated benefits. Employees unable to work because of job-related injuries are eligible for worker's compensation which pays a portion of a disabled worker's wages and provides medical and rehabilitation benefits. Unemployment compensation provides benefits in the form of a fixed level of pay for employees who were laid off or quit their jobs under certain circumstances and are actively seeking work. Worker's compensation is funded through employer contributions, and unemployment compensation is funded by a combination of federal funds and employer contributions. Public employees are covered under both of these programs.

The Family and Medical Leave Act of 1993 (FMLA) requires that employers with fifty or more employees permit employees to take up to twelve weeks of unpaid family and medical leave during any twelve-month period; thus, family leave became a mandated benefit. The leave may be used for birth or adoption of a child, foster care placement, care of a family member, or one's own care. There has been much litigation concerning what are appropriate circumstances for the leave. In what many hope will be a nationwide model, California adopted the first paid family leave in 2002, providing employees 55% of their pay for up to six weeks. The program is funded through a payroll tax. New Jersey and Washington also passed versions of paid FMLA, and several other states have considered it.

Public employers provide various benefits at their own discretion. These discretionary benefits are often heralded as being important in attracting and retaining good employees. Almost universally, public employers grant vacation and sick leave. They also often allow for educational leave, and they often reimburse employees for the cost of job-related courses and training programs. Day care is subsidized, and, increasingly support for eldercare programs has emerged as an important benefit to many employees with elderly parents or other relatives for whom they are responsible. Flexible work hours and job sharing are increasingly offered as incentives for employees to stay with an organization. Additionally, legal services are subsidized or provided in many benefits packages. The changing demographics of the workforce, especially the larger presence of women with dependent care responsibilities, are changing the array of benefits needed and provided.

Health care benefits have been among the most common discretionary benefits. They also are among the most costly, with costs rising at a rapid rate. Because of the rising costs of health care and the importance of health care, the nation has been engaged in a debate about how to deal with the issue for decades. Many support universal health care either through a nationalized health care system or by requiring all employers to provide it for employees (thus making it a mandated benefit). The irony is that as costs increase, many employers are reducing coverage, dropping coverage, or increasing costs to the employee. Public employers have been hit with the rising costs like any other employer. The result is that many public employers who previously paid all the premiums for employee coverage now require employees to share part of the cost. Employers who already require cost sharing are increasing the amount employees have to pay. Health care coverage shifted from indemnity plans, where patients had full choice in selection of health care providers, to health maintenance organizations (HMOs) and preferred provider organizations (PPOs), in which the plan limits the choices of providers. With these plans, patients also have co-pay requirements in which they are responsible for a fee each time they visit a provider. With the passage of the Affordable Health Act (also known as Obama Care) in 2010, employers who do not provide health care coverage will have to pay a per employee fee to the national government each year to help pay the cost of health care now required of all people.

Typically, health care plans include a variety of coverages. Traditionally, physical health was covered, including medication and hospitalization to maintain physical health and treat medical conditions. Gradually mental health was included, and dental benefits have become common. In 2008, the Mental Health Parity and Addiction Equity Act was passed, requiring that employers provide health care plans that cover mental health in the same way they cover other medical issues. To stem increasing coverage costs, many employers encourage preventive measures including regular physical examinations. Additionally, many employers have wellness programs to keep their employees healthy by teaching them about nutrition, diet, exercise, stress reduction techniques and ways to quit smoking.

Retirement benefits represent the other major benefit cost. Public employee retirement systems enroll some 18 million employees with assets exceeding 2.7 trillion dollars (Rhee, 2012; U.S. Bureau of the Census, 2012). During the 1960s, public pension systems grew rapidly, partly in response to the growth of collective bargaining and partly because pensions represented a benefit that public policy makers could grant while passing on the costs to future policy makers. During the late 1970s and

1980s, many of the systems experienced tremendous strain because employees were retiring and the systems had not been prefunded. Government generally responded by prefunding plans and establishing a two-tiered system in which new employees receive less generous benefits. With the good economic years of the 1990s , public pension systems became solvent but the recessions of 2000 and 2008 and the losses due to risky and bad fund investments resulted in severe underfunding again (Brown, Clark, & Rauh, 2011; Eucalitto, 2012; Munell, Aubry, & Quigley, 2010; PEW Center on the States, 2012).

One of the reasons government pension plans developed funding problems is that many were what is known as *defined benefits plans* in which the employee is guaranteed a specific benefit level (usually with cost-of-living adjustments) upon retirement and public employees could often retire as early as age fifty-five. As people live longer and receive larger payouts from cost-of-living increases, the cost of pensions often outstripped the funds. Because most government pension systems had been pay-as-you-go, current operating budgets had to include funds for retirement pensions. Now, most systems fund for the future thus relieving the problem. Nonetheless, most plans now face unsustainable costs.

Increasingly, governments use defined contributions systems, which is the standard practice in private industry. Defined contributions plans are those in which the employer and employee each contribute a specified amount to an account in the individual employee's name. The amount is usually a specified percentage of the employee's pay. When the employee retires, the benefit is a function of what was placed in the account and how well the investment of funds has fared. Thus, the system is funded up front and pension fund managers are responsible for investing the money and managing the retirement systems. Once the employee retires, the employer no longer has any funding obligation.

Adapting Benefits to the Changing Workforce

Because the demographics of the workforce are changing constantly, public employee benefits programs also adapt. Because the needs of all employees are not the same, flexible, or *cafeteria-style* benefit plans are now more common. With flexible plans, employees can choose which benefits they want, although there are usually restrictions. For example, health services and retirement must be covered through the employee's benefits or through a spouse's plan. In such a system, a fixed amount of money is set aside for each employee. The employee then can distribute the money across the benefits that are most meaningful for him or her. Thus, one employee may need child care services, whereas another may fund a legal services plan.

Domestic partnership policies emerged as a controversial issue in the 1990s (Gosset & Ng, 2008). Twenty-two states, including California, Connecticut, Maine, New York, Oregon, Rhode Island, Vermont, and Washington, offered some form of domestic partnership benefits as of 2010 (Human Rights Campaign Foundation, 2011) as do many municipalities. After meeting the criteria established by the policy, unmarried domestic partners of employees are accorded the same benefits as are spouses of married employees. Some jurisdictions limit the domestic partnership benefits to same-sex couples on the basis that, by law, they cannot marry and acquire the benefits whereas heterosexual couples can.

As health care has improved and people enjoy longer lives, eldercare has become an increasingly important issue. As a result, employers face increasing pressure to accommodate the needs of those responsible for eldercare. Many employees have responsibility for both children and elderly parents or other relatives. Called the "sandwich generation," these employees face particular challenges. To address their concerns, many employers have instituted benefits to allow time and resources for such care. The issue is particularly acute for women, as they are more likely than men to have eldercare responsibilities.

Strategies for Controlling Compensation Costs

In times of tight resources, public employers find themselves needing to contain compensation costs. They have several strategies available, and most employers use a combination of them. The typical strategies include pay freezes, furloughs, layoffs, attrition, privatization, and cutting benefits' costs. Pay freezes usually are used as a short-term strategy, and they tend to be politically popular. In the national government, pay was frozen between 2010 and 2013. The downside of pay freezes is that they create employee morale problems and often lead to higher recruitment and training costs as good employees leave for other opportunities. Furloughs require employees to take time off without pay to help the government reduce personnel cost. During 2008 and 2009, many state and local governments required their employees to take off a day or two a month to save money. Layoffs also help in the short run by quickly reducing costs. Attrition means not filling positions as employees leave. Layoffs and attrition can lead to increased workloads and stress for employees who remain as well as to reduced morale and productivity. In the long run, these strategies may be counterproductive because of the problems they create.

The Reagan administration's Grace Commission on reducing the costs of government and increasing productivity, and the reinventing government movement of the 1980s and early 1990s advocated for privatization as a way of increasing the efficiency and productivity of the public service by introducing business practices and strategies to accomplish their goals. Similar efforts emerged in most state and larger local governments. The first President Bush issued Executive Order 12803 in 1992, which required all federal agencies to pursue privatizing their infrastructure activities. Similarly, the second President Bush privatized many civilian activities of the military and attempted unsuccessfully to privatize Social Security. He was successful in privatizing the Transportation Security Administration (TSA), but it was later brought back into government. Although personnel costs may be initially reduced by privatization and the governmental jurisdiction may avoid encumbering benefits costs, there is scant evidence that long run costs are reduced. New costs arise for the administration of privatized functions when preparing requests for proposals, handling the bidding and contract negotiations, and monitoring the contract after it is consummated (Bel & Warner, 2008: Dilger, Moffett, & Struyk, 1997; Fernandez, Rainey, & Lowman, 2006).

Cutting benefits has become the most recent approach to cutting compensation costs (National Governors Association, 2012). Benefits costs may be cut by requiring greater employee contribution to benefits programs. Employees may be required to pay part, or more of their health care premiums and to pay larger copayments for services they access, thus reducing the cost of the contract for the employer. The Bureau of Labor Statistics reported in 2012 that the costs of benefits represented 35.3% of total compensation for state and local government employees with health care costs being the most significant part of the increase (U.S. Bureau of Labor Statistics, 2012). Smaller jurisdictions use consortia to help reduce costs. By joining together in a consortium, public employers can increase the number of employees for whom they bargain, thus benefit from economies of scale to use as leverage in their negotiations with service providers. Consortia are used particularly for health care coverage, but the same principle applies to retirement systems as local jurisdictions often join statewide systems rather than form their own. Another strategy to reduce benefits costs is to reduce the number of people eligible for benefits. Full-time employees are made part-time, part-time employees are dropped from eligibility and retired employees may no longer be covered under the health care plans (Clark & Morrill, 2010). The retirement age may be raised to help reduce retirement costs, at least in the short run. Conversely, in other situations providing incentives to retire early might be a better strategy to save on costs. This strategy is meant to reduce direct pay costs as more long-time employees retire and are replaced by younger, lower-paid employees. However, the costs are shifted to the retirement system. Of course, if the system uses the defined contributions approach, the employer does not bear any increased costs for retirees.

Benefits costs also are reduced by the introduction of two-tiered plans. In these plans, the generous benefits once given to employees may not be the same for new employees. The employer may reduce the level of benefits for newer employees and may require them to pay more for those benefits. Usually, this approach results from the legal principle that promises made to employees are considered contracts and it is difficult to change the terms of employment without sparking litigation. However, new employees can be hired under a different contract.

Summary

Human resources planning has become a major concern of human resources management as employers deal with constantly changing needs for employees with appropriate knowledge, skills, and abilities to achieve organizational goals.

Position classification and compensation are important functions in the management of human resources. Position classification defines jobs and places them according to the importance and lines of authority within the organization. Classification helps establish the value of the positions, and compensation plans differentiate pay among positions. Over time, the shortcomings of strictly adhering to position classification has led many organizations to adopt a system known as broadbanding. Broadbanding places positions in job families and gives departmental managers a great deal of flexibility in organizing positions within the job families and in setting their pay levels.

Compensation includes both direct pay and benefits. While generally offering lower levels of pay than the private sector, the public sector has traditionally been able to attract employees by offering better benefits. The increasing costs of benefits, especially health care coverage, has developed as a major concern in the past decade, thus pressuring public employers to be creative in offering benefits to accommodate the needs of the changing workforce while finding strategies for containing costs.

Once the classification and compensation systems are in place, jurisdictions can seek to find employees to fill positions. Chapter 5 deals with strategies for staffing the public service and for keeping the employees productive.

Exercises

1. Interview someone who works in a government job. Ask the person to explain exactly what he or she is required to do in the job. Get details on the person's specific duties and interaction with others in the organization. Also ask whether your interviewee is responsible for supervising others and for independent decision making.

> Based on your interview, write up a job description. Then ask for a copy of the individual's position description. Compare the two. What were the challenges in writing your description? What did you learn from the exercise?

2. Renee Porter has been the director of the Tech Shop for seven years and has always received excellent reviews for the shop's performance. She is proud of her employees, who are all hard workers and they take pride in their efforts. Rarely is there a complaint from the agencies that use the Tech Shop's services.

Jeremy Perrill is one of the best employees at the Tech Shop. He has been a leader in keeping abreast of the latest developments in technology, especially information-processing equipment and software. He regularly receives accolades from those for whom he provides services. His performance evaluations have always been the highest they can be. Renee has been concerned about losing Jeremy because the compensation policy of the organization does not allow her to reward him for his outstanding work. Instead, he gets the same pay increases all the other employees get.

During the past three years Jeremy has asked Renee to reclassify his position. Each time Renee has sent the request to the human resources department, it has been denied. Jeremy has requested a reclassification once again. Renee is sympathetic to Jeremy's request but believes it is a futile effort.

> (A) You are Renee Porter. What will you consider in making a decision about whether to make the request to human resources? Are there any other options? What will your final decision be, and why?

(B) Assume that the request has been made and that you are the classification specialist from human resources assigned to this request. What will be your considerations in examining the request? Are there any suggestions you will make to Renee if you deny the request?

3. John Purcell spent twenty-five years as a police officer and retired with a full pension. During his years as a police officer, numerous disciplinary actions were taken against him. Each one was minor enough to warrant no more than a day or two of suspension. He would go long periods with no disciplinary actions and then would have two or three in a short period. This cycle continued throughout his career.

After three years of retirement, his colleagues were surprised to learn that he had been arrested as one of three people who had held up an armored car and made off with $1.5 million. As news of the arrest and Purcell's background became public, questions were asked about his pension and whether he could continue to draw it after being arrested. State law allowed jurisdictions to take away pensions in such cases so that victims could be compensated. However, there was no provision requiring such action. Purcell's wife is unable to work and will be left without resources if the pension is taken away.

You are a benefits analyst for the pension fund and have been asked to make a recommendation to the pension board concerning whether Purcell's pension should be taken from him. What will you consider in making your recommendation? Explain the rationale for what you will consider and for the recommendation you will ultimately make.

4. Find a meeting of a legislative committee, city council, school board, county commission, or tribal council in which employee pay or benefits are on the agenda. Attend the meeting and observe the discussion.

What issues are raised? Who participates in the discussion and what arguments do they use to support their positions? What was decided? If you were voting on the issue, how would you vote? Why?

Selected Websites

Bloomberg BNA. Publisher of reference products on personnel and other management and financial issues. Includes a section on human resources issues including employee benefits. Primary focus is on private sector but has some public sector material.

www.bna.com

Center for Retirement Research at Boston College. Conducts and publishes research on retirement issues.

crr.bc.edu

Center for State and Local Government Excellence (SLGE). Sponsors and publishes research on public sector human resources management issues.

www.slge.org

Employee Benefit Research Institute (EBRI). Nonprofit research and information dissemination organization on economic security and employee benefits.

www.ebri.org

International Foundation of Employee Benefit Plans (IFEBF). Nonprofit membership organization devoted to education about benefits.

www.ifebp.org

International Society of Certified Employee Benefit Specialists (ISCEBS). Organization devoted to information sharing and innovation on benefits administration.

www.iscebs.org

Kaiser Family Foundation. Conducts and publishes research on health care issues with an emphasis on health care costs including employer costs for health care.

www.kff.org

National Institute on Retirement Security. Conducts and publishes research on retirement issues.

www.nirsonline.org

The Occupational Information Network (O*Net). An online database created by the U.S. Department of Labor. It provides job descriptions for hundreds of standard occupations along with salary ranges.

www.onetonline.org

Recognition Professionals International (RPI). Dedicated to enhanced employee performance through recognition. Shares information and sponsors conferences on strategies for and programs on recognition.

www.recognition.org

U.S. Bureau of the Census. Publishes regular reports on aspects of employment including data on public employment issues.

www.census.gov

U.S. Bureau of Labor Statistics (BLS). Publishes statistics on all aspects of labor including wages and salaries and benefits.

www.bls.gov

WorldatWork. (Formerly American Compensation Association). Nonprofit focused on compensation, benefits, and rewards. Engages in publication of materials, networking, and certification programs.

www.worldatwork.org

References

Alonso, P., & Lewis, G. B. (2001). Public service motivation and job performance: Evidence from the federal sector. *Review of Public Personnel Administration, 31*, 363–380.

Arvey, R. D. (1986). Sex bias in job evaluation procedures. *Personnel Psychology, 39*, 315–335.

Ban, C. (1991). The navy demonstration project: An experiment in experimentation. In C. Ban & N.M. Riccucci (Eds.), *Public personnel management: Current concerns, future challenges* (pp. 31–41). New York: Longman.

Bel, G., & Warner, M. (2008). Does privatization of solid waste and water services reduce costs? A review of empirical studies. *Resources, Conservation and Recycling, 52*, 1337–1348.

Brown, J. F., Clark, R., & Rauh, J. (2011). *The economics of state and local public pensions.* Cambridge, MA: National Bureau of Economic Research.

Cayer, N. J. (2010). Managing employee benefits: From health care to pensions. In S.F. Condrey (Ed.), *Handbook of human resource management in government* (3rd ed.) (pp. 817–834). San Francisco: Jossey-Bass.

Center for State and Local Government Excellence (2012). Retrieved from http://slge.org/wp-content/uploads/2012/04/S-L-Govt-Workforce-2012_12-195_web.pdf.

Center for State and Local Government Excellence (2009). *Survey findings: A tidal wave postponed: The economy and public sector retirements.* Washington, DC: Center for State and Local Government Excellence.

Cipola, F. (1999, July 15). Time for classification system to go. *Federal Times*, p. 15.

Civil Service Assembly. (1941). *Position classification in the public service.* Reprinted in 1965 by the Public Personnel Association. Chicago: Civil Service Assembly,

Clark, R. L., & Morrill, M.S. (2010). *Retiree health plans in the public sector: Is there a funding crisis?* Northampton, MA: Edward Elgar.

Corbett, C., & Hill, C. (2012). *Graduating to a pay gap: The earnings of women and men one year after college graduation.* Washington DC: American Association of University Women.

County of Washington v. Gunther, 452 U.S. 161 (1981).

DeSanto, J. F. (1980). Higher pay for good performance—the average grade approach. *Public Personnel Management, 9,* 282–284.

Davidson, J. (2012, October 24). Federal Salary Council's call for 35 percent pay hike unrealistic. *The Washington Post*. Retrieved from http://articles.washingtonpost.com/2012-10-24/local/35500943_1_gap-issue-federal-employees-federal-salary-council

Dilger, R. J., Moffet,, R. R., & Stryuk, L. (1997). Privatization of municipal services in America's largest cities. *Public Administration Review, 57,* 21–26.

Eucalitto, C. (2012). How States underfund public pensions. *State Budget Solutions*. Retrieved from http://www.statebudgetsolutions.org/publications/detail/how-states-underfund-public-pensions.

Federal Salary Council. (2012). Level of Comparability payments for January 2014 and other matters pertaining to the Locality Pay Program, memo. Retrieved from http://www.opm.gov/oca/fsc/recommendation12.pdf

Fernandez, S., Rainey, H. G., & Lowman, C. (2006). Privatization and human resources management. In N.M. Riccucci (Ed.), *Public personnel management: Current concerns, future challenges* (4th ed.) (pp. 204–224). New York: Longman.

French, P. E., & Goodman, D. (2012). An assessment of the current and future state of human resource management at the local government level. *Review of Public Personnel Administration, 32,* 62–74.

Gosset, C. W. & Ng, E. S. W. (2008). Domestic partner benefits. In C. G. Reddick & J. D. Coggburn (Eds.), *Handbook of employee benefits and administration* (pp. 379–397). Boca Raton, Fl: CRC Press.

Human Rights Campaign Foundation (2011). *Equality from state to state.* Washington, DC: Human Rights Campaign Foundation.

Iberman, W. (2010). Viewpoint: How to end the era of public employee entitlements. *American City and County.* Retrieved from http://americancityand-county.com/commentary/entitlements-gainsharing-employees-20100217.

Ingraham, P. W. (1993). Of pigs in pokes and policy diffusion: Another look at pay for performance. *Public Administration Review, 53,* 348–356.

Institute of Women's Policy Research (2012). *The gender wage gap: 2011.* Retrieved from www.iwpr.org

International Personnel Management Association (2002). *Workforce planning resource guide for public sector human resource professionals.* Washington, DC: International Personnel Management Association.

International Public Management Association for Human Resources. (2012). IPMA-HR benchmarking committee releases variable pay survey results. *HR News, 78,* 27.

Jacobsen, W. (2010). Preparing for tomorrow: A case study of workforce planning in North Carolina municipal governments. *Public Personnel Management, 39,* 353–378.

Johansen, E. (1984). Managing the revolution: The case of comparable worth. *Public Personnel Management, 4,* 14–27.

Johnson, A. T. (1982). Cutback strategies and public personnel management: An analysis of nine Maryland counties. *Review of Public Personnel Administration, 3,* 41–55.

Johnson, G. L., & Brown, J. (2004). Workforce planning not a common practice, IPMA-HR survey finds. *Public Personnel Management, 33,* 379–388.

Kellough, J. E., & Lu, H. (1993). The paradox of merit pay in the public sector: Persistence of a problematic procedure. *Review of Public Personnel Administration, 13,* 45–64.

Kellough, J. D., & Selden, S. C. (2003). The reinvention of public personnel administration: An analysis of the diffusion of personnel management reforms in the states. *Public Administration Review, 63,* 165–176.

Ledbetter v. Goodyear Tire and Rubber Co., Inc., 550 U.S. 618 (2007).

Lunney, K. (2012). Survey: Feds have it good compared to private sector workers. *Government Executive.* Retrieved from http://www.govexec.com/pay-benefits/2012/12/survey-feds-have-it-good-compared-private-sector-workers/60054

Munell, A. H., Aubry, J. P., & Quinby, L. (2010). *The impact of public pensions on state and local budgets.* Chestnut Hill, MA: Center for Retirement Research at Boston College.

Naff, K. C. (2003). Why managers hate position classification. In S. W. Hays & R. C. Kearney (Eds.), *Public personnel administration: Problems and prospects* (4th ed.) (pp. 126–142). Upper Saddle River, NJ: Prentice-Hall.

National Academy of Public Administration (2003). *Broadband pay experience in the public sector.* Washington, DC: National Academy of Public Administration.

National Academy of Public Administration (1991). *Modernizing federal classification: An opportunity for excellence.* Washington, DC: National Academy of Public Administration.

National Academy of Public Administration (1995). *Modernizing federal classification: Operational broadbanding systems alternatives.* Washington, DC: National Academy of Public Administration.

National Governors Association. (2012). *Strategies for curbing health insurance costs for state employees: Benefit design, wellness programs, and data mining.* Retrieved fromhttp://www.nga.org/files/live/sites/NGA/files/pdf/1210StrategiesForCurbingHealthInsuranceCosts.pdf.

Neuse, S. (1982). A critical perspective on the comparable worth debate. *Review of Public Personnel Administration, 3*, 1–20.

Penner, M. (1983). How job-based classification systems promote organizational ineffectiveness. *Public Personnel Management, 12*, 268–276.

Perry, J. L. (1986). Merit pay in the public sector: The case for a failure of theory. *Review of Public Personnel Administration, 7*, 57–69.

Perry, J. L. (1993). Strategic human resource management. *Review of Public Personnel Administration, 13*, 59–71.

Pew Center on the States. (2012). *Pensions update: The widening gap update.* Washington, DC: The Pew Charitable Trusts.

Reddick, C. G. (2009). The importance of employee health benefits to public and private sector organizations. *Public Personnel Management, 38*(2), 49–68.

Reilly, T. (2012). *Rethinking public sector compensation: What ever happened to the public interest?* Armonk, NY: M.E. Sharpe.

Rhee, N. (2012). *On the right track? Public pension reforms in the wake of the financial crisis.* Washington, DC: National Institute on Retirement Security.

Risher, H. (2012, April 12). Job classification mess another reason to replace GS system. *Federal Times* http://www.federaltimes.com/apps/pbcs.dll/article?AID=2012204010301

Risher, H., & Wilder, W. (2007). *Pay for performance: The road to success.* Washington, DC: International Ciy/County Management Association.

Schulkind, G. (1976). Monitoring position classification: Practical problems and possible solutions. *Public Personnel Management, 4.* 32–37.

Selden, S. C., Ingraham, P. W., & Jacobson. W. (2001). Human resource practices in state government: Findings from a National Survey. *Public Administration Review, 61,* 598–607.

Shareef, R. (1994). Skill-based pay in the public sector: An innovative idea. *Review of Public Personnel Administration, 14,* 60–74.

Thompson, F. (1976). Classification as politics. In R. T. Golembiewski & M. Cohen (Eds.), *People in public service* (pp. 515–529). Itassca, Il: Peacock Publishers.

U.S. Bureau of the Census, (2012). *Summary of the quarterly survey of public pensions for 2012: Q2.* Retrieved from www.census.gov/newsroom/releases/archives/governments/cb12-tps63.html

U.S. Bureau of Labor Statistics. (2012). *Employer costs for employee compensation new release text.* Retrieved from http://stats.bls.gov/news.release/ecec.nr0.htm

U.S. Government Accountability Office. (2012). *Human capital management: Effectively implementing reforms and closing critical skills gaps are key to addressing federal workforce challenges.* Washington, DC: U.S. Government Accountability Office.

Waters, R. (2006). *Public sector's guide to skill-based pay system development & implementation* (3rd ed.). Dallas, TX: The Waters Consulting Group, Inc.

Weibel, A., Rost, K., & Osterloh, M. (2010). Pay for performance in the public sector—benefits and (hidden) costs. *Journal of Public Administration Research and Theory, 20,* 387–412.

Whalen, C., & Guy, M. E. (2008). Broadbanding trends in the states. *Review of Public Personnel Administration, 28,* 349–366.

Yoder, E. (2012, October 19) Federal workers are falling farther behind on pay, study shows. *The Washington Post Politics.* Retrieved from http://www.washingtonpost.com/blogs/federal-eye/wp/2012/10/19/federal-workers-are-falling-farther-behind-on-pay-study-shows

5

Staffing and Maintaining the Workforce

With close to one million federal employees eligible to retire by 2016, attracting and retaining employees continues to be an arduous task for the public sector. Staffing and maintaining a large workforce requires putting into place methods for recruiting, examining, selecting, evaluating, promoting, and disciplining employees. Staffing challenges are further compounded by a number of factors: the negative image of the public service, sector switching among public service employees, preference among public affairs graduates to work for the private sector, and the inflexibility of some government personnel processes (Chetkovich, 2003; Clerkin & Coggburn, 2012; Light, 1999; Ritz & Waldner, 2011). However, under the presidency of Barack Obama, the US Office of Personnel Management has launched several hiring reforms to promote and attract bright, talented, and well-trained individuals to careers in government.

Until the 1970s, the processes for staffing and maintaining the workforce were fairly simple, but with the passage of the Equal Employment Opportunity Act of 1972, which brought state and local governments under the provisions of the Civil Rights Act of 1964, those processes became more complex. Over time, other legislation and policies added to the work of public personnel systems. The Americans with Disabilities Act of 1990 (ADA) established the most sweeping requirements for employers, including those in the public sector. As a result, every process in the personnel system is scrutinized for its impact on people with disabilities. Litigation based on these and other acts have complicated the personnel process as well. Nevertheless, the first step in the staffing process still begins with recruitment.

Recruitment

Recruiting is one of the most critical and challenging activities performed by the personnel department. Recruitment is the process by which an employer seeks qualified applicants for vacant or potentially vacant positions. In times of high unemployment, such as in the early 1990s and post–2008, attracting a large pool of qualified applicants poses no problems. In times of low unemployment such as in the late 1990s and 2006–2008, the poor image of the public service makes it difficult for government agencies to compete with private industry in recruiting the best applicants. Also once hired, government employees take a lot of abuse from elected officials, the media, and the general public. As a result, many qualified people would rather work for private industry, in which they are relatively insulated from such pressures. Nonetheless, many people still prefer the excitement of the public spotlight and politics or have a strong commitment to public service. Thus, there are people in government service who are as highly qualified as those in private industry. The problem lies in continuing to attract and retain highly qualified people. To help government change its negative image and to hire and retain the best talent, in 2012 the Pathways program was founded to recruit students and recent graduates to the federal workforce.

In 2008, the Obama administration put into place the End-to-End (E2E) hiring initiative to effectively and efficiently fill the gap that will be created by impending retirements. This new initiative was aimed at improving the overall hiring experience of potential federal employees starting with workforce planning, recruitment, hiring, screening and security clearance, and orientation. The key goal was to reduce the hiring time from 180 days to 80 days and make the application process less cumbersome. At the time the initiative was put into place, the hiring time in government was reported to average between 93-109 days (Llorens, 2009). The initiative also eliminated the Knowledge, Skills, and Abilities (KSA) essay as an initial hiring requirement, simplied the language and the content of job announcements, and revamped the USAJOBS website to improve the application process for federal jobs.

New Recruitment Challenges in the Public Sector Since the 1970s

Beginning in the 1970s, governments found themselves under different pressures in the recruitment process. With the passage of the Equal Employment Opportunity Act of 1972, state and local governments became subject to antidiscrimination legislation. As a result, public employers had to recruit women and minority group members for all types of positions in government. Charges of discrimination could be brought against a jurisdiction by anyone who felt discriminated against in the personnel process. If the jurisdiction was found discriminatory in its practices, it could be required to make restitution to the individuals directly discriminated against and usually was forced to develop a plan to eliminate discrimination in the future. Many federal grants contained stipulations permitting revocation if a jurisdiction did not follow equal employment opportunity policies. Equal employment opportunity and affirmative action have been the two main approaches to expanding employment opportunities for women and minorities.

Affirmative action is a process by which an employer makes positive efforts to recruit people from groups underrepresented in the organization's work force. Affirmative action plans became common features of personnel policies across the country as federal agencies often required them to establish eligibility for grants and as monitoring agencies and courts ordered the development of such plans to reverse past discriminatory practices. However, the Reagan administration deemphasized affirmative action and equal opportunity during the 1980s, and the Supreme Court retreated on the issue as well; thus state and local governments were under less pressure to maintain equal employment opportunity. Equal opportunity and affirmative action nonetheless attained enough acceptance that jurisdictions continued such efforts because it was the just and fair thing to do.

Affirmative action programs have also been quite controversial given the conflicting rulings achieved in the University of Michigan lawsuits concerning race in admissions. In *Grutter v. Bollinger*, 539 U.S. 306 (2003) the Supreme Court upheld affirmative action in the admission policy of the law school arguing that race was a compelling factor in diversifying the student body. On the contrary, in *Gratz v. Bollinger*, 539 U.S. 244 (2003), the Supreme Court rejected the use of adding 20 points for undergraduate admission to every racial minority. Chief Justice William H. Rehnquist ruled that the use of the point system violated the Equal Protection Clause and Title VI, arguing that the use of race was neither narrowly tailored nor of compelling interest in the University of Michigan's freshmen admissions. The controversy continues in *Fisher v. University of Texas,* an affirmative action case that is being debated before the U.S Supreme Court in 2013. These issues are discussed in more detail in Chapter 9.

Though compliance with legal requirements is still a major factor in many organizations' efforts to increase the diversity of their workforces, strategic organizations recognize that diversity has much value for them. Diversity initiatives give employers a competitive advantage in recruiting the best employees. Diverse organizations also relate better to their increasingly diverse communities. The globalization of society also demands greater diversity in organizations so that they are better able to serve and interact with a widening array of cultures. As Audrey Mathews says "The payback ... will include employee retention, increased productivity, less absenteeism, better morale, an expanded market place and improved services rendered to customers" (Mathews, 1998, p. 177).

Although it is illegal for an employer to discriminate against applicants based on their race, color, religion, gender, pregnancy status, national origin, age (40 or older), disability or genetic information, women and minorities have had widely varying degrees of success in state and local governments. They have been employed in increasing numbers, but the types of jobs and levels of positions they have attained suggest continuing patterns of discrimination (Guy, 2003; Hale, 1999; Kellough, 2003). Moreover, in recent decades, protection has been extended against discrimination based on sexual orientation.

Protecting the rights of LGBT (lesbians, gay, bisexual and transgender) during the recruitment process has been in the works since the Employment Non-Discrimination Act (ENDA) was introduced in the 103rd Congress in 1994. Although several states offer protection based on sexual orientation, no federal law mandates such protection across the United States. Other laws that ensure fair recruitment practices are the 2008 Genetic Information Nondiscrimination Act (GINA), Americans with Disabilities Act (ADA), and Americans with Disabilities Amendments Act (ADAAA), (Kellough, 2000; Mani, 2003). GINA applies to organizations with 15 or more employees, and makes it illegal to discriminate against employees or applicants based on their genetic information. Under this law, the use of genetic information in hiring, firing, pay, job assignments, promotions, training, benefits, layoffs, or any other term of employment is considered illegal except under certain permissible conditions that relate to work. Under ADA and the 2008 ADAAA, qualification requirements must focus on essential job functions. The definition of disability is expanded under the 2008 amendment to include physical or mental impairment that substantially limits one or more major life activities.

Recruitment processes can be discriminatory in themselves because of the qualifications required for a position or because of the recruitment market. Public employers often exaggerate the credentials needed for a position because they feel that higher requirements lead to hiring a better quality of employee. This rationale has other implications, however. It may result in the hiring of an overqualified employee who will not be satisfied with the position. It also may mean that people who could do the job well are not considered because they lack the required credentials. Thus, some requirements can, in effect, be discriminatory because some groups have been systematically denied opportunities to gain certain credentials, whether educational or experiential. Equal employment opportunity policy prohibits using a qualification requirement unless it can be shown to be relevant to the position.

Recently, efforts to overcome discriminatory recruitment policies have included job sharing and the employment of dual-career couples. Job sharing permits an organization to hire two or more people to do what ordinarily would be done by one. The job sharers work reduced hours and share one position. With such an arrangement, the focus can be on accommodating people's unique scheduling problems (e.g., caring for children) or dividing the position along the lines of the skills needed. Thus, if part of the job requires a specific highly developed skill, it is possible that one part-time employee will have that skill and that another, less skilled individual can be employed to fulfill the job's other functions. In poor economic times, job sharing serves as a viable alternative for employees to keep their jobs with partial benefits and prorated compensation. However, job sharing is still an underutilized benefit in the federal government (Partnership for Public Service, 2010).

Dual-career couples are another important element of the labor market. Often spouses have difficulty finding employment in their specializations in the same labor market, especially in small communities. In the past, nepotism rules often prohibited married couples from being employed in the same organization. Increasingly, employers recognize that it may be to their advantage to make adjustments to accommodate the needs of such couples, including job-sharing, in which the couple share one position. With two people in one position, the organization often is much more productive than it would be with one individual in that position. At the same time, the couple can pursue their professional interests together. Such flexible employment situations promote happier employees and can also aid in recruitment by widening the applicant pool.

The recruitment process, if successful, results in a number of applicants who meet the minimum standards for a position. In situations where there are a large number of applicants, examinations provide one method for narrowing the field of applicants.

Examinations

Examinations were the mainstays of traditional public sector selection processes and they continue to dominate in most jurisdictions. Ideally, exams help identify applicants who are best able to perform the job for which the exam is used. The exam may be either assembled or unassembled. An unassembled exam normally is an evaluation of an applicant's background, experience, and references. The information comes from the application and other documentation required in the application process, along with follow-ups on recommendations from former employers. These exams are most useful for managerial and professional positions, but many small jurisdictions without extensive resources also use them for most of their positions. Tests are most commonly used when hiring for the foreign service, customs, traffic control, the postal service, and some clerical positions.

An assembled exam is employed more commonly on the state level and in large local jurisdictions. At the national level, the exam previously used for general entry-level recruitment (PACE, or the Professional and Administrative Careers Examination) was abandoned in 1982 after it was found to be discriminatory. For entry-level positions, OPM now uses six exams under the banner of Administrative Careers with America (ACWA). In 2009, OPM recommended using ACWA but did not require agencies to use written tests as long as the assessments used were valid (job related). Examples of assessments include, but are not limited to the following:

- Job knowledge tests
- Rating schedules
- Ability tests
- Work samples
- Situational judgment tests
- Structured interviews

The exam that is selected depends on the entry-level position being filled. For some positions, agencies can develop their own exams with assistance from OPM. Assembled exams are usually written but also may include a combination of any aforementioned evaluation. In some cases, assessment-center procedures are used in which applicants are placed in a highly structured situation and engage in some form of simulation exercise. Assembled exams also may require some type of performance test, such as taking shorthand or running a computer program. Many jurisdictions use some combination of these types of exams. The written exam is often used as a preliminary screening device, and then other exams may be used as appropriate.

It is important to make sure that the exams are valid and that they test the appropriate skills. Although the relevance (validity) of general knowledge or aptitude exams is debatable, they are still frequently used. There are three main types of validity: content, criterion, and construct.

Content validity means that an exam measures factors that are directly related to the duties and responsibilities of the position. Content validity is particularly useful in positions calling for a definable and measurable skill. For example, the content validity of word-processing tests for word processors is easy to verify.

Criterion validity refers to whether an exam is a good predictor of performance on the job. Thus employees may be selected, and then later a comparison is made between their scores on the exam and their performance evaluations or other criteria. Another way of testing for criterion validation entails giving an exam to those already in these positions. If the exam is valid, those who score well on it should be successful employees whose performance is rated high by their superiors.

Construct validity is more difficult to achieve because it applies to tests that measure more elusive qualities, such as ability and flexibility. Construct validation is useful for managerial decision-making positions whose precise job content is difficult to establish.

The validity of examinations has become a major issue in the wake of equal employment opportunity. The Americans with Disabilities Act puts even more pressure on employers to ensure that exams measure factors that are relevant to performing the essential functions of a position. Further, the ADA and ADAAA require accommodation in the testing process so that the disabled can compete for positions in which they can perform. To make sure the personnel system is not discriminatory, employers must make sure their examination procedures are valid. The courts may invalidate an examination if it is found to have an adverse impact on the disabled, minorities, and women. Adverse impact means that the members of such groups have a smaller chance of being selected than do others. According to federal guidelines, adverse impact is assumed if the selection rate for a protected group is less than 80 percent of the rate for the group with the greatest selection success. This selection rate is widely used, but the Supreme Court has demonstrated flexibility, indicating that the overall employment record and the particular content of the employer's actions should be considered in deciding such cases (*Albermarle Paper Co. v. Moody,* 1975; *Brunet v. City of Columbus,* 1995; *Connecticut v. Teal,* 1982; *Griggs v. Duke Power Co.,* 1971; *Washington v. Davis,* 1976). Although examinations will continue to have to meet the relevance criterion, it seems that the employer's total personnel system is being given more consideration.

In the federal service, the trend has been toward decentralizing the responsibility for testing potential employees since the early 1980s. With greater responsibility for making hiring decisions, agencies have been moving away from written exams and have been relying on practices such as promoting from within, making provisional appointments, and converting classified positions to exempt status where competitive rules do not apply (Ban, 2002). Pressure for state and local decentralization of the hiring responsibility has also resulted in reforms allowing agencies greater flexibility. Georgia, for example, gives agencies almost complete freedom in hiring.

Selection

Most personnel offices certify applicants to the unit doing the hiring after reviewing their applications and, where appropriate, administering exams. Certified applicants are those the personnel office has selected as eligible for hiring by the unit. While still used in some state and local governments, the Rule of Three, meaning that any of the top three applicants can be selected, is a thing of the past. John Berry, Director of OPM said at the first anniversary of the new federal hiring reform, "We're hiring based on resumes and cover letters 91% of the time, up from 39% in 2009." Most of the job announcements do not require KSA essays. He further pointed out that: "Hiring managers now have more choices—they get to see more resumes, because 89% of our announcements have category rating, up from only 12% in 2009. No more Rule of Three" (Berry, 2011). Under the new hiring reform, a category rating system is used instead of ranking individuals on numeric scores. Eligible candidates are rated based on prequalified categories developed by identifying tasks critical to successfully perform the job. For example, if there are 15 highly qualified applicants for the job, the manager can select from any of the 15 candidates instead of selecting from the top three.

Further, OPM developed two new methods of selecting career appointees, one is the Accomplishment Record and the other is résumé-based. Both methods are based on the 5 Executive Core

Qualifications: Leading Change, Leading People, Results Driven, Business Acumen, and Building Coalitions. The core qualifications are required for entry into the Senior Executive Service (SES) by most agencies.

The selection process becomes even more complicated when veterans are involved. Politically powerful and influential veterans' groups have been effective in persuading Congress and state legislators to enact veterans' preference. Not all veterans are given preference; only veterans honorably discharged or released from active duty are eligible for the preference. Traditionally, the federal service gave a bonus of five points to all veterans and a ten-point bonus to disabled and Purple Heart veterans who pass the general competitive exam. As the federal service has disbanded its general exam and allowed the individual departments to draw up their own exam, the regulations now apply to departmentally developed and administered exams. In some jurisdictions veterans get absolute preference; that is, they go to the top of the list if they receive a minimum passing score. The preference given to veterans thus may interfere with the appointing official's ability to select the best candidate, because top scorers are pushed aside by veterans who receive bonus points. In most instances they perform ably, but there is always a chance that more capable people are being turned away. The absolute preference system used at some state and local levels and at the entry level in the federal service for disabled veterans represents the most extreme examples of preferential treatment. Some jurisdictions even extend the same preferences to spouses and children of veterans.

Although veterans' preference laws have been under strong attack for many years, little change has been forthcoming. As part of the Civil Service Reform Act of 1978, President Carter attempted to reduce the preference and limit the time during which veterans could ask for preferential treatment. However, veterans' groups mobilized their members and mounted an effective counterlobby to the proposal. Ironically, instead of reducing preference, the legislation offered additional benefits to veterans with disabilities, allowing them appointments without competitive examinations and retention rights during reductions in force. Challenges at the state level have been taken to the courts. Helen Feeney challenged Massachusetts's absolute preference law, which put veterans who passed the exam ahead of anyone else. She had taken the civil service promotion exam three times during the twelve years she was employed by the state. Each time veterans were put ahead of her because of the absolute preference system. By a seven-to-two decision, the court upheld that state statute, noting that the law did not discriminate on the basis of sex, even though the veterans at that time were almost always male (*Personnel Administrator of Massachusetts v. Feeney,* 1979). Thus, all efforts to change such provisions have been directed to legislative bodies. The implications for public service go beyond equality as such, preferential treatment remains an obstacle to women and thus to equal opportunity. In 2011, President Obama signed the VOW (Veterans Opportunity to Work) Act to give preference to active duty service members who are expected to be discharged or released from active duty.

If the position is a temporary one, competitive exams may not be required by personnel rules. Nonetheless, there is often abuse in using temporary appointments. Employers may use temporary appointments to retain people who might not qualify for a permanent position. Some employers continually reappoint "temporary" employees, renewing the appointments each time they expire. Temporary employees thus become permanent employees for all intents and purposes. Of course, such employees can be easily intimidated by the threat of not renewing the appointment.

Selection may be limited to candidates from within an agency, thus excluding outsiders from consideration. In a closed system, appointments are open only to those inside the organization. Promotion is the common method of filling positions from within and will be discussed later. Selection from within often is favored by employee organizations as a way of ensuring employees an opportunity for advancement. Management may favor outside recruitment to bring in new ideas, but collective bargaining has tended to increase the prevalence of selection from within.

Once an agency receives the list of those eligible for hire, it follows further procedures for making a final choice. An interview is common. The agency manager or supervisor may conduct the interview, or in some cases a panel of workers, supervisors, or managers may do so. These interviews are structured, with the same questions being asked of all candidates to avoid discrimination. Interviewers should be trained by the equal employment office of the agency or jurisdiction to keep them from asking inappropriate questions that could give the appearance of discriminatory intent. Once the interviews are completed, the position supervisor or manager usually makes the final selection and checks the references. Pre-employment queries should all be job related. The ADA does not allow employers to ask applicants to take a medical exam or to reveal their medical history or type of disability. The employer may ask the applicant if he or she can perform the essential job functions with or without reasonable accommodations.

A final step in the selection process often is a probationary period in which the employee is observed on the job. A probationary period is most often six months, but it can be as long as two years for some positions. During the probationary period, the employee can be terminated for any reason, and this sometimes leads to arbitrary decisions. If it is used correctly and if managers are well trained in its use, the probationary period can lead to better selection decisions and provide an opportunity for on-the-job training.

Promotion

Promotion, which is a type of selection, provides an opportunity for employees to advance in the organization. Through promotion, they gain status in the organization and ordinarily improve their salary levels. Management also uses promotion as a way of keeping valuable employees and increasing their input into the organization's activities. Ideally, promotions are based on the employee's merit and the organization's needs. As in all decisions in which human beings are involved, however, merit is not always the major consideration. Both management and employee organizations have an interest in the process, and they structure promotions to serve their interests. From management's perspective, merit is important, but so too is the employee's attitude and ability to work within the organization. Thus, promotion often is used to weed out those who may challenge the organization's values and goals and to reward those who show the "proper respect" for the agency's policies and values (Downs, 1967; Perrow, 1970). Employee organizations such as unions usually prefer seniority as the basis for promotion, as it is quantifiable, and it leaves little to management's discretion. Promotion from within can be a motivator and morale builder for employees who see opportunity for advancement. Many unions favor and protect promotions based on seniority. However, such a system runs the risk of promoting mediocrity and protecting poor performers.

Promotions may hamper an organization if they reward those who accept the agency's perspective on everything. Because promotions go to those who agree with management, new ideas are unlikely to be introduced, and service and productivity may suffer because the agency's problems probably will not be resolved and new ways of doing things will not be considered. Protection of the status quo or accretion of power may become more important than providing high-quality service to the public. To prevent such stagnation, open competition for positions by people inside and outside the organization can be used.

Except for seniority, the criteria for promotion are difficult to establish. Managers frequently promote an employee who has demonstrated outstanding performance in a specific job. Supervisory responsibility, however, requires skills different from those needed for the work supervised. As a result, employees often are promoted to positions for which they are not suited. Public sector agencies increasingly recognize the problem of unskilled supervisors and try to resolve it through better selection processes and through supervisory training. Assessment centers have become popular methods for evaluating employees' supervisory and managerial potential, but because they are expensive, their use is limited. Another alternative is to have employees rated by selected associates. Because the raters are familiar with the organization and the job, the process is organization-specific. Once employment decisions are made, supervisors need to conduct various activities to maintain the workforce. Among the most important activities are performance evaluation and discipline.

Performance Evaluation

Performance evaluation or appraisal is an essential yet difficult part of the personnel process. Performance evaluation serves different purposes, depending on whether it is viewed from the perspective of management or that of the employee (Cogburn, 1998; Glendinning, 2002; Kellough, 2002; Roberts 1998). Management or the organization uses performance evaluation to help make decisions about compensation, training needs, promotion, on whether to retain probationary employees, and on how to improve performance and management. Viewed from the individual perspective, however, performance evaluation assumes importance in regard to considerations of equity, employee growth and development, and participation and support of human resources in the organization. These sometimes conflicting perspectives can lead to a misunderstanding of the performance evaluation system and can cause anxiety for the employee and supervisor alike (McGregor, 1957; Sherwin, 1957).

The basic responsibility for performance evaluation rests with the supervisor or manager, though recent trends have also included the employee in the evaluation process. Employees' participation in the design and implementation of appraisal systems appears to increase their trust in those systems (Maroney & Buckley, 1992). Employees are often asked to rate their own performance and then discuss their evaluation with the supervisor and compare it with the supervisor's appraisal. In many cases, the employee actually sets up goals and objectives with the supervisor and then is evaluated against them. Increasingly the public sector uses 360-degree evaluation, in which feedback is obtained from supervisors, colleagues, and subordinates (De-Leon & Ewen, 1997; Edwards & Ewen, 1996; Pollack & Pollack, 1996). All the information is used to arrive at a final evaluation.

Regardless of how evaluations are made, they tend to cause anxiety. Supervisors often have difficulty explaining exactly what is expected of their employees, and when evaluation time comes, they have difficulty measuring performance against what they see as the organization's goals. It usually is assumed that the supervisors' anxiety arises because of their not wanting to deliver bad news to an employee, but John Nalbandian (1981) found that supervisors are actually most uncomfortable with their subordinates' reactions to evaluation. Thus, supervisors often rate employees as satisfactory. Klingner and Nalbandian (2003) report that about 99% of federal government employees are given a rating of "fully successful." It is to be expected that employees will be defensive about their evaluations and that supervisors will be uncomfortable dealing with those reactions.

The tendency in recent years has been to formalize the evaluation process. Whereas in years past, informal approaches with little record keeping sufficed, more documentation is required today. Thus, annual evaluations are common, with a formal report being kept in the employee's personnel file. With increasing requirements from employee organizations, the law, and the courts that performance evaluation and other personnel functions be based on valid job-related criteria, supervisors must document the process and results to protect both the organization and the employee (Holley & Fields, 1975; Rosenbloom & Bailey, 2003).

Performance ratings can take various forms, such as measurements of output and examinations. Numerical ratings on various trait-based characteristics, such as punctuality, attitude, and ability to work with others, are common, as are narrative or essay evaluations. Each of these approaches has variations and negative and positive features. For example, output measurement may be effective in evaluating performance when an identifiable product is made but inappropriate when a service or policy is the output. Examinations are useful in measuring potential or capacity but may be ineffectual in judging actual performance.

Rating employees on various qualities and narrative evaluations can be effective if they are carefully constructed and properly used. The checkoff, or objective evaluation, assigns employees a score on qualities such as promptness, courteousness, writing ability, and initiative. The narrative approach permits supervisors to describe employees' strong and weak points. In some narrative evaluations, specific items must be discussed. These kinds of narrative evaluations are unpopular because they are difficult to compare, and there is little control over which qualities are evaluated. The narratives also depend on the supervisor's writing ability. Rating people on specific qualities is easier and provides for greater comparability. Unfortunately, the qualities rated often have little relevance to performance; instead, they relate to personal traits. Although personality factors may be important in some jobs, that is not the case for all or even most positions. Consequently, governments have been shifting toward performance-based evaluation systems.

The Civil Service Reform Act of 1978 requires each federal department to develop a performance-based appraisal system. Consistent with the strategic role of personnel management in organizations, performance appraisal increasingly ties performance to the organization's mission and pay. Pay-for-performance, a concept borrowed from the private sector, gained momentum, especially in at-will employment states such as

Georgia, Florida and Texas (Battaglio & Condrey, 2006; Condrey & Battaglio, 2007; Hays & Sowa, 2006). Nevertheless, the U.S. Government Performance and Results Act of 1993 (GPRA) and the Program Assessment Rating Tool (PART), used by the Office of Management and Budget, requires every federal agency to establish goals and provide evidence of performance relative to the goals established.

Several methods of evaluation incorporate elements of both the rating and the narrative approaches. The critical incident type of evaluation has the supervisor record specific behaviors of the employees that are indicative of good or poor performance and that contribute to organization mission. This method highlights performance-related activities and thus conforms to one of the major criteria necessary for effective evaluation. However, it tends to focus on behavioral extremes and thus may ignore general, less visible aspects of performance that might say more about the employee's role in the organization. Thus an employee who does well consistently but seldom does anything spectacular may be at a disadvantage.

The narrative approach has many variations as well. It may require the supervisor to write an overall evaluation of the employee's performance, or it may require an explanation of the employee's most significant contribution to the organization and most serious weakness. Also it may call for a description of specific factors such as quality of work, ability to get along with others, innovativeness, and potential for growth. As was noted above, narrative approaches are usually not good for comparing employees, but they offer flexibility and an opportunity for supervisors to stress individual contributions and provide a broader perspective on performance. One drawback is that supervisors vary in their ability to identify strengths and weaknesses and then write about them. The employee then benefits or suffers according to the supervisor's evaluative skills.

Forced-choice evaluation is another approach. In this method, a supervisor may be required to choose a certain percentage of employees who deserve recognition for meritorious performance. Such an approach often is used in decisions in which a limited number of a supervisor's subordinates may be singled out for merit pay increases. It usually forces the supervisor to develop specific criteria by which the decisions are made. It is not, however, an easy process to administer, and it can create morale problems.

In recent years, many organizations have used group and peer appraisal. Peer appraisal may use any of the forms suggested above but frequently requires a numerical rating on specific characteristics. It often also entails a simple listing of individuals who should be considered good or poor workers. This method can offer illuminating perspectives on employee performance, though it may produce inflated evaluations. In the self-appraisal system, employees examine their own performance relative to specified criteria. In most instances, they then discuss their evaluations with the supervisor and set goals for the future. Employees tend to either over- or underestimate their contributions and cannot always see themselves in relation to the total organization; thus their evaluations can be inaccurate. Nonetheless, used in combination with other techniques, these systems can provide a useful examination of employee activities.

Performance evaluations can distort the importance of particular activities to the organization. For instance, when output is the major criterion on which employees are evaluated, it is not surprising that employees neglect concerns such as coordination of effort and quality of output. The likelihood is that employees will focus on the activities that gain them favorable evaluations (Blau, 1963).

Perhaps the greatest problem with performance ratings is that they often are made hurriedly, and periodically resulting in several rating errors. When the deadline for evaluations approaches, the supervisor does them quickly, often remembering only the exceptional or most recent occurrences (the recency effect). The result is a distorted view of the employee. An ongoing evaluation in which the supervisor discusses the strong and weak aspects of performance as they occur probably is the most effective approach. The employee can then make adjustments as needed rather than finding at the end of a year that he or she has not lived up to expectations. Adequate record keeping is also necessary. If an employee does not correct unsatisfactory performance over a reasonable period of time, disciplinary action is in order. Similarly, when an employee feels that he or she has been unfairly judged, a review process should be available. Most important, evaluations should have as their goal the best perfor-

mance possible, and punishment should be a last resort. Typically, an evaluation interview concludes the appraisal process. This
interview permits discussion of the strengths and weaknesses of
employee performance and provides an opportunity to plan for
improvement and set performance goals.

In recent years performance evaluations have served to protect employees from capricious action by their superiors. A record of periodic evaluations makes it difficult for a supervisor
to suddenly dismiss an employee who is out of favor. In the days
when employees were not regularly evaluated, they could be told
after a number of years of service that they did not meet the
(often unspecified) standards of the agency. Similarly, a record of
inadequate performance can be used in counseling, disciplining,
and terminating employees.

Discipline

Disciplining employees is a major task of supervisors and one
they usually would rather avoid. If the organization has effective
personnel policies in general, discipline should be needed only on
rare occasions. Because of the spotlight in which the public service must operate, however, public employers often must judge
their employees by higher standards of conduct than are used
in the private sector. An effective discipline policy is one that is
clearly stated, clearly understood by employees, and uniformly
applied. It also requires documentation of every action. If discipline is not timely, any later actions are likely to be ineffectual.
In addition, unjust disciplinary actions are likely to be resented
and to be destructive to morale. However, once such actions are
imposed, the employee should have access to an appeals process
to review the action to provide protection against capricious action by supervisors.

The most commonly used forms of discipline are reprimands,
suspensions with or without pay, demotion or other reassignment, and termination. Others used to a lesser degree include
loss of salary increases, seniority rights, and overtime work and
demerits on the employee's personnel record. These forms of
discipline once were used extensively but now are considered
demeaning and not particularly productive. Reprimands, both
oral and written, should be sufficient to correct most problems,

particularly if the employee and supervisor have good communication and mutual respect. The purpose of the reprimand should be to correct the employee's actions, not to embarrass or humiliate the employee. The supervisor's training and personality are important in making this type of disciplinary action effective. Fumbling and inconsiderate use of reprimands can cause irreparable harm to employee–supervisor relations.

Suspension, demotion, and reassignment are more severe types of discipline. They should be used with care and only when reprimands are ineffective. Suspension often leaves an employee with a loss of pay and may kindle hostility. Demotion and reassignment are appropriate when an employee has demonstrated a lack of ability in a particular position. The change of job ordinarily is made on the basis of more effectively utilizing the employee's capabilities. Using it as a disciplinary action is humiliating to employees, and it makes them more resistant to the organization and its needs. Reassignment may result in pawning off incompetent employees on other units of the organization, thus weakening the organization.

Termination is the most extreme form of discipline and should be used only as a last resort. Termination usually occurs only after other efforts to correct the behavior in question have failed. Thus, normally the other forms of discipline are applied first, moving from the least to the most severe. This process is known as progressive discipline. At each step, the employee is warned about the consequences of failure to correct the behavior in question. However, for some behaviors, such as theft, termination is the initial discipline.

Once a decision to terminate is made, it normally is reviewed by the personnel and legal departments and higher-level supervisors and/or managers before it is implemented. The employee usually is entitled to procedural due process or a pretermination hearing and can appeal the decision after it is made. The appeal may be heard by higher-level administrators or by an independent personnel board or commission. In the appeal step, the issue of whether employees understand the policy and understand the consequences of their behavior become important. Thus, it is critical to document how and whether the employee was aware of agency policy and the consequences of violating that policy. Those hearing the appeal will be concerned with fairness to the employee, and their decisions will hinge on the written record. Dismissal policies should be clearly stated and understood, as with all disciplinary policies. Employees' appeal rights are routine parts of such policies. Too much procedural detail, however, may lead to inflexibility for the manager. A balance between employee rights and the public's expectations for high-quality service often is difficult to achieve. Managers often feel frustrated at the difficulties of disciplining employees. Public sector employees not in a collective bargaining environment settle their grievances by an internal appeals system or a personnel board. However, in collective bargaining situations, the terms of grievance settlements are established in collective bargaining agreements (Haraway, 2005).

At the same time, there are many problems with managers harassing employees for disagreeing with them or with agency policy. The Civil Service Reform Act of 1978 attempted to protect employees from such badgering and contains a provision to protect "whistle-blowers" or people who reveal the wrongful behavior of their supervisors and agencies. The act prohibits reprisals against whistle-blowers and provides for bringing disciplinary charges against those who institute such reprisals. However, many employees who have availed themselves of the whistle-blower protection have found that life in the organization can be made difficult for them. The Whistleblower Protection Act of 2009 and Whistleblower Protection Enhancement Act of 2012 were addopted to provide better protection for employees who engage in whistleblowing.

Effective discipline is really self-discipline. A successful supervisor considers discipline a form of teaching in which employees are coached to perform in the most productive way possible (Lee & Cayer, 1994). When a problem arises, the supervisor is there to discuss the problem and suggest remedies. In the rare instances in which this approach does not work, the formal discipline process must be invoked.

Summary

To ensure adequate numbers of capable staff members, public service agencies must have a system in place for several processes. In particular, it is necessary to recruit qualified individuals. Historically, recruitment was a fairly simple process because the skills needed were not complicated. With the increasing complexity of government and technology, governments face the challenge of recruiting for a variety of skills; thus, the recruitment process has become more formal. In recent times, several hiring reforms have been instituted to attract and retain younger generations to the government.

Selection procedures also have become more complex as instruments such as exams have been challenged for being inappropriate or discriminatory. Once selected, employees are given protection against discrimination in performance evaluation, promotion, and disciplinary actions. As a result of various non-discrimination laws and rules, the processes for administering the public personnel system have become highly formalized.

Exercises

1. Javina Jobe applied for a position as a police officer in the small town of High Mount. After taking the exam for police officers, she felt optimistic but never got a call back for an interview. When she inquired about the results, she was told she scored too high. She filed a suit alleging discrimination based on intelligence.

The police department and city legal counsel explained that candidates who score too high on the exam may not be challenged by the work and may get bored. They tend to leave before long, and the city loses the $25,000 it spent on training.

You are a member of the jury. How would you argue that the jury consider deciding? Explain why you take the position you do.

2. Design a Recruitment and Selection Plan

Great news! Just as expected, Grand Prairie, TX is growing! The City Manager has approved hiring five new positions: Human Resources Intern, Assistant Superintendent for Recreation, City Engineer, Budget Manager, and Assistant Administrator. Design a recruitment and hiring plan that includes the following:

A brief job description of the positions.

The plan and activities for recruitment, including where to find applicants.

A discussion of how to sort the applicants to determine who and how many will get an interview.

A plan for the interview process.

Who will do the interviews?

What is your interview format?

Include some sample interview questions.

The selection criteria.

3. Rachel Wells was excited about being called in for an interview for a job as the liaison between the city planning department and the city council staff. The job also involved working with community-based groups interested in planning and zoning issues. Her interview was with John Jameson, the planning director.

As the interview began, Jameson made small talk about the terrible weather and how it would be nice when it warmed up a bit. Then he turned to specific questions concerning Rachel's potential employment by the city. He asked the following questions:

(1) Why do you think you are the person we should hire for the job?

(2) What skills do you have that would make you effective in performing the job's tasks?

(3) What is your political affiliation?

(4) When did you graduate from high school? College?

(5) Do you have small children?

(6) Have you ever been arrested?

(7) To what social and professional organizations do you belong?

(8) What is the general state of your health?

(9) Where does your spouse work?

(10) How long have you lived in the city?

(11) Are there any questions you would like to ask me?

After Rachel asked a few questions about the planning department and its personnel policy, the interview ended, and Rachel left. She felt that the interview had gone well and that she made a good impression. However, she had been uncomfortable with some of the questions. She felt that she had to answer them to have any chance at getting the job but also believed that many of them were inappropriate.

> Was Rachel overreacting? Explain. Examine each question, and identify any that were inappropriate and explain why that question should not have been asked during an interview for a government job. Are there any inappropriate questions which Jason asked Rachel that if rephrased, could have elicited legitimate information? If your answer is yes, which question(s)? How might the question(s) be rephrased to get the legitimate information?

(*Hint:* You can refer to the EEOC's website for examples on discriminatory interview questions: http://www.eeoc.gov/facts/qanda.html)

4. Brandon Alexander is the Supervisor in the Public Works Department for Athens, Iowa. The division that Brandon heads consists of five sections: Project Development, Construction Management, Flood Control, Utilities, and Waste and Environmental Management. Brandon directly supervises 50 employees. Brandon is an extrovert, and he likes when his employees

come to him with innovative ideas. Ryan Scholl, an engineer in the Utilities and Waste Environmental Management section, is bright and outgoing, and he often meets with Brandon to discuss his ideas. However, none of his ideas have been adopted by the department.

Rita Parker, another engineer in the Utilities Division, is a good employee who is diligent but reserved, and she often keeps to herself. She came up with a brilliant recycling idea that, if successful, would save the department $500,000 over the next five years. Her plan was put to the test, and it failed during the pilot phase. Rita's performance evaluation was ten days after the failed pilot test. Brandon gave Rita a low rating on her annual performance evaluation. Ryan, on the other hand, was given an exemplary rating and received a 3.0 percent merit increase, Rita received none.

> Based only on the information above, do you agree with Brandon's evaluations of Ryan and Rita? Discuss the type of rating errors that are in play in this situation? If you were the supervisor, how would you conduct the performance evaluation of your employees? Should supervisors be given training before they can conduct performance evaluations? Discuss the key components of such training.

5. Jason Sanders worked for fourteen years for the city of Slippery Slope, where he advanced to Division Manager in the Parks and Library Department. He enjoyed his job and colleagues. To supplement his income, he worked as a bartender in a neighborhood sports bar a couple of nights a week. One day the owner of the bar asked if he would be able to work a day shift two weeks later. Jason agreed to do it. When the day came, he called in sick to his city job and went to work at the bar.

Another city employee went to the bar for lunch and recognized Jason. He did not think much about it but later that afternoon, this employee happened to have a meeting with Jason's supervisor and mentioned seeing Jason working at the bar.

When Jason arrived at work the next day, there was a message telling him to report to his supervisor immediately. Jason's supervisor told him that he was terminated immediately for conduct unbecoming a city employee and for defrauding the city by taking sick leave when he was not sick. The supervisor relayed what he had learned from the other city employee. Jason was given a termination notice to sign, indicating that he understood the action being taken and the reasons for it. He was also notified that he had the right to appeal to the Personnel Appeals Board.

You are a member of the Personnel Appeals Board. Jason has asked the board to reinstate him with a three-day suspension, admitting that he violated city policy. What information would you want to have before you made a decision? How would this information affect your decision? What would you decide if you only had the information provided above?

Selected Websites

Bloomberg (Bloomberg BNA). Publishes materials on all aspects of employment including federal laws and the rules and regulations implementing them.

www.bna.com

Conference of Minority Public Administrators (COMPA) – A section of the American Society for Public Administration (ASPA) sharing information and holding conferences on issues of concern to minority administrators in government.

www.compaonline.org

Disability.gov. The federal government web portal for comprehensive information on disability programs and services in communities nationwide.

https://www.disability.gov/

Human Rights Campaign. Publishes reports on policies affecting employment of lesbian, gay, bisexual, and transgender community members.

www.hrc.org

National Council on Disability. Advocates for people with disabilities and publishes reports on their status. Also provides information and guides for accommodating people with disabilities in the workforce.

www.ncd.gov

Office of Personnel Management. End-to-End hiring initiative.

http://www.opm.gov/publications/EndToEnd-HiringInitiative. pdf

Recruitment and Selection of Senior Executive Service, Executive Core Qualifications (ECQ).

www.opm.gov/ses/recruitment/ecq.asp

Section on Women in Public Administration (SWPA). Section of the American Society for Public Administration (ASPA) that shares information and provides networking on issues related to women in government.

http://www.aspaonline.org/swpa/

U.S. Bureau of the Census – Collects data and publishes reports on all aspects of U.S. society and economy including labor force characteristics and government employment by various categories.

www.census.gov

U.S. Department of Labor (DOL). Bureau of Labor Statistics – Collects data and publishes reports on all aspects of the labor force. Many of the reports focus on the impact of government on the labor market.

www.bls.gov

elaws Advisors. Web site containing interactive tools providing information about federal employment law.

www.dol.gov/elaws

U.S. Equal Employment Opportunity Commission (EEOC). Enforces non-discriminatory and equal employment opportunity laws. Also publishes reports and statistics on the demographics of the labor force and government employment.

www.eeoc.gov

U.S. Government Accountability Office (GAO). Publishes reports on government agencies including their compliance with employment policies.

www.gao.gov

U.S. Merit Systems Protection Board (MSPB). Serves as the appeals board for federal government employees and issues regular reports on the federal merit systems.

www.mspb.gov

References

Albermarle Paper v. Moody, 422 U.S. 405 (1975).

Ban, C. (2002). Hiring in the federal government: The politics of reform. In C. Ban & N.M. Riccucci (Eds.), *Public personnel management: Current concerns, future challenges* (pp. 166–180). New York: Longman.

Battaglio, R. P., & Condrey, S. E. (2006). Civil service reform examining state and local government cases. *Review of Public Personnel Administration, 26,* 118–138.

Berry, J. (2011). Remarks of OPM Director John Berry Hiring Reform First Anniversary Event National Press Club. Office of Personnel Management http://www.opm.gov/news/speeches-remarks/hiring-reform-first-anniversary-event/.

Blau, P. (1963). *The dynamics of bureaucracy: A study of interpersonal relationships in two government agencies* (2nd ed.). Chicago: University of Chicago Press.

Brunet v. City of Columbus, 58 F. 2d 251 (1995).

Chetkovich, C. (2003). What's in a sector? The shifting career plans of public policy students. *Public Administration Review 63,* 660–74.

Clerkin, R. M., & Coggburn, J. D. (2012). The dimensions of public service motivation and sector work preferences. *Review of Public Personnel Administration, 32,* 209–235.

Coggburn, J.D. (1998). Subordinate appraisal of managers: Lessons from a state agency. *Review of Public Personnel Management, 18,* 68–79.

Condrey, S. E., & Battaglio, R. P. (2007). A return to spoils? Revisiting radical civil service reform in the United States. *Public Administration Review, 67,* 425–436.

Connecticut v. Teal, 457 U.S. 440 (1982).

De Leon, L., & Ewen, A.J. (1997). Multi-source performance appraisals: Employee perceptions of fairness. *Review of Public Personnel Administration,* *17,* 22–36

Downs, A. (1967). *Inside bureaucracy.* Boston: Little Brown.

Edwards, M., & Ewen, A. (1996). *360 degree feedback: The powerful new model for employee appraisal and performance improvement.* New York: Amacon Books.

Genetic Information Nondiscrimination Act (2008). U.S. Equal Employment Opportunity Commission, http://www.eeoc.gov/laws/types/genetic.cfm.

Glendinning, P.M. (2002). Performance measurement: Pariah or messiah. *Public Personnel Management, 31,* 161–178.

Griggs v. Duke Power Co., 401 U.S. 424 (1971).

Guy, M.E. (2003). The difference that gender makes. In S.W. Hayes & R.C. Kearney (Eds.), *Public personnel administration: Problems and prospects* (pp. 256–270). Upper Saddle River, NJ: Prentice-Hall.

Hale, M. (1999). He says, she says: Gender and worklife. *Public Administration Review, 59,* 410–424.

Haraway, W. (2005). Employee grievance programs: Understanding the nexus between workplace justice, organizational legitimacy and successful organizations. *Public Personnel Management, 34,* 329–342.

Hays, S. W., & Sowa, J. E. (2006). A broader look at the "Accountability" movement some grim realities in state civil service systems. *Review of Public Personnel Administration, 26,* 102–117.

Holley, W.H. & Field, H.S. (1975). Performance appraisal and the law. *Labor Law Journal, 26,* 423-430.

Kellough, J.E. (2000). The Americans with Disabilities Act – A note on personnel policy impacts in state government. *Public Personnel Management, 29,* 211–224.

Kellough, J.E. (2002). Employee performance appraisal and pay for performance in the public sector: A critical examination. In C. Ban & N.M. Riccucci (Eds.), *Public personnel management: Current concerns, future challenges* (pp. 181–193). New York: Longman.

Kellough, J.E. (2003). Equal employment opportunity and affirmative action in the public sector. In S.W. Hays & R.C. Kearney (Eds.), *Public personnel administration: Problems and prospects.* (pp. 209–224). Upper Saddle River, NJ: Prentice Hall.

Klinger, D. E., & Nalbandian, J. (2003). *Public personnel management: Contexts and strategies.* Upper Saddle River, NJ: Prentice Hall.

Lee, D.S., & Cayer, N.J. (1994). *Supervision for success in government: A practical guide for first in line supervisors.* San Francisco: Jossey-Bass.

Light, P. C. (1999). *The true size of government.* Washington, DC; Brookings Institution Press.

Llorens, J. J. (2009). A renewed emphasis on hiring A closer look at the federal Government's end-to-end hiring roadmap. *Review of Public Personnel Administration, 29,* 373–381.

Mani, G.M. (2003). Disabled or not disabled: How does the Americans with Disabilities Act affect employment policies? In S.W. Hays & R.C. Kearney (Eds.), *Public personnel administration: Problems and prospects* (pp. 271–286). Upper Saddle River, NJ: Prentice-Hall.

Maroney, B.P., & Buckley, M.R. (1992). Does research in performance appraisal influence the practice of performance appraisal? Apparently not! *Public Personnel Management, 21,* 185–196.

Mathews, A. (1998). Diversity: A principle of human resource management. *Public Personnel Management, 27,* 175–185.

McGregor, D. (1957). An uneasy look at performance appraisal. *Harvard Business Review, 35,* 89–94.

Nalbandian, J. (1981). Performance appraisal: If only people were not involved. *Public Administration Review, 42,* 392–396.

Partnership for Public Service (2010). On demand government: Deploying flexibilities to ensure service continuity. http://ourpublicservice.org/OPS/publications/viewcontentdetails.php?id=144

Perrow, C. (1970). *Organizational analysis: A sociological view.* Belmont, CA: Brooks/Cole.

Personnel Administrator of Massachusetts v. Feeney, 442 U.S. 256 (1979).

Pollock, D.M., & Pollock, L.J. (1996). Using 360 degree feedback in performance appraisal. *Public Personnel Management, 25,* 507–528.

Ritz, A., & Waldner, C. (2011). Competing for future leaders A study of attractiveness of public sector organizations to potential job applicants. *Review of Public Personnel Administration, 31,* 291–316.

Roberts, G.E. (1998). Perspectives on enduring and emerging issues in performance appraisal. *Public Personnel Management, 27,* 301–320.

Rosenbloom, D.H. & Bailey, M. (2003). What every public personnel manager should know about the constitution. In S.W. Hays & R.C. Kearney (Eds.), *Public personnel administration: Problems and prospects* (pp. 29–45). Upper Saddle River, NJ: Prentice-Hall.

Sherwin, D.S. (1957). The job of job evaluation. *Harvard Business Review, 35,* 63–71.

Washington v. Davis, 426 U.S. 229 (1976).

6

Keeping Employees Motivated and Productive

The ultimate test of the public service and its personnel system is performance. Performance and efficiency in the public sector have been at the heart of the public management debate. There is general consensus that the private sector is more efficient and that it performs better than the public sector. However, empirical research has found otherwise (Downs & Larkey, 1986; Goodsell, 2004). The constant pressure placed upon the public sector to perform resulted in the passage of the Government Performance and Results Act of 1993 (GPRA), which instituted private sector practices such as cutback management, reduction-in-force, pay-for-performance, contracting out, and employment-at-will—all aimed at improving performance. Faced with shrinking resources, inflation, and collective bargaining, government agencies are being asked to do more with less. In such an environment, motivating employees to improve performance while reducing turnover is vital. This chapter examines the role of supervisors, motivation techniques, performance management, and training and development in securing optimal performance. It also considers the aforementioned privatization measures as pressures on performance.

The Supervisor

Supervisors are generally considered the key to better employee performance in the public sector (Brewer, 2005; Light, 1999, 2002; National Academy of Public Administration, 2003; National Commission on the Public Service, 2003). Although some evidence suggests that supervision contributes little to the organization's productivity, it is still important in establishing the organization's smooth operation so that work can be accomplished (Homans, 1965). Ironically, in efforts to save costs, middle management is often eliminated by outsourcing public sector jobs (Brewer, 2005). Using data from the 2000 Merit Principles Survey, Brewer (2005) found that frontline supervisors played a major role in the success of federal agencies. In fact, high-performing organizations have skillful employees who embrace the organization's goals and values. The author concludes that "outsourcing public jobs to improve governmental performance also seems paradoxical: the very elements that need to be strengthened to improve federal agency performance are those that seem to be most lacking in the private sector" (Brewer, 2005, p. 520).

Supervisors carry out several tasks related to the performance of those under them (Lee & Cayer, 1994). They must see that the job gets done, keep work areas safe, encourage teamwork and cooperation, assist in developing employee skills, and maintain records. Because employees and work situations vary from agency to agency, supervisory approaches must vary as well. Supervisors need training if their organizations are to avoid the pitfalls of the Peter Principle, which states that "in a hierarchy, every employee tends to rise to his level of incompetence" (Peter, 1972). Performing well as a supervisor thus calls for many skills.

Henry Mintzberg has suggested three categories of supervisor roles, which encompass a total of ten roles (Mintzberg, 1973). The categories are interpersonal, informational, and decisional. *Interpersonal roles* require the supervisor to be a leader, to serve as a liaison for individual workers and groups, and to handle symbolic and ceremonial activities. Each of these activities can help motivate workers to be productive and to take pride and an interest in the organization. The *informational role* involves monitoring and disseminating information and being a spokesperson for the organization. In each of these activities, the supervisor helps keep the organization productive by being aware of what is taking place and by providing information to the appropriate people so that decisions can be made to maintain operations or change things when necessary. In *decisional roles,* supervisors serve as entrepreneurs, disturbance handlers, negotiators, and resource allocators. Again, a successful supervisor must be adept in activities that keep the organization functioning and changing as needed.

The supervisor's job requires dealing with a wide variety of employee needs and types. Some employees are motivated primarily by the money a job pays, and they work only to earn the resources needed to enjoy their desired standard of living. Such employees are not motivated by their work, and they need relatively structured supervision to be productive. Others are more concerned about being in a friendly workplace; they enjoy the company of associates, and they are motivated by the organization's social norms and congeniality. Still others need to feel they have control over their careers, and they require independence to work within the constraints of their jobs. Assuming that they have the ability, these people can be given responsibility, and they respond favorably to incentives. Still other employees are motivated by the work itself. They are concerned with whether the work is socially meaningful and whether it contributes to a goal to which they are committed. A particular challenge for the twenty-first century supervisor is that employees have different expectations of their work experiences (Green, 2000; Light, 1999; Mir & Mosca, 2002). Employees now anticipate changing jobs more frequently than they did in the past, and they expect employers to be more flexible in accommodating their needs. Additionally, supervisors are faced with motivating different generations of workers and workers with different personal circumstances.

With four generations in the workforce—the Silent Generation or traditionalists (born 1925–1945), the Baby Boomers (born 1946–1964), Generation X (born 1965–1980), and Generation Y or millennials or iGen or GenMe (born 1981–2000)—the task of motivation becomes challenging. Research has found several generational differences in motivation, commitment, and attitude toward work (Tang et al., 2012; Twenge & Campbell, 2008). In general, Gen X and Gen Y are more individualistic and self-focused when compared with the traditionalists and the baby boomers (Twenge, 2006; Twenge & Campbell, 2008). Gen X and Gen Y also value leisure more than the traditionalists and Baby Boomers did at a similar age (Downing, 2006; Ng et al., 2010; Tang et al., 2012; Twenge et al., 2010).

Using time lapse data, Twenge et al. (2010) found interesting results, indicating that, compared with Boomers, Gen X and Gen Y (which they refer to as GenMe) are motivated by extrinsic rewards. GenY value intrinsic and social rewards (jobs that help them connect with people and make new friends) less than the Baby Boomers did. The authors argue that with the rise of dual-income families, increased working hours, and limited vacation, the value placed on additional leisure time is considerably stronger in Gen X and Y. Given these differences, managers can offer more work–life balance programs and opportunities for leisure to Gen X and Gen Y generations as a form of motivation. The federal government has paid close attention to this research and offers programs that help with employees' work–life balance. These include child care subsidies, eldercare support groups, employee assistance programs, fitness assistance, leave sharing, lactation centers, alternate work schedules such as flexible and compressed work schedules, telecommuting, and health and retirement benefits.

Generational difference is just one factor affecting the motivation and personality of employees. Additionally, supervisors must realize that some employees need detailed instructions and that others need a great deal of independence. Some need to be left alone, and others need to be stroked constantly. Supervisors must use various techniques to obtain performance from different people. Some of the resources needed for motivating employees are available to the supervisor, but others are outside her control. Certainly a supervisor can create a friendly, open, and authority-sharing work situation. However, the supervisor alone cannot determine monetary rewards, advancement, and the work situation; upper management usually has the final say in these and other matters.

The supervisor's approach depends on his knowledge of the employees and their needs. It also depends on the technology available and his authority to make changes. In addition, employee organizations and unions are having an increasing effect on management's ability to use performance improvement techniques.

Approaches to Motivation

Because people are motivated by different factors, approaches to motivation must vary. Nonetheless, people are generally motivated by *extrinsic* (external) and *intrinsic* (internal) factors. Extrinsic rewards include pay and benefits; intrinsic rewards include satisfaction and psychological fulfilment. In consideration of these factors, motivation theories can be divided into three different approaches: needs theory, expectancy theory, and equity theory.

Needs Theory

Needs theory posits that individuals are motivated by needs, and every individual has different needs. Needs also vary over time for an individual. Perhaps the clearest expression of needs theory is Maslow's (1954) hierarchy of needs: physiological, safety, social, ego, and self-actualization. The needs are listed in order from the most basic to the highest level need. As one level of need is satisfied, it no longer motivates the individual.

- Physiological needs include air, food, and clothing. These needs are indirectly satisfied in the workplace primarily through compensation.

- Safety needs include security, shelter, and freedom from physical harm. The pay and benefits of a job help satisfy safety needs.

- Social needs include love, affection, and acceptance. Support from supervisors and managers provides part of the satisfaction of social needs, but friendly informal groups and interactions with co-workers are the primary satisfiers of social needs within an organization.

- Ego needs include a feeling of achievement, accomplishment, and self-worth. Workplaces help satisfy ego needs by offering recognition, respect, and status.

- Self-actualization needs involve the fulfillment and realization of one's potential. Self-actualization needs can be satisfied through increasing autonomy and independence in the work situation and through increasing levels of responsibility.

Approaches to motivation focus on different aspects of needs theory. Traditional motivation theorists viewed human beings as primarily rational and as motivated primarily by economic needs. Furthermore, traditional theory based its techniques on the belief that people dislike work but do it to satisfy their material (physiological and safety) needs. According to this view, the way to increase their productivity is to raise employees' salaries. In the industrial sector, where productivity usually was more easily measured, the emphasis on material incentives led to the use of piece-rate forms of compensation in which an employee could earn more by producing more. Gradually, theorists learned that money motivates employees to a certain point but then loses value as an incentive (Halachmi & Korgt, 1998; Whyte et al., 1955).

With the recognition that the appeal of monetary incentives was limited, attention turned to workers' physical environment. The Scientific Management school was at the forefront of this trend. This approach viewed the physical environment and monetary incentives as closely linked because morale could be improved by pleasant surroundings, thus leading to increased production, which in turn would lead to increased pay. Ironically, the concern with surroundings was responsible for the discovery of the importance of the human element in organization behavior. The well-known Hawthorne Studies at Western Electric were directed at finding the optimal physical conditions under which assembly line workers are the most productive. Experiments conducted for this study involving changing illumination levels and other aspects of the work environment led to the unexpected discovery that social and psychological factors are more important than are physical conditions in determining the level of productivity (Brown, 1962; Homans, 1951; Parsons, 1974).

The Human Relations approach to management, which focuses on people's social needs, grew out of the 1928 Hawthorne studies, although Mary Parker Follett had suggested similar ideas earlier (Follet, 1924). According to this approach, creating a work situation in which employees believe that management cares about them leads to increased productivity. Fostering interpersonal relationships and group dynamics became the fad in the immediate post-World War II era. Students of organizatal behavior emphasized informal groups and norms in organizations and frequently ignored the formal structure (Blau, 1963; Blau

& Mayer, 1976). Most studies in human relations concentrated on the way the requirements of the formal structure created unnatural specialization and led to the development of informal groups to overcome the tediousness of the work. Little attention was given to the need for reevaluating the work process itself; managers were supposed to become the friends of workers. Industrial psychologists were employed to help design the optimum working conditions to foster increased efficiency and productivity. Such approaches led to charges that human relations programs were manipulating employees, and workers saw through managers whose interest was still in increasing productivity and who accomplished this using psychological rather than monetary means. Although the human relations approach helped humanize the work situation, it still focused on the individual as a part of the organization's machinery.

One student of management, Chester I. Barnard, saw early on that the requirements of the individual and those of the organization had to match (Barnard, 1968). Nonetheless, his focus was on motivating workers by means of effective management techniques and leadership qualities. For some time, leadership traits and styles were seen as the principal factors in gaining employees' cooperation. Leadership styles were particularly important. Generally it was concluded that the democratic style is most effective over the long run, authoritarian leadership can be effective over the short term, and laissez-faire leadership appears ineffective. Barnard combined his research on leadership with the reactions of employees to their leaders. He was an early advocate of considering the personality of workers and managers, as well as the psychological factors in workers' reactions to commands and directives. It was therefore a short step to studies on the relationship between human personality and organizations.

Organizational humanists, typified by Chris Argyris, went beyond the manipulative approaches of human relations and identified the needs of individuals that affect their roles as members of organizations (e.g., ego and self-actualization needs) (Argyris, 1964). In essence, Argyris claimed that organizations require submissive and dependent workers who do as they are told; the incongruity between personality and organizational needs increases the lower one is in the hierarchy. Argyris called for organizations to adapt to promote greater responsibility for the well-being of their members.

Argyris argued that not all people react in the same way but that many of the needs of the mature human personality are inconsistent with the demands of organizations modeled on traditional principles. Robert Presthus pointed out that personalities differ in their adjustments to the needs of complex organizations (Presthus, 1978). Once the ground was broken, however, a new approach to maximizing individual potential was unleashed. People were no longer viewed as disliking their work per se but rather as disliking the way it was organized. People could be motivated to produce if they were permitted to develop themselves in the work situation. Behavioral scientists have built on these ideas to devise new approaches to human self-actualization in the workplace. The next section of this chapter summarizes some of their approaches.

The work of Presthus and others led to the recognition that different types of personalities are found at different levels of organizations. Those at the highest levels of management are usually concerned less with material rewards and the need to feel wanted by the organization than with recognition, prestige, titles, and the accumulation of the symbols of success. The relationship of the success of these persons in the organization to success or recognition in society as a whole can be much more of a driving force than it is likely to be for those in the middle and lower levels of the bureaucracy (Downs, 1967; Jurkiewicz & Massey, 1997; Rand, 1974).

The behavioral approach stresses the notion that human beings enjoy and need work as much as they do recreation; therefore, ways should be found to permit employees to use their capacities to the fullest extent in the work situation. The key to effective organization became what Douglas McGregor called the Theory Y form of organization, which stressed people's independence, creative intelligence, and willingness to perform what they view as useful tasks (McGregor, 1968). The realization that people (1) do not hate work, (2) are capable of making intelligent judgments, and (3) are motivated to achieve objectives that they help determine has led to the advocacy by many of democratic, or participative, administration.

Behavioral scientists base their analysis on Maslow's hierarchy of needs. Frederick Herzberg suggested that most organizations do not actually build on these needs as motivators; instead, they tend to focus on "hygiene" factors, physical surroundings, status, and the like, which all members of an organization expect anyway (Herzberg, 1966). Basing his analysis on the hierarchy of human needs, Herzberg recommended that organizations use positive growth factors as motivators because workers' motivation comes from things such as their own achievement, recognition, and increased responsibility.

Public Service Motivation (PSM) is also a needs-based approach to understanding motivation, particularly among public sector employees (Clerkin & Coggburn, 2012). Perry and Wise (1990) define PSM as an "individual's predisposition to respond to motives grounded primarily or uniquely in public institutions and organizations" (p. 368). Perry and Wise argue that individuals enter the public sector for one of the following reasons: (a) rational—when an individual identifies with an issue and is motivated by the possibility of bringing a policy change, (b) norm-based—an inherent desire to serve the public interest, or (c) affective—a personal attachment and commitment to advance a particular public program. PSM thus impacts one's occupational choice, job satisfaction, job performance, and work preferences (Alonso & Lewis, 2001; Brewer & Selden, 2000; Frank & Lewis, 2004; Kim, 2005; Naff & Crum, 1999). Studies also find that public service motivation varies by gender, age, education level, and level of managerial responsibility (Bright, 2005; Moynihan & Pandey, 2007; Naff & Crum, 1999; Perry, 1997). In recent years, it has been suggested that using PSM as a recruitment tool can help improve work attitudes, performance, and reduce turnover (Clerkin & Coggburn, 2012; Kim, 2012).

Expectancy Theory

Expectancy theory is based on the idea that people expect some type of outcome from a given action or level of effort. For motivation purposes, the outcome should be a reward that is valued by the individual and that results from effort expended (Vroom, 1964). Managers need to make clear linkages between effort and reward in order to motivate employees. Thus, employees must know exactly what is expected and what they will gain from the effort. For the expectations to motivate, the organization needs to fulfill the promised reward once the individual performs. Otherwise, the individual becomes demotivated.

Pay-for-performance, as discussed in Chapter 3, is based on expectancy theory. Presumably employees will increase performance levels to earn merit/performance pay increases or bonuses. As noted in the earlier discussion, the public sector's use of pay-for-performance also usually illustrates the demotivating nature of ill-conceived use of expectancy theory. Because governments usually do not fund pay-for-performance systems adequately, employees do not realize the reward they expect for increased performance and thus become demotivated.

Equity Theory

For rewards to motivate, they also must be perceived by employees as being fair (Adams, 1965). Fairness is judged on the basis of whether the reward is appropriate for the amount of effort needed to receive it. Employees also judge fairness on the basis of how the reward compares with that given to other employees. Thus, they look at other employees' levels of effort and rewards. If they are perceived as fair, the rewards can motivate, but if they are perceived as unfair, they can demotivate.

Motivation Techniques

Motivating employees involves using a variety of techniques, some specifically motivational in intent and others more generally concerned with humanizing and democratizing the organization. One of the most general and widely accepted behavioral conclusions is that employees are more committed and productive if they have an opportunity to participate in the organization's decisions, particularly those pertaining to the work situation.

The meaning of employee participation in the decision-making process is often vague, but it usually starts with the belief that individuals have the capacity and desire to assume responsibility. They are more likely to assume responsibility for achieving outcomes if they participate in deciding what the outcomes will be. Michael Smith (1976) suggests that participation also enhances the interpersonal, social, and political skills of employees, thus improving service as they interact with the public. He also believes that participative management results in less resentment of those in authority, thus focusing more energy on the work to be done.

Although arguments for participative management are strong, many factors work against it. Managers are reluctant to give up their power and blur the status distinction between them and their subordinates. They also tend to try to protect the organization from the uncertainty that change brings by sticking to traditional ways of doing things (Smith, 1976).

Vasu, Stewart, and Garson (1998) suggest other reasons for resistance to participative approaches. They believe that traditional approaches survive because of the cozy relationship of bureaucracies to clientele and other stakeholders in the political environment. Because goals of public organizations are unclear and are subject to constant change, evidence of participative management is difficult to demonstrate. Also, elected political leaders like to retain control over making policy and believe that bureaucracies are supposed to be implementing the policy, not making it.

The private sector more commonly uses participative management approaches, though many government bureaucracies also use them. Management by Objectives (MBO), for example, has been used by agencies at all levels of government. According to MBO, organization members participate in setting goals and choosing how to achieve them. It also involves participatory monitoring and evaluating progress toward goals (Drucker, 1954). Most MBOs in the public sector are a streamlined version focusing mostly on setting objectives. Strategic planning, now common in government agencies, builds on basic MBO processes.

Job enrichment is a motivational technique suggested by many behavioral scientists. Job boredom is a problem in all sectors and levels of society, particularly among lower-level employees. By making the job interesting, management increases employee commitment and motivation. Employees who have control over and responsibility for their work, see the results of their efforts. Moreover, employees who have diversified duties are likely to identify with the job and take pride in doing it well. They are also likely to be more productive than those who perform a highly specialized task with no idea about the end product (Ford, 1973; Zwerdling, 1973). Although there are many advantages to job enrichment, managers find the principle difficult to apply because of their lack of understanding of the technique and unfounded fears of loss of status or role.

Other approaches to building organization capacity and engaging employees more fully include organization development (OD) and its variations. OD literature focuses on adapting the organization to the changing environment and (particularly relevant to our considerations) to the changing needs of the people within the organization. OD strives to break down communication barriers. The hope is that through self-awareness, awareness of others, and awareness of the organization's needs, all individuals in the organization will become more trusting of one another, more committed to the organization's goals, and more self-directed and responsible in attempting to solve organizational problems (Golembiewski, 1969). In general, this approach is based on the assumption that people will change their attitudes and behavior for the better in an open, problem-solving atmosphere.

Managers must be adaptable and flexible in dealing with different employees. The task of accommodating differing needs of employees is a daunting one. Employees of organizations have varying values and attitudes that affect their motivation to work (Denhardt, Denhardt, & Aristigueta, 2008; Eddy, 1981; Van Wart, 1998). Some people have strong work ethics and cannot give anything less than their best effort, whereas others try to get away with doing the least amount of work possible. Some workers have a constant need for approval and ego stroking, whereas others desire autonomy and are motivated by their own achievements or by the need to exercise responsibility. Many crave symbols of success, such as titles, office accoutrements, or money. Managers need to use different approaches to motivate various employees who have differing needs. Nevertheless, even if managers were capable of understanding what was important to each employee, they rarely have the capacity and resources to act on such information. There is no magic formula for success. However, research consistently suggests that managers who combine a rational goal orientation with a sincere concern and support for their employees tend to be the most successful.

Another approach to management, which uses well-established behavioral principals, is total quality management (TQM). TQM has been used successfully in Japan since the Japanese imported the idea from the United States shortly after World War II. After seeing its success in Japan, many U.S. companies re-imported the concept during the 1970s, and the public sector experimented with it as well. TQM focuses on improving and maintaining quality throughout the organization. The ultimate focus is on high-quality service to the customer, whether the customer is external or internal to the organization. To improve quality, processes are instituted to identify practices that lead to errors or defects. The goal is zero defects. Catching and correcting errors as they occur enhances the quality of the end product or service. Money is saved because defective products and services should not occur, thus saving the cost of replacing them. Correcting errors early in the process costs less than does going back after the fact. TQM relates to motivation by involving everyone in the organization in the analysis of work processes and in efforts to improve them. Team building is a part of TQM, and it represents another approach to improving employee performance. Because it deals less with individual motivation and more with the productivity of a work group or unit, team building is discussed later in this chapter.

To better motivate employees, supervisors should provide feedback, set clear and attainable organizational goals, reduce red tape, and provide psychological contracts. These are also components of the performance management system, which are discussed in the next section. Providing fair and timely feedback can also serve as a great motivating tool (Kim & Rubianty, 2011; Selden, 2008). Too often the feedback provided via appraisals is inadequate, unclear, or unfair. Employees want feedback that will help them to meet organizational goals and to advance within the organization.

Setting clear organizational goals can also serve as a motivating factor, whereas having vague, ambiguous goals can detract and demotivate employees (Jung & Rainey, 2011). A motivated public servant can easily be demotivated and can become frustrated with the organizational systems and goal displacement (Moynihan & Pandey, 2007). Reinventing government is an effort to counter the challenges of the system. In fact, the mantra of President Clinton's administration was to move from "red tape to results." Other efforts to counter the problem of rigid personnel rules and red tape in the government are creating flatter organizational structures, performing red tape audits, and increasing citizen engagement (Bozeman, 2000; Moynihan & Herd, 2010).

𝓋 *Psychological contracts* are defined as "informal agreements between managers and individual workers that aim to increase worker commitment and alignment with the needs of the organization" (Berman & West, 2003, p.268). They can have a positive impact on an employee's motivation and can further job productivity. These contracts begin where formal agreements end; psychological contracts ensure a balance between what people want and what they get in return. For example, an employee can have a psychological contract with his supervisor about coming late every Wednesday so he can attend classes at a community college; in return, he works late on Fridays.

Over the last few decades, research has supported the positive relationship between *transformational leadership* style and employee motivation and satisfaction (Paarlberg & Lavigna, 2010; Park & Rainey, 2008; Trottier, Van Wart, & Wang, 2008; Wright, Moynihan, & Pandey, 2012). Transformational leadership is "a process that motivates employees by appealing to their higher ideals and moral values" (Paarlberg & Lavigna, 2010, p. 711). Transformational leadership is a concept formulated in 1978 by James MacGregor Burns, who proposed that the leadership process occurs in one of two ways—transactional or transformational. The transactional leader approaches his followers with the intent of "exchanging one thing for another" (p. 4). This style appeals to self-interest. The transforming leader attempts to understand the relationship between leaders and followers to raise each other's motivation and sense of higher achievement or purpose. This concept follows Maslow's (1954) hierarchy of needs, in which self-actualization is the highest order in the hierarchy. A transformational leader similarly addresses the highest-order needs of his or her followers. In the process, the leader and follower may emerge with a stronger and higher set of moral values. Having a supervisor with a transformative leadership style can create a productive and motivated workforce.

Performance Management

Performance management encompasses a set of functions aimed at improving individual performance and motivating employees. These functions include clarifying agency goals and adopting the actions that will achieve them, establishing clear expectations and providing feedback through employee appraisals, fair compensation, and training and development opportunities to address job-related weaknesses, and offering growth opportunities (Sowa & Selden, 2011). It also requires the development of credible performance data to measure achievement (Ammons, 1995; Greiner, 1996). Performance management relies on both individual and organizational aspects of performance. It also serves as a tool for holding organizations and management accountable.

The various incentives and behavioral techniques discussed in association with motivation are aspects of individual performance management strategies that organizations can use. Some of the commonly used efforts focused on improving performance include (1) pay-for-performance, in which salary increases are tied to performance, and (2) gainsharing, a concept commonly used in the private sector, and to a lesser extend in the public sector, in which the organization shares with employees its savings from improved performance. The productivity improvement programs of the 1970s and 1980s were also attempts at improving individual and organizational performance (Hayward, 1976; Horton, 1976; Newland, 1972).

In the 1980s, a new approach emerged called *new public management*, which emphasized reinvention of government through improved performance. By adapting a private-sector-market approach to the public sector, it was believed that government could become more efficient. Government agencies were viewed as businesses, and citizens were viewed as customers. The Clinton administration's National Performance Review embodied many of the principles of reinvention and focused on making government work better while using fewer resources (National Performance Review, 1993). Critics of new public management claim that the approach focuses on efficiency to the detriment of public service to citizens (Denhardt & Denhardt, 2000; King & Stivers, 1998). Denhardt and Denhardt proposed a different approach to public administration called "The New Public Service." The major tenets are as follows:

Serve rather than steer—help citizens articulate and meet their shared interests.

Make public interest the aim, not the by-product.

Think strategically, act democratically.

Serve citizens, not customers.

Recognize that accountability is not simple.

Value people, not productivity.

Value citizenship and public service above entrepreneurship (Denhardt & Denhardt, 2000).

These themes suggest that performance management assesses the quality of public service not only by its efficiency at serving citizens but also by how well it upholds the values on which the system is based. Noting that accountability is not simple, Denhardt and Denhardt (2000) recognize the complexity of measuring performance according to these values.

Most government jurisdictions now use *total performance measurement* to cope with the complexities of performance management (National Center for Productivity and Quality of Working Life, 1978). In this approach, data are first systematically collected; then a performance audit is conducted to examine productivity data, along with other information, to evaluate overall performance and improve productivity. Employees, clientele, and citizens can be surveyed to determine whether the organization is perceived to be productive and whether its service is effective and useful. Feedback to employees and managers is a central aspect of performance management. Such feedback permits everyone to understand what needs to change and encourages participation in making the changes.

Training and Development

In the past, governments assumed that they could acquire personnel in the labor market with the requisite skills and abilities; therefore, the training and development of public employees were not considered a high priority. However, rapid changes in technology, the need for employees to constantly acquire new skills and knowledge base, and the effects of a more diverse workforce (among other factors) have required government employers to provide training and development programs.

Even truer today than in 1993 when Paul Sandwith said it, "The triple threat of most organizations today...are the simultaneous demands for improved quality, reduced costs, and constant innovation" (Sandwith, 1993, p.43). To meet these demands, training and development (aka human resource development) are critical elements of human resources systems (Van Wart, Cayer, & Cook, 1993). Recognizing the need for human resource development (HRD), the federal government passed the Government Employees Training Act in 1958, requiring federal agencies to create programs for employee training. Subsequently, in 1970, the Intergovernmental Personnel Act (IPA) was passed, permitting the temporary assignment of federal agency personnel to state and local governments and vice versa. Since the elimination of IPA during the Reagan administration, state and local governments have assumed the responsibility for HRD themselves.

When instituting a training and development program, the personnel office and operating department usually work together, although in some government units the personnel office is not involved in employee training. The personnel office or HRD unit can provide expertise and advice, but the operating department is usually in the best position to determine the actual training needs. Training programs are often developed with the cooperation of a centralized training agency that possesses the needs-assessment capabilities and training competence.

The most elementary training program is a new-employee orientation program that can have a significant impact on employee behavior and productivity. Traditionally, agencies had spent only a short time introducing new employees and explaining the rules, regulations, and benefits of the job. Now, depending on the job of course, the orientation process often stretches over a longer period, and employees are encouraged to discuss their problems adjusting to their new job and learning their duties. They also learn what resources the employer offers to help them to adjust to and succeed in the agency. In some cases, employees are trained on-the-job. In this case, an individual without the needed skills is hired and learns the job from another employee. Often the new person serves an apprenticeship. Such training can also be used to help employees move up in their organization by learning new skills.

It has become common to encourage individual employee development through a variety of programs inside and outside the organization. These programs take the form of workshops, institutes, professional conferences, university and college programs, tuition reimbursement, and sabbaticals. The national government has sponsored such programs for a long time and permits state and local government employees to participate in many of the federal programs. State and local governments have also created their own programs along the same lines.

As training and development have evolved, HRD professionals have come to recognize that employees, supervisors, managers, and executives all have differing needs in regard to training and development programs. Catering to different constituents, these programs should focus on specific technical, interpersonal, or conceptual skills. Though all employees need each of these types of programs, the level of need for each varies with the type of role the individual plays in the organization. Employees have other needs that have to be addressed. For example, many employees become plateaued in the organization, meaning that they reach a level beyond which they cannot advance. Especially in today's environment in which organizational hierarchies are flat and downsizing is common, opportunities for promotion are greatly reduced. Plateaued employees may need special attention and perhaps some sort of accommodation if they are to remain contributing members of the organization. As with all employees, each plateaued employee will have a different reaction to the situation.

In addition to different substantive content, training and development programs employ different methods to deliver the material. Because training and development programs in the public service serve adults, they must be sensitive to the ways adults learn and must recognize that each employee has a different learning style. Traditional lecture methods tend to be ineffective. Successful HRD programs require teaching through a combination of lecture, discussion, role playing, and problem solving. Studies have shown that interactive learning increases the likelihood of comprehension and retention of the program content.

Not surprising, the national government has been a leader in many types of training programs. The Office of Personnel Management (OPM) sponsors a variety of programs and has training centers in each of its regions. Although the regional centers are primarily for middle- and upper-level federal officials, state and local personnel are accepted on a space-available basis. Executive Development Seminars throughout the country provide intensive training opportunities for management personnel. The Federal Executive Institute in Charlottesville, Virginia, offers small, intensive courses for high-level administrators and demonstrates the OPM's commitment to excellence in the public service. In addition to these programs, individual departments and agencies conduct their own training and development activities as a way to identify and groom future leaders. This is also a part of their succession planning activities. Ingraham and Getha-Taylor (2004) provide the following examples of various leadership programs in the federal government:

(USDA) Aspiring Leaders Program for GS 5 to 7

(EPA) Candidate Development Program for GS 14 to 15

(DOD) The Defense Leadership and Management Program for GS 13 to 15

(IRS) Leadership Development Program for front-line, senior, and executive employees.

Department of Veterans Affairs—Leadership Enhancement and Development Program

The National Aeronautics and Space Administration—Agency-wide Leadership and Management Development Program

Although state and local governments were slow to follow the national government's lead, most now have established some sort of ongoing training and development program. The Intergovernmental Personnel Act of 1970 provided the seed money for and demonstrated the value of many training and development activities. Of course, training and development programs often fall victim to budget cuts, and when finances are limited, these programs suffer. Nonetheless, training and development of employees have been recognized as essential in the public service at all levels of government.

Mobility programs are another kind of development program that trains employees in a broad area of activities. In the national government, for example, the Senior Executive Service (SES) is a mobility program. Although its emphasis is not on training, it permits those selected to be exposed to a large part of the federal bureaucracy and thus broaden their skills and knowledge base. Mobility programs were a significant part of Intergovernmental Personnel Act programs. Employees of state and local governments would often take temporary assignments in the federal bureaucracy, and federal governmental employees would do the same in state and local governments. Universities also participated in the program. Now individual federal government agencies maintain similar programs, and the private sector sometimes becomes involved. These programs help employees learn about the other organizations they deal with and offer opportunities to employees to develop new skills and expertise that can be important to their agencies. The participating organizations also benefit from the new perspectives of the people they host.

Another type of training aimed at new and prospective employees is the internship. Many institutions of higher education require public service internships as part of their undergraduate and graduate programs in public administration. Other disciplines have their own internships. Students gain experience in the practical application of what they learn in the classroom. The internship requires government agencies to be willing to budget money for them and supervise the interns they host. Of course, the agencies benefit along with the student if the internship is carefully planned and executed. The Presidential Management Fellowship Program at the national level is an example of a major internship program that recruits top students from across the country to spend two years with a federal agency with the expectation that the interns will become permanent employees. Several states, including New York, Texas, and Montana have copied this program. Dallas, Long Beach, Phoenix, and the Metropolitan Dade County government have similar programs at the local level.

Apprenticeship training is another type of training that the public sector sometimes uses. While it is common in many types of private organizations, apprenticeship training exists to a lesser extent in the public sector. This type of training combines classroom instruction with on-the-job training and is normally used in skilled crafts or trades. The U.S. Department of Defense is the largest user of apprenticeship training in the public sector. State and local governments use the approach mostly for fire fighters, correctional officers, and police officers, although some use it for occupations such as electricians and secretaries.

Regardless of the type of program, managers must take the following into account. Will the training meet the short- and long-term objectives of the agency and align with the agency's goals?

Managers must also seek input from employees and supervisors on their training needs and expectations. It is also necessary to determine the site and budget for the training program. After the training is complete, it is critical to assess whether the training met its goals (OPM, 2008).

Research suggests that simply having a policy (e.g., a diversity or sexual harassment policy) does not necessarily lead to positive outcomes (Reese & Lindenberg, 2003). Training employees and educating them about the policy can have a positive impact on employee conduct. Training and development are often mentioned together, but they have different meanings. *Training* is often given to improve the current level of knowledge, skills, and abilities required to do the job. *Development* refers to an employee's long-term growth (Berman et al., 2012). Organizations offering developmental opportunities signal to their employees that they care about their growth.

Unfortunately, training is often the first activity that gets slashed from the budget during poor economic times. Training is costly, and the costs lead to controversy over whether it should be undertaken. However, the long-term costs of not undertaking training may be greater than the costs of the programs themselves, and most governments have recognized the value of such programs. Despite the costs involved, investing in training can lead to long-term benefits. To save costs, web-based training programs are gaining in popularity. Despite the various shortcomings associated with online training (the primary one being lack of face-to-face interaction), it is seen as an effective way to disseminate information and enhance learning (Preusser, Bartels, & Nordstrom, 2011). Strong support from the top political leadership is critical to getting an agency to buy in to training and development and help fend off efforts to cut programs. In this ever-changing society, a lack of training leads to employees with only outmoded skills who become frustrated by the lack of advancement opportunities. The end result is turnover and a need to recruit new employees, which is a costly process.

Performance Under Fiscal Constraints

Fiscal constraints are facts of life for government at all levels. Tax revolts and other spending limitations became popular nationwide in the late 1970s and continue to the present, necessitating cutback management in government. To deal with these pressures, the personnel function has become a major concern because personnel costs are the single most expensive part of a government's operating costs. However, cutback management creates uncertainties and faces resistance from employees, unions, interest groups, and agency managers. Attempting to accommodate the varying interests of these actors in the process and satisfy the demands of the public and politically elected officials places the personnel function in a difficult position. Reductions in force (RIF) and contracting out for public services are two major strategies used in cutback management.

When faced with cutbacks in funds, most governmental units attempt to achieve some form of reduction in the workforce. RIF can be accomplished through layoffs or attrition. Layoffs mean that positions are identified as dispensable according to criteria on which the unit agrees, resulting in employees being dismissed. Attrition means that positions are eliminated or not filled as incumbents leave. Each method of achieving a RIF leads to positive and negative consequences for the organization.

Layoffs have the advantage of permitting an agency to reduce the size of its personnel force quickly by eliminating dispensable positions. Thus, if conducted with a clear evaluation of an agency's needs and resources, layoffs can lead to a streamlined agency that is better able to use the skills and expertise of the employees it retains. Unfortunately, the task is not as easy as it sounds. Establishing the criteria for layoffs can be a controversial process. Usually employee unions want seniority to be the criterion for layoffs, whereas management normally wants a criterion such as performance or contribution to the organization's needs. If the criteria depend on the evaluation of performance or the like, uncertainty is likely to develop among the employees, causing morale problems. Because of low morale and a feeling of insecurity among employees, performance is likely to decline.

Cutbacks through layoffs provide an opportunity for management to evaluate employee performance and to find ways to use the agency's resources more efficiently in achieving its goals. The evidence suggests, however, that layoffs usually do not occur as a result of such rational analysis and often lead to greater problems for the organization because of the anxiety and stress employees experience from the process. Neither the public service nor citizens benefit much from poorly planned and executed RIF systems.

Employees and their unions usually look upon attrition more favorably than layoffs because no one loses a job involuntarily. Instead, as people leave, their positions are not filled. Attrition can ease management's job in getting the cooperation of employees during workforce reduction, so managers seldom oppose the process. Some managers, however, recognize that attrition can cause problems for the organization if it is not well planned and implemented. A basic problem is that management cannot control which positions become vacant. Employees leave for a variety of reasons. Often the ones who elect to leave are the most valuable employees who have the most sought-after skills or best performance records and who are the ones best able to acquire new jobs. As a result, management could be left with employees with less impressive skills and job performance. Obviously, the organization's productivity will suffer if this occurs.

However, attrition can be an effective RIF method if the organization prepares for it. Employees can be cross-trained so that if some leave, others can pick up their responsibilities. Especially effective is the training of employees whose skills or operations are least valuable to the organization's work. They can be trained in more needed areas of activity and thus become more valuable to the organization. Similarly, internal training can be used to fill the gap of needed skills lost through attrition. The training also could have the advantage of making employees more loyal and enabling them to see the organization as caring about them. This could also cause the employees to become more committed to its goals.

Clearly, layoffs and attrition can accomplish the objectives of reducing the number of personnel in a governmental unit. The choice of system depends on the particular situation and the speed with which reduction is necessary. Given the more humanistic nature of most personnel systems these days, attrition seems to be the most common method to achieve RIF. The effects on employee performance usually loom large in the decision about which method to use.

Ironically, when governments face calls for austerity, they have to endure budget cuts while demands for services increase. Budget cuts usually occur when the overall economy is in a downturn, resulting in a corresponding decline in tax revenue. As the economy weakens, people are put out of work, and they rely on social services for a safety net. Thus, governments often find that they need to provide more services with fewer resources. Public employees face the pressure of an increased demand for their services while their workforce is shrinking. The increased demand on those left can lead to stress, burnout, and a deterioration of morale. The human resources system then must deal with the problem of keeping the retained employees motivated and productive.

Another method of achieving cutbacks in government spending is contracting out government services, often referred to as privatization or outsourcing. Contracting is often touted as a cost saver because it reduces the permanent personnel of a governmental unit and gives the unit flexibility to contract for exactly the amount of service required. Thus, it is unnecessary to maintain a large workforce either in anticipation of a heavy workload that may not materialize or for seasonal jobs such as snow removal or swimming pool attendants. Instead, the governmental unit can contract for the job, and the private employer bears the cost of the overhead for maintaining its payroll. Having a private employer perform the service for many government agencies or other private organizations also can result in an economy of scale, which can be reflected in the cost of the contract. It is also usually assumed that by contracting out services, governmental jurisdictions can save money because they are not tied into long-term benefit programs such as retirement for the employees providing these services. The private firm handles all of that. Of course, contracting could be done with other governmental jurisdictions, as well as with private firms.

Although contracting out for services has cost advantages, some disagree with proponents' rosy picture. The American Federation of State, County and Municipal Employees (AFSCME), for instance, believes that contracting for services costs more (AFSCME, 1984) in the long run. AFSCME points to problems in controlling the cost and quality of the services provided and the potential for collusion between public officials and contractors. The potential abuses can be costly for the taxpayer, who must also bear the costs of monitoring and making the contractors accountable. Obviously, AFSCME has a special interest in protecting the jobs of public employees, but it does raise some important issues that governments need to consider when they contract out for services. At any rate, contracting requires careful planning and does not guarantee efficiency or savings unless it is implemented properly and with realistic expectations (Bel, Fageda, & Warner, 2010; Chi and Jasper, 1998; DeHoog, 1997; Hefetz & Warner, 2012; Hodge, 2000; Seidenstat, 1999). As Donald Kettl points out, extensive contracting out also has implications for the nature of government work (Kettl, 2002). With contracting out, the government must have managers capable of keeping contractors accountable. Unfortunately, the resources for monitoring and assessment are not always forthcoming, and abuses which waste taxpayer's money have frquently come to light.

Privatization, that is often embraced as another way to reduce the public workforce and thus save money, has many implications for human resources management. Morale is likely to be negatively affected, and unionized employees may view privatization as a vehicle for union busting. There could also be a disparity between the treatment of public sector employees and that of the employees of the private firms providing the contracted service. Public sector employees have procedural rights and protections that do not apply to private sector employees. This leads to the issue of whether government has an obligation to ensure equitable treatment of employees who provide public services even if they work for a private firm.

The drive for creating an efficient government and for doing more with less has led several states to adopt private sector policies on the premise of saving costs and improving performance. The most sweeping changes in personnel were made by Florida in 2001 under the governorship of Jeb Bush, who introduced employment-at-will and pay-for-performance, following similar arrangements in Georgia (1996) and Texas (1985). "Employment at will (EAW) allows employers to terminate employees at any time, for any reason—good or bad—not contrary to the law, or for no reason" (Coggburn et al., 2010, p. 190). The impacts of EAW continue to be debated. Proponents of the reform argue that EAW increases managerial flexibility, reduces red tape, and provides the much needed impetus for improving performance (Bowman, Gertz, Gertz, & Williams, 2003; Green et al., 2007; Walters, 2003). However, opponents argue that eliminating the very pillar on which civil service was founded (job tenure) can lead to return of the spoils system (Kellough & Nigro, 2005). Battaglio and Condrey (2009) argue that "by exchanging job security in favor of managerial flexibility, reformers may have delivered a blow to employee commitment and organizational productivity" (p.703) Pay-for-performance, another strategy adopted from the private sector, has met with mixed responses from agencies. Public sector employees who are intrinsically motivated are less likely to favor performance-based systems (Soo Oh & Lewis, 2009).

Summary

Public employee performance is a key concern of governments because taxpayers demand high levels of service while taxes are held down. To ensure the highest level of service possible, public employers depend on the supervisor to create an environment in which employees wish to work. In addition, organizations use various theories of motivation to persuade employees to produce at their optimum effort. In recent years, behavioral approaches to organizing the work unit and job have acquired support as ways of improving performance. Governments also use performance management programs that utilize new technology, better management techniques, and employee participation. Evaluation systems test employee performance and the effects of techniques for improving performance. Performance management also helps assess training needs and create development programs to improve the skills and opportunities of employees in the organization.

Public employers are limited in their ability to use performance enhancement measures by the realities of the political environment. The political environment since the 1970s has been dominated by pressure for fiscal constraint. Thus, public employers must find ways to do the job better with fewer resources. Governments often must reduce their personnel but still meet the public's service demands. Government agencies therefore are caught between the demands of their employees and those of the citizens. Cutback management is accomplished through reduction-in-force methods (layoffs and attrition), contracting out for services, and employment-at-will strategies. Some services are eliminated and are accompanied by reductions-in-force.

Exercises

1. Make an appointment with the director or manager of a department in a state, county, municipal, or tribal government agency. Ask the manager what he or she believes is the most effective way to get people to be productive in the organization. Ask the manager to describe a situation in the organization in which there was an issue with the performance of an individual or group.

> How did he or she handle the situation? From what you have heard from the manager, how would you characterize his or her assumptions about human nature? How would you describe the manager's management style?

2. Interview a leader of an employee union or association in local or state government. Ask the leader to describe the role of the union or association in decision making within the organization.

> From the interview, what sense do you get of how much the group participates in managing the organization? Does the relationship between the government and its employees appear to be an open, communicative one? Explain. What are the implications for how the agency operates?

3. Motivating employees is an important management task. When people are motivated, they work with energy, enthusiasm, and initiative.

> Drawing on one of your job experiences, identify ways in which your immediate supervisor has knowingly and unknowingly affected your motivation. Which actions or policies by your supervisor increased your motivation? Which ones decreased your motivation? How would you like to be motivated? What are some techniques that employers can use to positively impact the motivation of their employees?

4. Gary Corbett worked for five years in the Utilities Department of Milltown. He was recognized as a hard worker and appeared to work well with everyone. When an opening occurred in the directorship of the customer service division, he applied and was appointed. The customer service division had always run relatively smoothly and had a relaxed atmosphere. Gary appreciated the fact that the work got done but thought the employees could be less social and more focused on their work. On his first day, he called a staff meeting, in which he said,

> I am very pleased to be joining the customer service division and look forward to working with all of you. The work of this division is very good, and with all your help we will make it even better. I want us to win the award for the most productive unit in the Utilities Department. Therefore, as time passes, there will be some changes. Again, I am pleased to be here, and I encourage you to communicate your ideas and concerns to me. I will have an open door. Working together, we can become the best.

Gary then outlined some new procedures and rules, including the requirement that each supervisor document the arrival time, break time, and departure time of each supervisee. Over the next few weeks, he established more rules to tighten procedures so that all employees knew exactly how to do their jobs and to ensure accountability.

To Gary's surprise, morale in the division deteriorated, and the unit's pleasant atmosphere disappeared. People began to take more sick leave, and customer complaints about service increased. People began handing in reports late. He also was surprised that few people took advantage of his open-door policy to talk with him about their ideas and suggestions.

> If you were called in as a consultant by Gary Corbett, what would you tell him? Explain the change in the employees' behavior. What was good and what was not good about the way Gary approached his responsibilities? How would you rectify the situation?

5. Mayor Carrie Campbell was elected on a platform to make city government more efficient and responsive to its citizens. Just after being elected mayor, and as owner of a real estate company, she went to a national real estate conference where she heard a motivational speaker make an inspiring presentation. The mayor was very impressed, made a point of introducing herself to the speaker, and indicated that she wanted the speaker to offer a training program to city department heads and managers. The mayor promised to contact the speaker later about the details.

When Mayor Campbell returned home, she called you, the director of training and development, into her office and informed you that you were to work with the conference speaker to arrange dates for her to offer her training and development program for all city employees.

How do you respond to the mayor? Is the mayor's idea good? Why or why not? If you were the mayor, what would you have done?

Selected Websites

Alliance for Innovation. Network of governments and other organizations devoted to developing and disseminating innovations in local governments. Encourages innovation through various activities including dissemination of research.

http://urbaninnovation.asu.edu/alliance-for-innovation

American Society for Training and Development (ASTD). Professional association of people devoted to learning through training and development in both the public and private sectors. Publishes journals and reports furthering training and development.

www.astd.org

Center for Accountability and Performance. Unit of the American Society for Public Administration (ASPA) that provides research, technical assistance, education, training, and advocacy on best practices in performance management.

www.aspaonline.org/cap

Section for Professional and Organizational Development (SPOD). Section of the American Society for Public Administration (ASPA) that advances continuing education and training for public service organizations. Sponsors a quarterly newsletter and the journal, *Public Administration Quarterly*.

http://www.aspanet.org/public/

Section on Public Performance and Management (SPPM). Section of the American Society for Public Administration (ASPA) that focuses on public organization performance. It sponsors panels at the ASPA annual conference and sponsors publications including the *SPPM Newsletter* and the journal, *Public Performance and Management Review*. http://www.aspanet.org/public/ASPA/Resources/ASPA_Chapters__Sections/ASPA/MemberTools/ChapterSectionListIPart. aspx?hkey=f2839f953bcc-4601-b4f6-113b6dc69aaa

References

Adams, J. S. (1965). Inequity in social exchange, In L. Berkowitz, (Ed.), *Advances in experimental social psychology, 2*. (267–299). San Diego: Academic Press.

Alonso, E, & Lewis, G. B. (2001). Public service motivation and job performance: Evidence from the federal sector. *The American Review of Public Administration, 31*, 363–380.

American Federation of State, County and Municipal Employees (AFSCME). (1984). *Passing the buck: The contracting out of public services.* Washington, DC: AFSCME.

Ammons, D. (1995). *Accountability for performance: Measurement and monitoring in local government.* Washington, DC: International City/County Management Association.

Argyris, C. (1964). *Integrating the Individual and Organization.* New York: Wiley.

Barnard, C. I. (1968). *The functions of the executive.* Cambridge, MA: Harvard University Press.

Battaglio, R. P., & Condrey, S. E. (2009). Reforming public management: Analyzing the impact of public service reform on organizational and managerial trust. *Journal of Public Administration Research and Theory, 19*(4), 689–707.

Bel, G., Fageda, X., & Warner, M. E. (2010). Is private production of public services cheaper than public production? A meta-regression analysis of solid waste and water services. *Journal of Policy Analysis and Management 29*(3), 553–77.

Berman, E. M., & West, J. P. (2003). Psychological contracts in local government A preliminary survey. *Review of Public Personnel Administration, 23*(4), 267–285.

Berman, E. M., West, J. P., Bowman, J. S., & Van Wart, M. R. (2012). *Human resource management in public service: Paradoxes, processes, and problems.* Thousand Oaks, CA: Sage Publications.

Blau, P. (1963). *The dynamics of bureaucracy: A study of interpersonal relationships intwo government agencies* (2nd ed.). Chicago: University of Chicago Press.

Blau, P., & Mayer, M. W. (1976). *Bureaucracy in modem society* (2nd ed.). New York: Random House.

Bowman, J. S., Gertz, M. G., Gertz, S. C., & Williams, R. L. (2003). Civil service reform in Florida state government, employee attitudes 1 year later. *Review of Public Personnel Administration, 23*(4), 286–304.

Bozeman, B. (2000). *Bureaucracy and red tape.* Upper Saddle River, NJ: Prentice Hall.

Brewer, G. A. (2005). In the eye of the storm: Frontline supervisors and federal agency performance. *Journal of Public Administration Research and Theory, 15*, 505–27.

Brewer, G. A., & Selden, S. C. (2000). Why elephants gallop: Assessing and predicting organizational performance in federal agencies. *Journal of Public Administration Research and Theory, 10*(4), 685–711.

Brown, J. A. C. (1962). *The social psychology of industry.* Baltimore, MD.: Penguin.

Burns, J. M. (1978). *Leadership.* NY: Harper & Row.

Chi, K. S., & Jasper, C. (1998). *Private practices: A review of privatization in state government.* Lexington, KY: Council of State Governments.

Clerkin, R. M., & Coggburn, J. D. (2012). The dimensions of public service motivation and sector work preferences. *Review of Public Personnel Administration, 32*(3), 209–235.

Coggburn, J. D., Battaglio, R. P., Bowman, J. S., Condrey, S. E., Goodman, D., & West, J. P. (2010). State government human resource professionals' commitment to employment at will. *The American Review of Public Administration, 40*(2), 189–208.

DeHoog, R. H. (1997). Legal issues in contracting for public services: When business does government, In P. J. Cooper & C. A. Newland (Eds.), *Public law and administration* (pp. 528–545). San Francisco: Jossey- Bass.

Denhardt R. B., & Denhardt, J. V. (2000). The new public service: Serving rather than steering. *Public Administration Review, 60*(6), 549–559.

Denhardt, R. B., Denhardt, J. V., & Aristigueta, M. P. (2008). *Managing human behavior in public sector and nonprofit organizations* (2nd ed.). Thousand Oaks, CA: Sage.

Downing, K. (2006). *Next generation: What leaders need to know about the millennials. Leadership in Action. 26,* 3–6.

Downs, A. (1967). *Inside bureaucracy.* Boston: Little, Brown.

Downs, G. W., & Larkey, P. D. (1986). *The search for government efficiency: From hubris to helplessness.* Philadelphia: Temple University Press.

Drucker, P. F. (1954). *The practice of management.* New York: Harper & Row.

Eddy, W. B. (1981). *Public organization behavior and development.* Cambridge, MA: Winthrop.

Follet, M. P. (1924). *Creative experience.* New York: Longman, Green.

Ford, R. N. (1973). Job enrichment lessons from AT&T. *Harvard Business Review, 51*(1), 96–106.

Frank, S., & Lewis, G. B., (2004). Government employees: Working or hardly working? *American Review of Public Administration, 34*(1), 36–51.

Golembiewski, R. T. (1969). Organization development in public agencies: Perspectives on theory and practice. *Public Administration Review, 29*(4), 367–377.

Goodsell, C. T. (2004). *The case for bureaucracy: A public administration polemic* (4th ed.).Washington, DC: CQ Press.

Green, M. E. (2000). Beware and prepare. *Public Personnel Management, 29*(4), 435–443.

Green, R., Forbis, R., Robinson, J., Nelson, S. L., Seelig, J., & Stefaniak, A. (2007). The attraction to at-will employment in Utah governments. In J. Bowman & J. West (Eds.), *American public service: Radical reform and the merit system* (pp. 175–192). Boca Raton, FL: Taylor & Francis.

Greiner, J. (1996). Positioning performance measurement for the twenty-first century, In A. Halachmi and G. Bouckeart, (Eds.), *Organizational performance measurement in the public sector* (pp. 11–50). Westport, CT: Quorum Books.

Halachmi, A., & Korgt, T. V. D. (1998). The role of the manager in employee motivation, In S.E. Condrey (Ed.), *Handbook of human resource management in government* (pp. 563–585). San Francisco: Jossey-Bass.

Hayward, N. S. (1976). The productivity challenge. *Public Administration Review, 36*(5), 544–550.

Hefetz, A., & Warner, M. E. (2012). Contracting or public delivery? The importance of service, market, and management characteristics. *Journal of Public Administration Research and Theory, 22*(2), 289–317.

Hodge, G. A. (2000). *Privatization: An international review of performance.* Boulder, CO: Westview Press.

Herzberg, F. (1966). *Work and the nature of man.* Cleveland: World Publishing.

Homans, G. C. (1951). The Western Electric research, In S. D. Hoslett, (Ed.), *Human factors in management* (pp. 210–241). New York: Harper & Row.

Homans, G. C. (1965). Effort, supervision, and productivity. In R. Dulin (Ed.), *Leadership and productivity* (pp.51–67). San Francisco: Chandler.

Horton, R. D. (1976). Productivity and productivity bargaining in government: A critical analysis. *Public Administration Review, 36*(4), 407–414.

Jurkiewicz, C. L., & Massey, Jr., T. K. (1997). What motivates municipal employees: A comparison study of supervisory vs. non-supervisory personnel. *Public Personnel Management, 26*(3), 367–377.

Kellough, J. E., & Nigro, L. G. (2005). Dramatic reform in the public service: At-will employment and the creation of a new public workforce. *Journal of Public Administration Research and Theory, 16*(3), 447–466.

Kettl, D. L. (2002). Privatization: Implications for the public workforce, In C. Ban & N. M. Riccucci, (Eds.), *Public personnel management: Current concerns, future challenges* (3rd ed.) (pp. 254–264). New York: Longman.

Kim, S. (2005). Individual-level factors and organizational performance in government organizations. *Journal of Public Administration Research and Theory, 15*, 245–261.

Kim, S. (2012). Does person organization fit matter in the public sector? Testing the mediating effect of person organization fit in the relationship between public service motivation and work attitudes. *Public Administration Review, 72*(6), 830–840.

Kim, S. E., & Rubianty, D. (2011). Perceived fairness of performance appraisals in the federal government, does it matter? *Review of Public Personnel Administration, 31*(4), 329–348.

King, C., & Stivers, C. (1998). *Government is us: Public administration in an anti-government era.* Thousand Oaks, CA: Sage.

Lee, D. S., & Cayer, N. J. (1994). *Supervision for success in government.* San Francisco: Jossey-Bass.

Light, P. (1999). *The new public service.* Washington, DC: Brookings Institution.

Light, P. (2002). *The troubled state of the federal public service.* Washington, DC: Brookings Institution.

Maslow, A. (1954). *Motivation and personality.* New York: Harper & Row.

McGregor, D. (1968). *The human side of enterprise.* New York: McGraw-Hill.

Mintzberg, H. (1973). *The nature of managerial work.* New York: Harper Collins.

Mir, A., Mir, R., & Mosca, J. B. (2002). The new age employee: An exploration of changing employee-organization relations. *Public Personnel Management, 31*(2), 187–200.

Moynihan, D., & Herd, P. (2010). Red tape and democracy: How rules affect citizenship rights. *The American Review of Public Administration, 40*(6), 654–670.

Moynihan, D. P., & Pandey, S. K. (2007). The role of organizations in fostering public service motivation. *Public Administration Review, 67*(1), 40–53.

Naff, K. C., & Crum, J. (1999). Working for America: Does public service motivation make a difference. *Review of Public Personnel Administration, 19*(4), 5–15.

National Academy of Public Administration. (2003). *First-line supervisors in the federal service: Their selection, development, and management.* Report of the 21st Century Federal Manager Series. Washington, DC: National Academy of Public Administration.

National Center for Productivity and Quality of Working Life (1978). *Total performance measurement: Some pointers for action.* Washington, DC: U.S. Government Printing Office.

National Commission on the Public Service. (2003). *Urgent business for America: Revitalizing the federal government for the 21st century.* Washington, DC: National Commission on the Public Service.

National Performance Review. (1993). *From red tape to results: Creating a government that works better and costs less.* Washington, DC: U.S. Government Printing Office.

Newland, C. A. (1972). Personnel concerns in government productivity improvement. *Public Administration Review, 32*(6), 807–815.

Ng., E. S., Schweitzer, W. L., & Lyons, S. T. (2010). New generation, great expectations: A field study of the Millennial generation, *Journal of Business Psychology, 25*, 281–292.

Oh, S. S., & Lewis, G. B. (2009). Can performance appraisal systems inspire intrinsically motivated employees? *Review of Public Personnel Administration, 29*(2), 158–167.

Paarlberg, L. E., & Lavigna, B. (2010). Transformational leadership and public service motivation: Driving individual and organizational performance. *Public Administration Review, 70*(5), 710–718.

Park, S. M., & Rainey, H. G. (2008). Leadership and public service motivation in U.S. federal agencies. *International Public Management Journal, 11*(1): 109–42.

Parsons, H. M. (1974, March 8). What happened at Hawthorne? *Science,* 922–932.

Perry, J. L. (1997). Antecedents of public service motivation. *Journal of Public Administration Research and Theory, 7*(2), 181–197.

Perry, J. L., & Wise, L. R. (1990). The motivational bases of public service. *Public Administration Review, 50*, 367–373.

Peter, L. J. (1972). *The Peter prescription.* New York: Morrow.

Presthus, R. (1978). *The organizational society.* New York: St. Martin's Press.

Preusser, M. K., Bartels, L. K., & Nordstrom, C. R. (2011). Sexual harassment training: Person versus machine. *Public Personnel Management, 40*(1), 47.

Rand, P. (1974). Collecting merit badges: The White House fellows. *Washington Monthly, 6,* 47–56.

Reese, L. A., & Lindenberg, K. E. (2003). The importance of training on sexual harassment policy outcomes. *Review of Public Personnel Administration, 23*(3), 175–191.

Sandwith, P. (1993). A hierarchy of management training requirements: The competency domain model. *Public Personnel Management, 22*(1), 43–62.

Seidenstat, P. (1999). *Contracting out government services.* Westport, CT: Praeger.

Selden, S. C. (2008). *Human capital: Tools and strategies for the public sector.* Washington, DC: CQ Press.

Sowa, J. E., & Selden, S. (2011). Performance management and appraisal in human service organizations: Management and staff perspectives. *Public Personnel Management, 40*(3), 251.

Smith, M. P. (1976). Barriers to organizational democracy in public administration. *Administration and Society, 18*(3), 275–317.

Tang, T. L. P., Cunningham, P. H., Frauman, E., Ivy, M., & Perry, T. L. (2012). Attitudes and occupational commitment among public personnel: Differences between Baby Boomers and Gen-Xers. *Public Personnel Management, 41*(2): 327–360.

Trottier, T., Van Wart, M., & Wang, X. (2008). Examining the nature and significance of leadership in government organizations. *Public Administration Review, 68*(2), 319–33.

Twenge, J. M. (2006). *Generation Me: Why today's young Americans are more confident, assertive, entitled—and more miserable than ever before.* New York: Free Press.

Twenge, J. M., Campbell, S. M., Hoffman, B. J., & Lance, C. E. (2010). Generational differences in work values: Leisure and extrinsic values increasing, social and intrinsic values decreasing. *Journal of Management, 36*(5). 1117–1142.

Twenge, J. M., & Campbell, S. M. (2008). Generational differences in psychological traits and their impact on the workplace. *Journal of Managerial Psychology, 23,* 862–877.

U.S. Office of Personnel Management (OPM). (2008). *Guide for collection and management of training information.* http://www.opm.gov/policy-data-oversight/training-and-development/reference-materials/

Van Wart, M. (1998). *Changing public sector values.* New York: Garland Publishing.

Van Wart, M., Cayer, N. J., & Cook, S. (1993). *Handbook of training and development for the public sector.* San Francisco: Jossey-Bass.

Vasu, M. L., Stewart, D. W., & Garson, G. D. (1998). *Organizational behavior and public management.* New York: Marcel Dekker.

Vroom, V. (1964). *Work and motivation.* New York: Wiley.

Walters, J. (2003). Civil service reform tsunami. *Governing, 16*(8), 34–40.

Whyte, W. F. (1955). *Money and motivation.* New York: Harper & Row.

Wright, B. E., Moynihan, D. P., & Pandey, S. K. (2012). Pulling the levers: Leadership, public service motivation and mission valence. *Public Administration Review, 72*(2): 206–215.

Zwerdling, D. (1973). Beyond boredom: A look at what's new on the assembly line. *Washington Monthly, 5*(July/August), 80–91.

7

Rights and Duties of Public Employees

Public employees have a responsibility to perform their jobs in a manner that provides effective public service. In return, public employees often enjoy more rights and greater job protection than do private sector employees. For example, because the due process clauses of the Fifth and Fourteenth Amendments to the U.S. Constitution apply to governments and not to private organizations, government employers are required to extend protections subsumed under due process (e.g., dismissals can occur only based on just cause) to their employees. At the same time, because government depends on the support of the general public, it often attempts to limit behavior that may be controversial or unpopular and thus infringes on the rights of employees. Moreover, being in the public eye imposes restrictions on one's conduct both on and off the job. The following discussion deals with off-the-job conduct as well as the internal rights associated with public employment.

Off-The-Job Conduct

The off-the-job conduct of public employees receives more attention than does that of employees in the private sector. In its eagerness to offer high-quality public service devoid of public controversy, the government often restricts the rights of those providing that service. Balancing the need for an impartial, fair, and high-quality public service with protecting the individual rights of employees creates controversies and difficulties in public personnel systems. Such problems are most likely to occur in a democratic system in which individual rights are many and are highly valued.

Restrictions on public employees have stemmed from the doctrine of privilege as applied to public employment. The courts have long held that privileges and gratuities are not subject to the same protection as rights are (Hartman, Homer, & Menditto, 1998; Rosenbloom & Bailey, 2003). Thus, if something is determined to be a privilege, no one has a right to it, and protections such as due process may not apply in the same way as they would if a right were involved. Over the years, the courts have held that government employment is a privilege, and if people want the privilege, they must abide by the conditions imposed on it. Since the 1960s, the courts have modified their stand on this issue by dispensing with the rights–privilege distinction (*Pickering v. Board of Education*, 1968) and by recognizing that employees can have a property right in employment or in continued employment (*Board of Regents v. Roth*, 1972; *Cleveland Board of Education v. Loudermill,* 1985). They also have liberty interests that can be affected by the employment situation (*Board of Regents v. Roth*, 1972).

Instances of intentional or unintentional abuses by public employees using e-mail and social media, have increased, leading many government agencies to enact policies restricting their use by public employees (Ahmed, 2008). In analyzing the email policies for 50 states, Ahmed (2008) reported that most states have an e-mail usage policy to prevent employees from abusing the system by spending a large portion of their work day checking personal e-mails and or sending inappropriate text/e-mail messages to co-workers or others. Some of the abuses reported in the various cases analyzed were intentional, whereas some were unintentional, owing to the lack of employee knowledge "about the rights and responsibilities in the workplace" (Ahmed, 2008, p. 2). As the following discussion demonstrates, legislatures and the courts continue to struggle with the balance between the constitutional rights of employees and the legitimate interests of public employers.

General Employee Conduct

Administrators in the public sector are usually forced to demand a higher standard of behavior of their employees than are administrators in the private sector. Public employees are scrutinized by taxpayers and the media, and any misstep is likely to result in a public outcry. Being less dependent on the public's good will and facing fewer consequences from the behavior of their employees, private sector employers can be more understanding of their employees' behavior. The support of the public and especially that of the elected political leaders are crucial to a public agency's existence. Sensitivity to potential consequences leads many public employers to take the expedient route of restricting employee rights or imposing discipline for non-work activities that would not be a concern in the private sector.

In recent decades, lifestyle has become a controversial issue in public employment. The emotional fervor associated with the issue is illustrated by the controversy surrounding the rights of lesbian, gay, bisexual, and transgender (LGBT) employees. As of 2012, fifteen states and Washington, DC, had laws protecting both public and private sector employees against discrimination based on both sexual orientation and gender identity. These states are California, Colorado, Connecticut, Hawaii, Illinois, Iowa, Maine, Massachusetts, Nevada, New Jersey, New Mexico, Oregon, Rhode Island, Vermont, and Washington. Five other states (Maryland, Minnesota, New Hampshire, New York, and Wisconsin) have provisions to protect against discrimination based on the sexual orientation of public and private sector employees but not gender identity. Delaware provides similar protections, although gender identity protection is guaranteed only for state employees (Hunt, 2012).

Nonetheless, jurisdictions across the country have adopted non–discrimination policies that include sexual orientation as a protected category. As of 2011, more than 175 cities and counties have outlawed employment discrimination based on sexual orientation, and more than 135 cities and counties ban discrimination based on gender identity (Human Rights Campaign, 2011). Even as gays continue to press for protection, in the hope of winning the kind of recognition given to other minorities, the controversy over this issue reached new heights in the 2012 presidential election. Maine, Maryland, and Washington passed ballot measures legalizing same sex marriage, whereas Minnesota voters rejected a ban on same-sex marriage. Wisconsin became the first state to elect an openly gay U.S. Senator Tammy Baldwin.

Issues affecting the LGBT community have been widely debated in American politics, and they became visible in the 1984 election campaign as the Democratic Party ticket endorsed gay rights. In 1992, the issue again attained high visibility as presidential candidate Bill Clinton pledged to reverse the ban on homosexuals in the military. Bowing to political realities, President Clinton eventually backed down on his pledge and agreed to a "don't ask, don't tell" policy, which essentially maintained the ban as it was enforced by the military departments. However, after nineteen years, on September 20, 2011, President Barack H. Obama signed the law repealing the discriminatory policy banning gay, lesbian, and bisexual military personnel. For the first time in U.S. history, LGBT men and women are allowed to openly serve in the military.

As of 2013, the federal government has not yet passed the Employment Non-Discrimination ACT (ENDA), which will end discrimination in hiring and employment on the basis of sexual orientation and gender identity for all federal, state, and local government agencies; employment agencies; unions; and private employers with fifteen or more employees. However, as gay political organizations demonstrate their political clout, gays will eventually be accorded the same consideration as other groups, and employment policies will reflect that political power. Additionally, the courts are increasingly ruling in favor of according homosexuals the same rights as other citizens.

Loyalty and Security

There is probably no aspect of public personnel administration that has been more directly affected by forces in the political environment than the issues of loyalty and security. At times, officials and the public alike have reacted out of hysteria by restricting the activities of public employees. Loyalty and security are separate concepts that are often perceived as one. *Loyalty* refers to an employee's support of the system, and a *loyalty risk* is one who would be likely to knowingly subvert the political system. A security risk is someone who, without malicious intent, might divulge information or act in a way detrimental to the system. Thus, someone can be a security risk without being disloyal and may be a security risk in one position but not in another.

Similarly, loyalty cannot be generated by offering more pay, benefits or programs such as work–life balance or membership to fitness clubs—these are all extrinsic to the job. Researchers argue that loyalty can be attained by more intrinsic factors such as recognition of the work done by employees, organizational justice, and autonomy provided by supervisors (Cho & Sai, 2012; Lukacs et al., 2012), which further reduce turnover (Daley, 2008; Lee & Whitford, 2008; Moynihan & Landuyt, 2008). Loyalty and freedom are competing objectives that have created numerous problems for the political system.

President Washington demanded loyalty to the new federal system from his public servants, and Lincoln required loyalty to the Union. However, specific tests of loyalty did not become formalized until 1939, when the Hatch Act (Section 9A) prohibited employees from being members of organizations advocating the overthrow of the government. Every period of crisis in our history, however, has produced policies that try to ensure the loyalty of public servants. After World War II, the anticommunist frenzy led to a variety of loyalty and security programs in the public service and research on employee loyalty. For the most part, the issue attracts much less attention today, but 9/11 brought attention back to the issue, and some of the discussion surrounding the creation of a Homeland Security Department raised issues about the loyalty and security of its employees.

Federal government employees are subject to an investigation of their backgrounds to determine their suitability for the public service, although for workers in nonsensitive positions, the investigation may be conducted after placement. Those appointed to sensitive positions are investigated before appointment and are subject to in-depth investigations. At the state and local levels, the tendency has been to require employees to sign loyalty oaths as a condition of employment, but the courts have invalidated many of these oaths for being too vague and unenforceable. A 1972 Supreme Court decision upheld the Massachusetts loyalty oath; loyalty oaths can still be used (*Cole v. Richardson*, 1972).

Although it may seem reasonable that those disloyal to the system should not be employed by the government and that security risks should not be employed in sensitive positions, there is little agreement on what constitutes a loyalty or security risk. In the post-9/11 era, loyalty oaths are increasingly being used under the guise of patriotism. In 2005, Ohio passed its version of the Patriot Act, which requires anyone seeking government employment, certain licenses and contracts or seeking to do business with the government worth $100,000 or more, to sign an oath stating that they are not terrorists, do not employ terrorists and have never materially supported terrorist groups (Heins, 2009). The law was finally repealed in September 2012, following acute criticism from the American Civil Liberties Union (ACLU) of Ohio and other groups. In California, Marianne Kearney-Brown, a math teacher and a graduate student at California State University, East Bay, was fired for refusing to sign a similar oath. California's oath read:

> I, _____, do solemnly swear (or affirm) that I will support and defend the Constitution of the United States and the Constitution of the State of California against all enemies, foreign and domestic; that I will bear true faith and allegiance to the Constitution of the United States and the Constitution of the State of California; that I take this obligation freely, without any mental reservation or purpose of evasion; and that I will well and faithfully discharge the duties upon which I am about to enter.

Kearney-Brown refused to sign the oath unless she could add the word "nonviolently" before the phrase "support and defend the Constitution." She filed for grievance with the help of the United Auto Workers Union and was eventually reinstated (Inside Higher Education, 2008).

Loyalty and security programs have been subject to much abuse. Many of them virtually ignore employees' individual rights, partly because of the privilege doctrine discussed earlier (*Bailey v. Richardson*, 1951). Gays and lesbians were particularly victimized by such policies during the Cold War. The most insidious invasion of individual rights occurs among those applying for jobs. A person may be denied a position on the basis of background information acquired during the investigation. Whether the information is accurate may never be determined because unsuccessful applicants are rarely told why they are unsuccessful. Thus, people may be denied jobs in the public service on the basis of information they have no chance to see or challenge.

Political Activity Restrictions

Some restrictions on public employees date from the English common law tradition, asserting that certain offices or activities are incompatible with one another (Kirchheimer, 1941). Conflict-of-interest statutes, orders and rulings, and legislation and constitutional provisions prohibiting holding certain public offices concurrently are the principal methods of putting this tradition into practice. The belief that politically active public servants cannot provide service free from bias led to the prohibition of certain political activities as well. In a democratic society, there may be a conflict between the rights of public employees as individuals and the right of the public to impartial service. For the most part, the United States has given priority to the public's right to service and placed limits on the rights of public employees as a legitimate cost of the political neutrality of the public bureaucracy.

The political activity of federal government employees is restricted by the Hatch Act of 1939 (Jones, 1969; Martin, 1974; Masters and Bierman, 1985). In 1940, the Act was amended to restrict the political activities of state and local government employees whose salaries are paid in part or in full by federal funds. The Federal Election Campaign Act amendments of 1974 repealed many of the restrictions on state and local government employees, although state and local level jurisdictions have their own restrictions. In 1993, the Act was amended again, removing many of the restrictions on federal employees (Bowman & West, 2009). Before the Hatch Act was passed, the Civil Service Commission drew up a body of rules and regulations pursuant to a 1907 executive order of Theodore Roosevelt, barring activity in "political management or in political campaigns" for those covered by the civil service. In implementing its rules and regulations, the commission ruled on some three thousand cases involving restrictions on political activity before 1940. It is generally believed that Congress intended the Hatch Act to incorporate those decisions as established precedents for interpreting the act's political activity prohibitions. Thus Congress would effectively deny the commission the authority to interpret the legislation differently. There has been some disagreement about congressional intent, but the effect was to hamper the flexibility of the Office of Personnel Management in dealing with the issue (Rose, 1962).

Regardless of Congress's intent, the Office of Personnel Management administers the Hatch Act which covers all civilian employees in the executive branch of the federal government, except the President and Vice President; part-time workers; and employees of the U.S. Postal Service and the District of Columbia, "except for the Mayor of the District of Columbia, the District of Columbia's City Council and the District's Recorder of Deeds" (U.S. Office of Special Counsel, 2010). Under the Hatch Act, federal employees are classified into (a) Further Restricted Employees and (b) Less Restricted Employees, placing limitations and permitting certain political activities for each group. Most federal employees fall under the "less restricted" group and enjoya greater range of permissible political activities. Tables 7.1 and 7.2 list the permitted and prohibited activities for these two groups of employees under the Hatch Act.

The rationale for the restrictions listed on Table 7.1 is that they help protect public employees from being coerced into working for particular candidates or parties, protect the beneficiaries of public services from such coercion, and prevent public officials from using public monies and positions to further their political careers. A more immediate political reason for the passage of the Hatch Act was a fear that the New Deal bureaucracy could be mobilized as a vast political machine in support of the administration. A similar concern among many legislators, that the party in power might take political advantage of politically active career servants, was a major factor in Congress's reluctance to liberalize the restrictions until 1993. At any rate, the Hatch Act was passed as a response to overindulgence in spoils politics.

The constitutional rights to freedom of expression, assembly, and petition were at the heart of the opposition to the Hatch Act. Because these rights were limited by the act, public employees argued that they were doomed to second-class citizenship (Martin, 1974; Thurber, 1993). Assaults on the Hatch Act and similar state legislation surfaced in the courts. For a while, it seemed that the courts would invalidate many of the restrictions—as some lower courts did—but in 1973, the Supreme Court, by a six-to-three decision, upheld the constitutionality of the Hatch Act and a similar state law reaffirming a 1974 decision (*U.S. Civil Service Commission v. National Association of Letter Carriers,* 1973; *United Public Workers of America v. Mitchell, 1947*). The coverage of the restrictions was extended in some places, such as in Arizona, where in 1983 the attorney general issued an opinion that the state law even prohibited participation in nonpartisan elections. Consequently, public employees focused their efforts for change on legislative bodies.

Finally, after years of effort, supporters of liberalizing the Hatch Act got Congress to revise it in 1993. Whereas employees in some sensitive agencies (Table 7.3) are still covered by the restrictions noted above, other federal civil service employees have had many restrictions lifted (see Table 7.2). Now most federal employees may hold a particular party office, participate in managing political campaigns while off duty, distribute campaign literature and solicit votes, participate in voter registration drives, participate in phone banks for political parties or candidates, stuff envelopes for candidates, and publicly endorse political candidates.

Table 7.1
Prohibited Activities under the Hatch Act

Less Restricted Employees	Further Restricted Employees (These employees are covered by the same restrictions as the less restricted plus those mentioned in this column)
May not be candidates for public office in partisan political elections.	May not be a candidate for nomination or election to public office in a partisan election

May not use their official authority or influence to interfere with or affect the result of an election. For example: • May not use their official titles or positions while engaged in political activity • May not invite subordinate employees to political events or otherwise suggest to subordinates that they attend political events or undertake any partisan political activity.	May not use their official authority or influence to interfere with or affect the result of an election. For example: • May not use their official titles or positions while engaged in political activity. • May not invite subordinate employees to political events or otherwise suggest to subordinates that they attend political events or undertake any partisan political activity
May not engage in political activity – i.e., activity directed at the success or failure of a political party, candidate for partisan political office, or partisan political group – while the employee is on duty, in any federal room or building, while wearing a uniform or official insignia, or using any federally owned or leased vehicle. For example: • May not distribute campaign materials or items. • May not display campaign materials or items. • May not perform campaign related chores • May not wear or display partisan political buttons, T-shirts, signs, or other items • May not make political contributions to a partisan political party, candidate for partisan political office, or partisan political group. • May not post a comment to a blog or a social media site that advocates for or against a partisan political party, candidate for partisan political office, or partisan political group. • May not use any e-mail account or social media to distribute, send, or forward content that advocates for or against a partisan political party, candidate for partisan political office, or partisan political group.	May not engage in political activity – i.e., activity directed at the success or failure of a political party, candidate for partisan political office, or partisan political group – while the employee is on duty, in any federal room or building, while wearing a uniform or official insignia, or using any federally owned or leased vehicle. For example: • May not distribute campaign materials or items. • May not display campaign materials or items. • May not perform campaign related chores • May not wear or display partisan political buttons, T-shirts, signs, or other items. • May not make political contributions to a partisan political party, candidate for partisan political office, or partisan political group. • May not post a comment to a blog or a social media site that advocates for or against a partisan political party, candidate for partisan political office, or partisan political group. • May not use any e-mail account or social media to distribute, send or forward content that advocates for or against a partisan political party, candidate for partisan political office, or partisan political group.

May not solicit, accept or receive a donation or contribution for a partisan political party, candidate for partisan political office, or partisan political group. For example: • May not host a political fundraiser • May not invite others to a political fundraiser. • May not collect contributions or sell tickets to political fundraising functions.	May not solicit, accept or receive a donation or contribution for a partisan political party, candidate for partisan political office, or partisan political group. For example: • May not host a political fundraiser • May not invite others to a political fundraiser. • May not collect contributions or sell tickets to political fundraising functions.
May not knowingly solicit or discourage the participation in any political activity of anyone who has business pending before their employing office.	May not take an active part in partisan political campaigns. For example: • May not campaign for or against a candidate or slate of candidates. • May not make campaign speeches or engage in other campaign activities to elect partisan candidates. • May not distribute campaign material in partisan elections. • May not circulate nominating petitions.
	May not take an active part in partisan political management. For example: • May not hold office in political clubs or parties. • May not organize or manage political rallies or meetings. • May not assist in partisan voter registration drives.

Source: U.S. Office of Special Counsel, http://www.osc.gov/hatchact.htm

Table 7.2:
Permitted Activities under the Hatch Act

Further Restricted Employees	Less Restricted Employees
• May register and vote as they choose • May assist in nonpartisan voter registration drives. • May participate in campaigns where none of the candidates represent a political party. • May contribute money to political campaigns, political parties, or partisan political groups. • May attend political fundraising functions. • May attend political rallies and meetings. • May join political clubs or parties. • May sign nominating petitions. • May campaign for or against referendum questions, constitutional amendments, or municipal ordinances. • May be a candidate for public office in a nonpartisan election. • May express opinions about candidates and issues. If the expression is political activity, however – i.e., activity directed at the success or failure of a political party, candidate for partisan political office, or partisan political group – then the expression is not permitted while the employee is on duty, in any federal room or building, while wearing a uniform or official insignia, or using any federally owned or leased vehicle.	• May be candidates for public office in nonpartisan elections. • May register and vote as they choose. • May assist in voter registration drives. • May contribute money to political campaigns, political parties, or partisan political groups. • May attend political fundraising functions. • May attend and be active at political rallies and meetings. • May join and be an active member of political clubs or parties. • May hold office in political clubs or parties. • May sign and circulate nominating petitions. • May campaign for or against referendum questions, constitutional amendments, or municipal ordinances. • May campaign for or against candidates in partisan elections. • May make campaign speeches for candidates in partisan elections. • May distribute campaign literature in partisan elections. • May volunteer to work on a partisan political campaign. • May express opinions about candidates and issues. If the expression is political activity, however – i.e., activity directed at the success or failure of a political party, candidate for partisan political office, or partisan political group – then the expression is not permitted while the employee is on duty, in any federal room or building, while wearing a uniform or official insignia, or using any federally owned or leased vehicle.

Source: U.S. Office of Special Counsel, Hatch Act.
http://www.osc.gov/hatchact.htm

Collective bargaining in the public sector has numerous implications for political activity. Unions exert a great deal of pressure in the political realm when they are permitted to engage in partisan political activity. As a result, direct public employee organizational activity in politics usually is restricted. Nonetheless, unions support their friends through endorsements and campaigning by their political action committees. Collective bargaining also undermines one of the justifications for prohibiting political activity in that it tends to reduce the likelihood that employees can be coerced or intimidated into engaging in the political activities desired by a supervisor. Because unions give workers leverage with management, employees have greater independence from their managers and have union support in resisting attempts by management to coerce them into political activity.

Table 7.3 Agencies Still Covered by Original Hatch Act Prohibitions

Federal Elections Commission
Federal Bureau of Investigation
Secret Service
Central Intelligence Agency
National Security Council
Defense Intelligence Agency
Merit Systems Protection Board
Office of Special Council
Internal Revenue Service Office of Criminal Investigation
Department of Justice Criminal Division
U.S. Customs Office of Investigative Programs
Bureau of Alcohol, Tobacco, and Firearms Office of Law Enforcement

Some governments impose general restrictions on the freedom of expression, privacy, residency, and personal appearance of public employees. However, freedom of expression is protected by the First Amendment. Thus restrictions on freedom of expression are subject to the courts' determination of whether the expression is a matter of public concern. If so, the court will then balance the employee's rights with the interest of the employer in taking action that undermines the mission of the organization (*Rankin v. McPherson*, 1987). Employee free speech also is protected when the employee engages in whistleblowing--the revelation of wrongdoing in the organization (*Pickering v. Board of Education,* 1968).

Another type of restriction is that placed on "moonlighting." Prohibiting the taking of a second job, especially when combined with low salaries in many jurisdictions, may create hardships for some employees or difficulty in recruiting for a jurisdiction. The employer's concern is that an employee's ability to perform a full-time job may be affected by the holding of another job; if such is the case, the employer does have a legitimate worry. Today, if the second job poses no conflict, however, most employers do not object.

Employees also enjoy constitutional protections of association, meaning that they cannot be prohibited from associating with whomever they want nor can they be forced to associate with anyone. (However, there are exceptions; e.g., most police departments prohibit their officers from associating with known criminals). This issue arose when loyalty and security policies led to the creation of lists of organizations that employees were prohibited from joining, such as the Communist Party. The courts have been consistent since the 1960s in striking down such policies (*Elfbrandt v. Rissell,* 1966; *Elrod v. Burns,* 1976; *Shelton v. Tucker,* 1960).

The issue of freedom of association also arises in the relationship between employees and labor unions. To undermine labor unions some employers tried to prohibit their employees from joining them. However, the courts struck down such prohibitions (*AFSCME v. Woodward,* 1969). Unions for their part, sometimes also acted heavy-handedly and insisted that all employees who worked for an agency whose employees were represented by the union, pay union dues. Right-to-work laws which exist in twenty-four states (most recently in Michigan since 2012) allow employees the right to opt out of paying union dues. While the Supreme Court affirmed that fees can be collected from non–union members in the organization who benefit from the union activities (*Abood v. Detroit Board of Education,* 1977; *Chicago Teachers Union v. Hudson,* 1986), it also ruled that employees cannot be forced to pay the portion of fees that go to support political causes and candidates with whom they disagree (*Chicago Teachers Union v. Hudson,* 1986).

The courts also have been chipping away at requirements for employees to be members of a particular political party. In places where the spoils system remains, elected political leaders now have less flexibility to remove people for reasons of party affiliation (*Branti v. Finkel*, 1980; *Elrod v. Burns*, 1976; *Rutan v. Republican Party of Illinois*, 1990). In order for public agencies to use party affiliation as a reason for dismissal, they must be able to demonstrate that "party affiliation is an appropriate requirement for the effective performance" of the job (*United States v. National Treasury Employees Union*, 1995).

Liberty rights of public employees also have occasioned court review. The Fifth and Fourteenth Amendments prohibit government deprivation of life, liberty, or property without due process. The Supreme Court also has ruled that school districts cannot require unpaid maternity leaves for teachers and may not interfere with reproductive decisions (*Cleveland Board of Education v. LaFleur*, 1974). Liberty pertains to a wide range of freedoms. Employers often require their employees to engage in activities such as public service projects or to contribute to specific charities; the courts have accepted such requirements when they are reasonably related to the interests of the employer (*United States v. National Treasury Employees Union*, 1995).

Employers may impose residency requirements upon employees (*McCarthy v. Philadelphia Civil Service Commission*, 1976). Jurisdictions justify such restrictions, especially for public safety and emergency personnel, on the need to be quickly available. Some agencies might want their high profile employees to live and pay taxes in the jurisdiction that pays their salaries and serve as role models for the community. On a similar issue, some jurisdictions have policies on personal appearance. They justify these policies on the basis of the need to put forth a good image and, for public safety personnel, as a way of encouraging discipline and ensuring respect from those they deal with. The Supreme Court has allowed such rules unless the employee can demonstrate that the rule has no rational connection to the agency's mission (*Kelley v. Johnson*, 1976). However, the issue of "physical appearance" in the workplace is controversial, given that it is not covered under Title VII of the Civil Rights Act. Courts have generally upheld dress code requirements for public employees. In *Riggs v. City of Fort Worth* (2002), a police officer, Mr. Riggs, with extensive tattoos on his arms and legs, was ordered to wear long sleeves and long pants at all times. The plaintiff argued that his tattoos are an expression of his race, sex, national origin, and statements of expression. The courts, however, did not see his tattoos as a form of protected free expression. The issue of tattoos and body piercings is an important issue when dealing with Generation X and millennials, as many among them have embraced self-expression via body art (Hoffman, Mc Vicker, & Radojevick-Kelley, 2009). Employers cannot ignore this issue, and they should clearly lay out their policies regarding appearances in their employee handbook.

On-the-Job Conduct and Rights

Public employees are expected to conduct themselves professionally on the job. To deal with instances in which public employees may be tempted to act in a nonprofessional way or in a manner contrary to public interest, policies have been established to delimit and ensure the rights of employees in the implementation of those restrictions.

Ethics and Public Employees

Ethical behavior is expected of public employees, but a problem arises when one attempts to define what is meant by ethical behavior because ethics involves making choices among competing values. Ultimately, ethics means doing what is right. However, this depends on many factors. In the public sector, doing what is right means doing what is in accordance with the laws, rules, and regulations; what is in the public interest; and what maintains one's integrity and the organization's integrity. These elements of ethical action often conflict with one another, and individuals need to balance values in making choices.

In the public sector, questions of ethics arise all the time. Any decision or action of the government has an impact on someone, and those affected will try to influence that decision or action. As a result, public employees and employers are likely to be subject to pressure or efforts to influence them (Svara, 2007; Van Wart, 1998). Problems often arise in regard to the appearance of being unduly influenced by those interested in the outcome of a decision or action. Whereas in the private sector decision makers usually are courted by those who are likely to benefit from a decision, this generally is not permitted in the public sector.

Although entertaining or providing private benefits to a decision maker is common practice in the private sector, it can create the impression of impropriety in the pbulic sector. Many scandals involving public officials occur because these officials come from the private sector, and they do not understand how public employment is different. Because public officials and employees are paid from public tax money, they are subject to much more scrutiny than are their private sector counterparts.

Because of periodic scandals involving high-level public officials, people tend to think of ethics issues as involving big decisions. Efforts to develop the civil service system go back to the Jacksonian period. The abuses of that era led people to develop rules for the public personnel system to curb abuses. Passage of the Hatch Act of 1939 resulted in part from concerns about ethical lapses in the public business. In every presidential administration, there has been some abuse that has led to concern about the ethics of some of the members of the administration. These concerns extend to the kind of example the officials provide for the rest of the public sector.

In the 1990s, ethics once again became a major issue for the public sector. The Clinton administration had difficulty governing partly because of questions of character arising from some activities of Clinton and his wife in their business dealings before he became president. Additionally, some of the activities of Clinton administration officials after the issue began to become public raise other questions of propriety. Three scandals involving cabinet members were particularly embarrassing to the president: Secretary of Agriculture Mike Espy resigned after revelations that he had accepted gifts from Tyson Foods, a corporation affected by agricultural policy. Secretary of Housing and Urban Development Henry Cisneros was sued by a former mistress for breach of contract over promised cash support. Secretary of Commerce Secretary Ron Brown was investigated for questionable business dealings that occurred before he joined the cabinet. Of course, the impeachment charges brought against Clinton, himself for his conduct with Monica Lewinsky, an intern, raised the issue to a new high.

The George W. Bush administration had its own ethical problems. As corporate scandals arose over accounting and executive insider trading, both Bush and his Vice President Dick Cheney faced questions about their dealings and windfalls as corporate executives and board members before they were elected. Several high ranking members of the Bush administration had been part of the Enron management team and got caught up in the scandal surrounding the collapse of Enron. Harvey Pitt, the Chair of the Securities and Exchange Commission (SEC), was pressured to resign when he embarrassed the administration with numerous lapses of judgment and the appearance of being too close to those the SEC regulates. The state legislatures of Arizona, Kentucky, Rhode Island, and South Carolina were rocked by bribery and influence-peddling scandals in the 1990s.

In 2001, a member of Congress was investigated in the disappearance of a congressional intern after it was learned he had an affair with her. The next year another member of Congress was expelled after his being convicted of fraud and corruption. Cases involving high school teacher–student sexual relations across the country highlighted issues of inappropriate behavior among teachers. A housing official and his aide in Tampa, Florida, were investigated over the romantic relationship between them and its connection to the aide's rapid rise in the organization. The Attorney General of Arizona and one of his employees were similarly investigated in 2012.

The Obama administration has also faced scandals. On April 11, 2012, prior to President Obama's summit in South America, several Secret Service officers in Colombia were involved in a prostitution scandal. Following the scandal, Mark Sullivan, the director of the Secret Service, issued new ethical conduct regulations for agents traveling abroad. Officers are now barred from "disreputable establishments, drinking heavily or within 10 hours of a shift. The new rules also bar employees from bringing foreigners to their hotel rooms" (Caldwell, 2012). Another ethical scandal, involving CIA director David Petraeus, resulted in his resignation on November 9, 2012, following an extramarital affair. In 2012, a watchdog group reported that a 2010 Las Vegas conference cost the General Services Administration (GSA) $823,000. The scandal resulted in the resignation of the GSA administrator, the firing of two top aides, and the placing of nine officers on administrative leave.

One of the reasons ethical considerations are so important to public administration is that public employees have a great deal of discretion in deciding on numerous issues that can benefit or hurt different parties. This discretion also puts public servants under pressure to act in ways that benefit the parties affected by the agency. Public employees often find themselves on the spot, and it is up to them to decide what is right and what is wrong.

Ethical behavior is influenced by both internal individual factors and external controls. The internal factors refer to the degree to which individuals perceive themselves as responsible for their actions. Theoretically, employees who are carefully chosen and who embrace democratic and professional values control their own conduct because of their dedication to the public, professional group standards, and peer pressure (Chandler, 1999; Friedrich, 1940). Unfortunately, the pressures faced by public servants are too complex and contradictory to allow an easy formulation of right or wrong responses. It is difficult to decide when a conflict between personal values and official duties warrants resignation or protest and to decide whether actions such as leaking or withholding information are valid. In other words, internal controls are usually not enough.

Because internal controls are inadequate, external controls become necessary (Finer, 1941). Individual leaders have a responsibility for ethical behavior in their organizations and should serve as a model of behavior for their subordinates. If the supervisor has lax standards of behavior, the subordinates can hardly be expected to maintain high standards in their performance.

Codes of conduct commonly regulate behavior, but there are differences of opinion about their effectiveness. For example, in 1965, Lyndon B. Johnson issued Executive Order 11222, "Prescribing Standards of Ethical Conduct for Government Officers and Employees," but no mention of it was made during the Watergate proceedings, suggesting that no one took it seriously. Codes of conduct provide guidelines for behavior, but often they are so general that they have little meaning. Without enforcement efforts, these codes are of little value—and enforcement rarely is pursued.

Besides identifying specific prohibited behaviors, codes of conduct usually require employees to avoid even the appearance of unethical behavior. Thus, something that might appear to be a conflict of interest should be avoided. However, what constitutes the appearance of a conflict of interest? What seems like a conflict of interest to some people may not appear so to others. Accepting lunches or gifts from the people one normally deals with may influence an employee's decisions or actions even if he or she insists otherwise. Even though the individual may resist any temptation, others may not be convinced. Therefore, temptation must be avoided to protect the integrity of the public service. Employees who come to government from the business community often find themselves confused by these rules because behavior that is standard in private dealings is frowned upon or prohibited in the public sector.

Because of these difficulties with codes of ethics, other methods of prohibiting certain practices also are used. Specific legal prohibitions on various practices are common. Most states have passed legislation on ethical behavior for public employees in recent years, and the Ethics in Government Act of 1978 cited specific legal prohibitions for federal employees. It also mandated the Office of Personnel Management to spell out specific rules and regulations to implement the act, and it established an Office of Government Ethics (OGE) within the OPM.

The Ethics Reform Act of 1989 gave the OGE statutory authority to issue ethics regulations and made OGE the sole executive branch authority for establishing ethical standards. To make standards uniform, new standards were established for almost all agencies, and agencies are not permitted to supplement those standards without permission from the OGE. Fourteen principles (Table 7.4) establish the foundation for the new standards. It is interesting to note that the last principle establishes the "reasonable person" criterion for judging whether an action is ethical, thus providing flexibility in applying the new standards to particular situations.

Table 7.4 General Principles of Public Service

1. Public service is a public trust, requiring employees to place loyalty to the constitution, the laws and ethical principals above private gain.

2. Employees shall not hold financial interests that conflict with the conscientious performance of duty.

3. Employees shall not engage in financial transactions using nonpublic government information or allow the improper use of such information to further any private interest.

4. An employee shall not, except as permitted, solicit any gift or other item of monetary value from any person or entity seeking official action from, doing business with or conducting activities regulated by the employee's agency, or whose interests may be substantially affected by the performance or nonperformance of the employee's duties.

5. Employees shall put forth honest effort in the performance of their duties.

6. Employees shall not knowingly make unauthorized commitments or promises of any kind purporting to bind the Government.

7. Employees shall not use public office for private gain.

8. Employees shall act impartially and not give preferential treatment to any private organization or individual.

9. Employees shall protect and conserve Federal property and not use it for other than authorized activities.

10. Employees shall not engage in outside employment or activities, including seeking or negotiating for employment, that conflict with official Government duties and responsibilities.

11. Employees shall disclose waste, fraud, abuse, and corruption to appropriate authorities.

12. Employees shall satisfy in good faith their obligations as citizens, including all just financial obligations, especially those--such as Federal, State or local taxes--that are imposed by law.

13. Employees shall adhere to all laws and regulations that provide equal opportunity for all Americans regardless of race, color, religion, sex, national origin, age, or handicap.

14. Employees shall endeavor to avoid any actions creating the appearance that they are violating the law or the ethical standards set forth in this part. Whether particular circumstances create an appearance that the law or these standards have been violated shall be determined from the perspective of a reasonable person with knowledge of the relevant facts.

Source: U.S. Office of Government Ethics, Retrieved from. http://www.oge.gov/Laws-and-Regulations/Employee-Standards-of-Conduct/Employee-Standards-of-Conduct/

The aforementioned principles are general guidelines that apply to every public service employee, which are further formalized in the Ethics Reform Act of 1989 (Table 7.5). These provisions represent an effort to bring uniformity to federal government agencies. State and local governments already have statutes and rules and regulations that apply across-the-board. The difficulties with this type of law illustrate the problems inherent in attempting to ensure the integrity of public employees.

Obviously, government expects its employees not to use their positions for personal gain. The questions are how far government should go in controlling its employees' behavior and what serves the public interest.

Table 7.5 Regulations under the 1989 Act apply to seven general areas of behavior

1. Gifts from outside sources. Clearly, gifts from those doing business with an employee's office may create the impression of influence. While things such as refreshments during meetings may not create such an impression, most other types of gifts are prohibited. Employees may accept gifts with a market price of less than $20 per occasion, aggregating to no more than $50 in a calendar year from any single source.

2. Gifts between employees. An employee may not give or solicit gifts or contributions for a superior or accept such gifts from another employee who receives less pay. Occasionally, employees can exchange gifts amounting to no more than $10 per instance.

3. Conflicting financial interest. Employees must demure from participating in any decision affecting a direct personal interest. In some cases, employees may be prohibited from having a personal financial interest if such an interest would lead to an appearance of a conflict of interest.

4. Impartiality in performing official duties. Employees must avoid the appearance of conflict by not participating in situations in which a reasonable person might question their impartiality and involving former employers who awarded the employee highly valuable pay after deciding to take government employment.

5. Seeking other employment. Employees may not seek employment with employers who might be affected by the decisions or actions of those employees in their official duties.

6. Misuse of position. Employees are prohibited from using their positions, government property, or nonpublic information for private gain for themselves, relatives, friends, or nongovernment associates. On official time, they may not perform other than official duties or officially sanctioned activities such as doing the work of a union representative or attending professional conferences.

7. Outside activities. Employees may not participate in employment or volunteer activities which conflict with their official duties.

Source: U.S. Office of Government Ethics, http://oge.gov/Laws-and-Regulations/Employee-Standards-of-Conduct/Employee-Standards-of-Conduct

To ensure ethical behavior, it is not enough to have policies to regulate employees' activities. It is necessary to provide role models and provide training in ethics on a regular basis (Bowman & Knox, 2008). Training reminds employees what the policies are and assists them in working through situations that might pose ethical dilemmas. By being reminded of the ease with which appearances of wrongdoing arise, employees may be more cautious in their activities.

It also is necessary to integrate ethics into all aspects of the personnel and management functions (Huberts, Maesschalck, & Jurkiewicz, 2008; Keller, 1998; Kellough, 1999; West, 2003). Employees need to understand the importance of ethics from the time they are hired (orientation) through the time they retire. Managers also need to constantly be reminded of the need for ethical behavior in all the decisions they make and all actions they take. Ethical values need to be part of the organizational culture if the organization is to act ethically.

Harassment-Free Workplace

Harassment has been defined as "repeated and persistent attempts to torment, wear down, frustrate, or get a reaction from another. It is treatment that persistently provokes, pressures, frightens, intimidates, or otherwise discomforts another person" (Brodsky, 1976). Unfortunately, harassment has occurred and continues to occur in many, if not most, workplaces. Clearly ethnic and racial minorities were subject to harassment as workplaces were integrated. Women have been harassed since they began participating in the workplace. Lesbians and gays suffer the same fate as do religious and other minorities.

Efforts to address harassment in the workplace stem primarily from the Civil Rights Act of 1964 and the Equal Employment Opportunity Act of 1972 (an amendment to the 1964 Civil Rights Act). Although these laws cover harassment of many kinds, sexual harassment has become the arena of most controversy and attention. The National Organization for Women (NOW) was formed in 1966 and began the effort to get public officials to recognize that discrimination against women falls within the scope of the Civil Rights Act. In the 1970s, women's groups began to focus on the sexual exploitation of women in the workplace and eventually succeeded in having the Equal Employment Opportunity Commission (EEOC) define sexual harassment as a violation of federal law. EEOC then published guidelines defining sexual harassment as "unwelcome advances, requests for sexual favors, and other verbal or physical conduct of a sexual nature...when submission to or rejection of this conduct explicitly or implicitly affects an individual's employment, unreasonably interferes with an individual's work performance or creates an intimidating, hostile or offensive work environment" (U.S. Equal Employment Opportunity Commission, 1980).

Through court decisions, sexual harassment has come to be viewed as a consequence of either *quid pro quo* or a hostile environment. Quid pro quo harassment is a situation in which employment decisions are dependent on sexual favors. Thus, a promotion may be given or denied based on whether an individual submits to a request or demand for sex. Hostile environment harassment refers to the situation in which the work environment is uncomfortable or intimidating because of things such as suggestive comments, touching, leering, and offensive materials on bulletin boards. Both victim and harasser can be of either sex.

In 1986, the U.S. Supreme Court used these two definitions of sexual harassment in *Meritor Savings Bank v. Vinson* (1986) in which the Court for the first time found sexual harassment illegal. Lower courts had dealt with the issue during the 1970s and had articulated many of the principles that were validated by the Meritor case. *Ellison v. Brady* (1991), a Ninth Circuit case, resulted in a ruling that the perspective of the woman claiming harassment must be taken into consideration rather than simply using the rule of a "reasonable person" to determine whether a hostile environment exists. In *Harris v. Forklift Systems* (1993), the Supreme Court held that the victim's perception of a hostile and abusive environment is sufficient to establish cause for legal action. In 1998, in *Oncale v. Sundowner Offshore Services, Inc.*, the Supreme Court ruled that same-sex harassment is also covered under the Civil Rights Act.

The policy emerging from *Meritor* and subsequent cases establishes employer liability for sexual harassment. Particularly in quid pro quo harassment, the employer tends to be held automatically liable. In hostile environment harassment, the employer may escape liability if it can demonstrate good faith efforts to correct the behavior that led to complaints of harassment. The Civil Rights Act of 1991 allows harassed employees to sue for punitive damages up to $300,000, in addition to back pay and attorney's costs.

The extent of sexual harassment is difficult to document. Different opinions of what constitutes sexual harassment and the reluctance of employees to file sexual harassment complaints makes it difficult to know the full extent of the problem (Hoyman, 1998; Reese & Lindenberg, 1997; Selden, 2003). Sexual harassment is not always about gender; creating a hostile work environment with offensive remarks about an individual's race, age, and national origin also constitutes harassment (Mann & Goodman, 2008). Nonetheless, surveys of employees indicate that the problem is widespread in both genders—as many as fifty percent of women and nearly forty percent of men reporting that they experienced some form of sexual harassment (Gutek, 1985; U.S. General Accounting Office, 1995; U.S. Merit Systems Protection Board, 1995). In 2011, men filed 16.3% of all sexual harassment charges filed with EEOC (EEOC, 2011). Surveys have yielded widely varying statistics, but sexual harassment is clearly a major problem for employers, and it places employees in untenable situations.

Employers may be sued if they do not protect their employees from sexual harassment. If employers take steps to prevent harassment and respond quickly to complaints, they may avoid liability. To prevent sexual harassment, employers need to develop a policy prohibiting it and communicate that policy clearly to all employees. Sexual harassment policies should address electronic communication as well. With the advent of the smart phone and social media, "sexting," a form of sexual harassment via text messages and emails, is providing newer challenges to employers. In 2012, 13 states introduced bills aimed at "sexting." Four states—Hawaii, New York, Pennsylvania and South Dakota—enacted legislation in 2012.

Regular training to update and remind everyone about the policy also is important. Investigation of any complaints and speedy and appropriate remedial action are necessary. Retaliation against the employee making the complaint rather than correction of the action, which was common in the past, cannot be tolerated. At the same time, employers must be sensitive to the due process rights of the accused.

Privacy Rights

Because public employers are subject to the provisions of the Fourth and Fifteenth Amendments, employees must be accorded protection against unreasonable search and seizure, and due process must be followed. Thus, the public sector is more limited than is the private sector in invading individual privacy. For public personnel administration, the issue has particular relevance in regard to testing applicants for employment; searching employee offices; and using drug tests, polygraphs, and medical exams (Cayer, 1998; Terpstra, Kethley, Foley, & Limpaphayon, 2000).

Applicant screening exams usually are assumed to focus on relevant job skills. Thus, administering skill tests to demonstrate proficiency is a commonly accepted practice. In recent years, psychological testing has become prevalent in the private sector and is being increasingly used in parts of the public sector as well. In particular, psychological tests may be used in sensitive areas of employment, such as public safety, and in positions involving national security. These tests are administered to assess personality characteristics, the ability to deal with stress, attitudes, interpersonal skills, patterns of dealing with conflict, leadership styles, and personal preferences. In the private sector, psychological tests may be used to evaluate all of these qualities, but in the public sector, testing is allowed only for qualities demonstrated to be relevant to job performance for the position in question.

Employers also use background screening and reference checking as part of their hiring processes. Although such devices can be helpful, most employers find the reference checks provide questionable information. People generally do not ask for a reference from someone who is not going to give them a positive evaluation. Most affirmative action policies in the public sector limit the contacting of references to those who the applicant has approved. Former employers often will not provide negative information for fear of lawsuits. Increasingly, employers will only verify dates of employment, salary, and eligibility for rehire. More than thirty states now have reference immunity laws, which shield former employers from liability as long as their references are factual and without malicious intent.

Background investigations are usually relatively perfunctory, except with particular types of positions. Teachers and law enforcement applicants usually undergo in-depth background checks. Similarly, applicants for jobs involving handling of money or controlled substances are likely to be subject to criminal investigations. The courts have so far placed few restrictions on the type of information that can be solicited for background checks.

Medical exams also have been fairly standard for people employed by most organizations, including governments. However, medical conditions cannot generally be a basis for denying employment. If a medical exam is required, employers normally request one after an offer of employment is tendered. Even then, employers cannot deny employment if the medical condition can be addressed by "reasonable accommodation" (Equal Employment Opportunity Commission, 2002). Of course, reasonable accommodation becomes a matter of litigation in many cases.

As the cost of employee health care benefits has increased, employers have attempted to use medical exams and genetic tests to screen out people with existing health issues or who have a high probability of future health problems. However, the Genetic Information Non-Discrimination Act of 2008 (GINA) now prohibits employers from using genetic information when it comes to any aspect of employment, including hiring, firing, pay, job assignments, promotions, layoffs, training, benefits, or any other condition of employment. Particularly controversial has been screening out applicants with HIV/AIDS. Employers also have used HIV/AIDS tests to assess eligibility for medical insurance. The Americans with Disabilities Act (ADA) identifies AIDS as a protected disability; thus, individuals cannot be terminated or discriminated against because of HIV or AIDS. ADA also makes it illegal to screen for any disability unrelated to job performance. The ADA Amendments Act of 2008 made it easier for people with HIV/AIDS to demonstrate that they are disabled because the virus impairs their immune system (Benfer, 2009).

Because drug use has become a serious problem in our society, public employers conduct drug testing to weed out employees who use drugs and may be liabilities. The standards for such tests vary with the groups subject to them. Applicants generally do not have any protections because they do not have a property right in a job. Consequently, drug screening is very common. When it comes to people who already are employed, however, drug testing policies must conform to the due process rights accorded to public employees. Basically, the courts have ruled that blanket drug testing is not consistent with the Constitution. However, in some cases, blanket testing of some employees is constitutional, such as cases in which employees are in positions where public safety could be affected. Thus, police and fire employees, transportation workers, and military personnel may be tested randomly or on a regular basis without violating their constitutional rights. General service public employees, however, usually cannot be subjected to blanket testing. Instead, such employees may be tested if there is a reasonable basis for suspicion of illegal drug use.

Executive Order 12564 (1986) prohibits the use of drugs by federal employees and requires agencies to take steps to ensure a drug-free workplace. The Drug-Free Workplace Act of 1988 requires all organizations that receive federal grants or contracts with federal agencies exceeding $100,000 to maintain a drug-free workplace. A public employer with a drug test policy has several concerns to consider. The first is who to test: applicants, current employees, all employees, or only those suspected of using illegal drugs. Policies also must address the chain of custody of the substances tested so that all samples tested and reported on are the ones taken from the individuals identified with them. The issue of which substances to test for also must be addressed. The employer also must decide what use is to be made of the information and who will have access to it. For example, discipline may be appropriate for certain results.

Additionally, because of the due process rights of public employees, courts have determined that employees with substance abuse problems cannot automatically be terminated. Instead, employers may be required to provide counseling and support, and continued employment may depend on overcoming the problem. Thus, employers must provide the employee an opportunity to address the issue. Clearly, because of public outrage surrounding drug abuse, drug testing in the workplace has much popular support, but the rights of individual employees have to be weighed in public employment.

In some government agencies, polygraphs (commonly known as lie detectors) are used in the employment screening process. Generally the polygraph cannot be used as the sole factor in making a hiring or other personnel decision. The Defense Department and Central Intelligence Agency (CIA), among other agencies, use the polygraph for employees with access to classified information, and state and local government law enforcement agencies routinely use them. For the public sector, the polygraph raises constitutional questions of illegal search and seizure. The questionable reliability of the polygraph is also an issue. Because courts allow only limited use of the polygraph, employers also are challenged by some of the reasoning used in court trials as explained in the discussion of cases that follow.

In 1923, the District of Columbia Appeals Court ruled that polygraph results were inadmissible as evidence in a criminal trial because of the lack of agreement by the scientific community regarding its accuracy (*Frye v. U.S,* 1923). In 1984, the Supreme Court let stand a circuit court decision that found polygraph questions about a police department applicant's sexual relations with someone already on the department force too intrusive to be constitutional (*Thorne v. City of El Sugundo,* 1983). On the other hand, in a fire department case, the use of a polygraph was acceptable to a federal circuit court in a drug use investigation in the department (*Hester v. City of Milledgeville,* 1985).

In 1993, the Supreme Court ruled that the polygraph is admissible but that federal rules of evidence must be met, resulting in varying decisions by lower courts (*Daubert v. Merrell Dow Pharmaceuticals, Inc.,* 1993). The court also ruled in 1998 that defendants have no constitutional right to have a polygraph admitted in evidence, even if it favors their case (*U.S. v. Scheffer,* 1998). In that decision, the court expressed doubts about the reliability of the polygraph.

The Employee Polygraph Act of 1988 prohibits most private employers from using the polygraph for pre-employment screening, discipline, or discharge. However, federal, state, and local employers are exempt. Public organizations continue to use the polygraph even amid questions about its appropriateness (White, 2001). A major issue for employers is to make sure it is used fairly. Many employee organizations press to have the polygraph outlawed as a device for personnel decisions, but they have been unsuccessful so far. Litigation is likely to continue and may be the best hope for employees to eliminate public sector use of polygraphs.

Courts have also been called upon to rule upon privacy issues as they relate to employees' right to freedom from search of their office, desk, and computer files. Generally, the courts consider whether the employee has a legitimate expectation of privacy in deciding on these searches. Courts have ruled that employees have an expectation of privacy if they have an office with a lockable door. That expectation of privacy extends to the property in that office, such as their desks and computers. However, if the employer has a stated policy allowing searches, that nullifies any expectation of privacy. Even where there is an expectation of privacy, the courts generally allow searches pursuant to an investigation of misconduct. *City of Ontario v. Quon* (2010) is a recent case on privacy rights of an employee. Quon, a police officer for the city of Ontario, was given an alphanumeric pager to send and receive text messages. When he exceeded his monthly limit, the police chief ordered transcripts from the wireless company providing the service. It was discovered that many of Quon's messages were not work related, and some were sexually explicit. He and his associates involved in the text messaging were disciplined, following which they filed a lawsuit alleging that their Fourth Amendment right to privacy was violated. In a 9–0 ruling, the justices found that the police chief did not violate the constitutional rights of the officers when he read the transcripts containing sexually explicit text messages sent from his work pager.

Summary

While employees have certain duties and responsibilities as members of the public service, they also have rights as citizens. Balancing these rights with the expectations of supervisors and the public is a difficult task. Management and the public expect public employees to be models of integrity. As a result, public employees often are held to a higher standard of behavior than are private sector employees. Public sector employees must be more concerned than private sector employees about not giving even the appearance of inappropriate behavior. Moreover, they often are called upon to refrain from activities, such as political activities, that citizens take for granted. At the same time, managers and supervisors can exert pressure on employees which would not be possible in the private sector; thus, protections from such coercion are also elements of public personnel policy.

Employees have the right not to be pressured to join organizations they do not want to join and the right to belong to any they do want to join. They also are protected from intimidation and harassment. Public employees also enjoy constitutional protections against intrusion into their privacy. Thus, public employers are limited in the use of medical, drug, and polygraph testing.

Exercises

1. Tanya Blackburn is a captain in the Fire Department and has been with the department for twenty years. This year, the city instituted random drug testing for all firefighters. In the past, testing was used only when there was a suspicion of drug use. Tammy and many of her colleagues objected to the new policy; they felt that it violated their constitutional rights against unreasonable searches and seizures. Nonetheless, all but Tammy went along with the tests. Tammy refused, and she was terminated under the new policy.

The city believes that random testing is necessary for reasons of public safety which override the privacy interest of the employee.

> You are a member of the Civil Service Board that will hear the appeal. What issues will you consider? How do you think the appeal should be decided? Why?

2. Min Patel applied for a position as deputy sheriff with her county sheriff's department. She was pleased to learn that she had passed all the exams and that the department wanted to hire her. She would have the job if she passed the medical exam.

During her medical exam when questioned about her medical history, Min explained that she had lung cancer three years earlier but was in complete remission. Otherwise, everything checked out fine. The department informed her that she could not be employed because she did not pass her medical exam.

Min filed a complaint saying that she was discriminated against based on a past medical condition which was no longer a factor. The county responded that there was a possibility the cancer could return and that as a deputy sheriff, Min would be exposed to situations where she could be breathing substances that could reactivate her condition.

> Do you think the county is right? Does Min have a legitimate complaint? Explain.

3. Cory Paul has been president of the state Public Labor Council for fifteen years during which he has been on leave from his job at the Department of Transportation. The 2010 gubernatorial election was a very spirited one, with the Republican incumbent eventually winning. Because the incumbent had been very antilabor in her first administration, the Public Labor Council, at Paul's urging, endorsed and worked for the election of the Democratic candidate. There was nothing unusual about the activity, as the council had done the same thing during its fifty-year history in the state.

Three months after the election, Cory Paul received a certified letter from the state personnel director informing Paul that he had violated the state's little "Hatch Act," which prohibits political activity by state employees. Specifically, Cory was charged with endorsing and campaigning for the election of the Democratic nominee for governor, contrary to the provisions of the law, which had been in effect for twenty-five years.

Cory was angry and confused. In his fifteen years as president of the Public Labor Council, he could not remember such a thing happening. In fact, no such case had occurred during the history of this state law.

The options for Cory were limited. The letter informed him that he would be prosecuted for violating the law and would be given a punishment ranging somewhere from suspension to termination. He was also offered to opportunity to resign, in which case the charges would be dropped.

Cory decided to fight the charges and filed an appeal with the Personnel Appeals Board, which handles disputes over personnel activities. His appeal requested that the charges be dismissed and that his record be expunged of any wrongdoing.

You are the hearing examiner. What do you want to know? What is your tentative decision? Why?

4. Cape City had a public beach with a café owned and operated by the city. Terry Talbert was employed as a food server at the café. On a couple of occasions, two rowdy men came to the café, and Terry waited on them. Each time, they made sexually suggestive comments to her, and she walked away. She complained to her manager, who told her to ignore their comments.

One day the men came in and sat in Terry's section. She told the manager she did not want to wait on them. He ordered her to wait on them and she complied. The men started their harassing comments, and she again complained to the manager, who told her to ignore the comments. When she brought their food, one of the customers grabbed her and touched her breast. Terry quit and walked out.

The next day her manager's supervisor called to find out what happened and offered Terry a job at another location. She declined the offer. She filed a complaint with the EEOC, charging the manager and department with sexual harassment.

Does Terry have a case? Explain.

5. In the summer of 2012, two sisters, Delsey Richards and Sarah Richards, applied for positions as police officers for the City of Lancaster, Ohio. Both passed the written and physical examination and possessed all the desired qualifications. When the city conducted a background check, they found that Sarah was convicted of a petty theft in 2008. The hiring committee, though impressed with both the sisters' qualifications, decided not to hire either of them, on the pretext that moral values are shared by family members.

Do you agree with the outcome of the hiring decision? Do you think that Delsey Richards should file a discrimination case with the EEOC?

6. A'idah Nur, a 911 operator, has been working for the State of Minnesota since 2000. She is a dedicated and hardworking employee. She is originally from Iran but moved to the United States in 1995. She follows her religious beliefs and wears a head scarf to work. She is bright and is pursuing a Bachelor's degree from the University of Minnesota. One afternoon, during her break, she is speaking on the phone to a family member in Persian. Her boss eavesdrops on her conversation. After she hangs up the phone, in a sarcastic tone, he asks her, "So are you planning the next attack?" A'idah was shocked, and she decided to confront her supervisor right away. She told him that she did not appreciate his condescending remarks. Her boss apologized and said he was just joking.

Should A'idah file a case under harassment based on her national origin? Does this one-time incident constitute harassment? Explain. What would you do if you were in A'idah's position?

Selected Websites

American Polygraph Association (APA). Professional association of polygraphers devoted to advancing the field of polygraphy. Conducts research and advances training and education to improve polygraph testing.

www.polygraph.org

Bloomberg BNA. Publisher of materials on legal, managerial, and regulatory aspects of organizations and on government employment issues.

www.bna.com

Ethics and Compliance Officer Association (ECOA). A world-wide membership organization of ethics officers of business, government, and non-profit organizations. Sponsors conferences and publications devoted to ethics concerns.

www.theecoa.org

Genetic Information Non-Discrimination Act (GINA).

www.eeoc.gov/laws/types/genetic.cfm

National Organization for Women (NOW). Advocacy organization for women. Publishes reports on the status of women in employment and on harassment.

www.now.org

National Partnership for Women and Families. Founded as the Women's Legal Defense Fund. The Partnership is an advocacy organization for women and families. Promotes fairness and the legal rights of women and families in employment.

www.nationalpartnership.org

Section on Ethics. A section of the American Society for Public Administration (ASPA) that seeks to increase understanding of ethics in government and the nonprofit sectors. Publishes a journal and newsletter and sponsors presentations at conferences.

www.aspaonline.org/ethicscommunity

Section on Personnel Administration and Labor Relations (SPLAR). A section of the American Society for Public Administration (ASPA) that promotes public human resource management and labor relations from both an operational and a theoretical perspective.

www.aspaonline.org/spalr/index.html

U.S. Department of Labor elaws Advisors. Agency that provides interactive tools on federal employment laws.

www.dol.gov/elaws

U.S. Equal Employment Opportunity Commission (EEOC). Monitors employer compliance with non-discrimination and equal employment law. Investigates and decides on complaints of discrimination brought to it. Also conducts studies and publishes reports on issues related to equal employment.

www.eeoc.gov

U.S. Office of Government Ethics (OGE). Agency whose mission is to foster high ethical standards for federal government employees and build confidence in government integrity. Helps prevent conflict of interest.

www.usoge.gov

U.S. Merit Systems Protection Board (MSPB). Monitors the federal government's merit-based employment system and serves as the appeals board for federal employees on major personnel actions. Conducts studies and publishes reports on merit systems.

www.mspb.gov

References

Abood v. Detroit Board of Education, 431 U.S. 209 (1977).

AFSCME v. Woodward, 406 F2D 137 (1969).

Ahmed, S. (2008). E-mail policies of the 50 states: A content analysis. *Public Personnel Management, 37*(1), 1–13.

Bailey v. Richardson, 341 U.S. 918 (1951).

Benfer, E. A. (2009). *The ADA amendments act: An overview of recent changes to the Americans with disabilities act.* Washington DC: American Constitution Society for Law and Policy.

Board of Regents v. Roth, 408 U.S. 564 (1972).

Bowman, J. S., & Knox, C. C. (2008). Ethics in government: No matter how long and dark the night. *Public Administration Review, 68*(4), 627–639.

Bowman, J. S., & West, J. P. (2009). To "Re-Hatch" public employees or not? An ethical analysis of the relaxation of restrictions on political activities in civil service. *Public Administration Review, 69*(1), 52–63.

Branti v. Finkel, 445 U.S. 507 (1980).

Brodsky, C. M. (1976). *The harassed worker.* Lexington, MA: Lexington Books.

Caldwell, A. (2012). *US interviews Colombian prostitute in Madrid.* Associated Press Report. Retrieved from http://cnsnews.com/news/article/us-interviews-colombian-prostitute-madrid

Cayer, N. J. (1998). Privacy and integrity testing for public employees. In P. J. Cooper, & C. A. Newland (Eds.), *Handbook of public law and administration.* (pp. 287–298). San Francisco: Jossey-Bass.

Chandler, R. C. (1999). Deontological dimensions of administration ethics revisited. *Public Personnel Management, 28,* 505–514.

Chicago Teachers Union v. Hudson, 475 U.S. 292 (1986).

Cho, Y. J., & Sai, N. (2012). Does organizational justice matter in the federal workplace? *Review of Public Personnel Administration,* published online before print September 13, 2012, doi:10.1177/0734371X12458126

City of Ontario v. Quon, 130 S. Ct. 2619, 560 U.S. ___ (2010).

Cleveland Board of Education v. LaFleur, 414 U.S. 632 (1974).

Cleveland Board of Education v. Loudermill, 470 U.S. 532 (1985).

Cole v. Richardson, 403 U.S. 917 (1972).

Daley, D. M. (2008). The burden of dealing with poor performers wear and tear on supervisory organizational engagement. *Review of Public Personnel Administration, 28*(1), 44–59.

Daubert v. Merrell Dow Pharmaceuticals, Inc., 509 U.S. 579 (1993).

EEOC (2011). *Sexual Harassment Charges EEOC & FEPAs Combined: FY 1997 –FY 2011*. Retrieved from http://www.eeoc.gov/eeoc/statistics/enforcement/sexual_harassment.cfm

Elfbrandt v. Rissell, 384 U.S. 11 (1966).

Ellison v. Brady, 924 F2d 872 (1991).

Elrod v. Burns, 427 U.S. 347 (1976).

Finer, H. (1941). Administrative responsibility in democratic government. *Public Administration Review, 1*, 335–350.

Friedrich, C. J. (1940). Public policy and the nature of administrative responsibility. *Public Policy, 1,* 3–24.

Frye v. U.S., 293 F. 1013 (1923).

Gutek, B.A. (1985). *Sex and the workplace*. San Francisco: Jossey-Bass.

Harris v. Forklift Systems, 114 S. Ct. 367 (1993).

Hartman, G. S., Homer, G. W., & Menditto, J. E. (1998). Human resource management legal issues, an overview. In S. E. Condrey (Ed.), *Handbook of human resource management in government* (pp. 145–164). San Francisco: Jossey-Bass.

Heins, M. (2009). "A pall of orthodoxy": The painful persistence of loyalty oaths. *Dissent, 56*(3), 63–72.

Hester v. City of Milledgeville, 777 F. 2d 1492 (11th Cir., 1985).

Hoffman, D. L., McVicker, E., & Radojevick-Kelley, N. (2009). Tattoos, piercings, body art and small business to hire or not hire? *Small Business Institute National Proceedings, 33*(1), 245–254.

Hoyman, M. M. (1998). Sexual harassment in the workplace. In S.E. Condrey (Ed.). *Handbook of human resource management in government* (pp. 183–198). San Francisco: Jossey-Bass.

Huberts, L., Maesschalck, J., & Jurkiewicz, C. L. (2008). *Ethics and integrity of governance: Perspectives across frontiers.* Northampton, MA: Edward Elgar Publishing.

Human Rights Campaign. (2011). *Employment non-discrimination laws on sexual orientation and gender identity*. Retrieved from http://preview.hrc.org/issues/workplace/equal_opportunity/4844.htm

Hunt. J. (2012). *A state-by-state examination of nondiscrimination laws and policies.* Washington, DC: Center for American Progress Action Fund.

Inside Higher Education. (2008). *A Loyalty Oath Firing in 2008*. Retrieved from http://www.insidehighered.com/news/2008/03/03/loyalty#ixzz2FRqP4IJW

Jones, C. O. (1969). Reevaluating the Hatch Act: A report on the commission on political activity of government personnel. *Public Administration Review, 29*(3), 249–254.

Kelley v. Johnson, 425 U.S. 238 (1976).

Keller, E. K. (Ed.). (1988). *Ethical insight/ethical action perspectives for the local government manager.* Washington, D.C: International City Management Association.

Kellough, J. E. (1999). Reinventing public personnel management: Ethical implications for managers and public personnel systems. *Public Personnel Management, 28*, 655–671.

Kirchheimer, O. (1941). The historical and comparative background of the Hatch Act. *Public Policy, 2*, 341–373.

Lee, S. Y., & Whitford, A. B. (2008). Exit, voice, loyalty, and pay: Evidence from the public workforce. *Journal of Public Administration Research and Theory, 18*(4), 647–671.

Lukacs, E., Cristache, N., Nicolai, M., & Michael, S. (2012). Corporate loyalty versus whistleblowing—An ethical challenge in HRM. *Business & Leadership, 1*(9), 55–66.

Mann, S., & Goodman, D. (2008). Sexual harassment isn't always the issue appellate courts and other factors that contribute to a hostile work environment. *Review of Public Personnel Administration, 28*(2), 190–196.

Martin, P. L. (1974). The constitutionality of the Hatch Act: Second class citizenship for public employees. *University of Toledo Law Review, 6*, 78–109.

Masters, M. F. & Bierman, L. (1985). The Hatch Act and political activities of federal employee unions: A need for policy reform. *Public Administration Review, 45*(4), 518–526.

McCarthy v. Philadelphia Civil Service Commission, 424 U.S. 645 (1976).

Meritor Savings Bank v. Vinson, 477 U.S. 57 (1986).

Moynihan, D. P., & Landuyt, N. (2008). Explaining turnover intention in state government examining the roles of gender, life cycle, and loyalty. *Review of Public Personnel Administration, 28*(2), 120–143.

National Treasury Employees Union v. Van Raab, 489 U.S. 656 (1989).

Oncale v. Sundowner, 523 U.S. 75 (1998).

Pickering v. Board of Education, 391 U.S. 563 (1968).

Rankin v. McPherson, 483 U.S. 378 (1987).

Reese, L. A., & Lindenberg, K. E. (1997). "Victimhood" and the implementation of sexual harassment policy. *Review of Public Personnel Administration, 22*, 37–57.

Riggs v. City of Fort Worth, 229 F.Supp. 2d 572 D.Dist. TX, (2002).

Rose, H. (1962). A critical look at the Hatch Act. *Harvard Law Review, 75*, 510–526.

Rosenbloom, D. H., & Bailey, M. (2003). What every personnel manager should know about the constitution. In S. W. Hays, & R. C. Kearney (Eds.), *Public personnel administration: Problems and prospects* (4th ed.) (pp. 29–45). Upper Saddle River, NJ: Prentice-Hall.

Rutan v. Republican Party of Illinois, 497 U.S. 62 (1990).

Selden, S.C. (2003). Sexual harassment in the workplace. In S.W. Hays & R.C. Kearney (Eds.), *Public personnel administration: Problems and prospects* (4th ed.) (pp. 225–237). Upper Saddle River, NJ: Prentice-Hall.

Shelton v. Tucker, 364 U.S. 479 (1960).

Svara, J. H. (2007). *The ethics primer for public administrators in government and nonprofit organizations.* Sudbury, MA: Jones and Bartlett.

Terpstra, D. E., Kethley, R. B., Foley, R. T. & Limpaphayon, W. (2000). The nature of litigation surrounding five screening devices. *Public Personnel Management, 29,* 43–53.

Thorne v City of El Sugundo, 726 F. 2d 456 (9th Cir., 1983), cert. denied, 469 U.S. 979.

Thurber, K. T., Jr., (1993). Big, little, littler: Synthesizing hatch-act based political activity legislation research. *Review of Public Personnel Administration, 13,* 38–51.

U.S. Civil Service Commission v. National Association of Letter Carriers, 413 U.S. 548 (1973).

U.S. Equal Employment Opportunity Commission. (2002). *Enforcement guidance: Reasonable accommodation and undue hardship under the Americans with Disabilities Act.* Retrieved from www.eeoc.gov/policy/docs/accommodation.html

U.S. Equal Employment Opportunity Commission. (1980). *Final guidelines on sexual harassment in the workplace.* Washington, DC: U.S. Government Printing Office.

U.S. General Accounting Office. (1995). *NIH's handling of alleged sexual harassment and sex discrimination matters.* Washington, DC: General Accounting Office.

U.S. Merit Systems Protection Board. (1995). *Sexual harassment in the federal workplace: Trends, progress, continuing challenges.* Washington, DC: U.S. Government Printing Office.

U. S. Office of Special Counsel. (2010). *Hatch Act: Who is covered?* Retrieved from: http://www.osc.gov/haFederalwhoiscovered.htm

United Public Workers of America v. Mitchell, 330 U.S. 75 (1947).

United States v. National Treasury Employees Union, 513 U.S. 464 (1995).

U.S. v Scheffer, 118 S. Ct. 1261 (1998).

Van Wart, M. (1998). *Changing public sector values.* Hamden, CT.: Garland Publishing.

West, J. P. (2003). Ethics and human resource management. In S. W. Hays, & R. C. Kearney (Eds.), *Public personnel administration: Problems and prospects* (4th Ed.) (pp. 301–315). Upper Saddle River, NJ: Prentice-Hall.

White, R. D. Jr. (2001). Ask me no questions, tell me no lies: Examining the uses and missuses of the polygraph. *Public Personnel Management, 30,* 483–493.

8

Labor–Management Relations

Traditionally, labor–management relations were vastly different in the public and private sectors. Whereas private sector employees achieved full collective bargaining rights by the 1940s, many public employees did not achieve the same rights until the 1960s. However, since the 1980s, the two sectors have appeared increasingly similar in their labor–management relationships (Kearney, 2008; Sulzner, 2002). The drive by public employees to unionize and bargain produced labor–management relations modeled on the private sector experience. The rapid increase in privatization since the 1980s also has blurred the distinction between public and private sector employees relative to labor relations. The preference by many public managers for the term labor–management relations over collective bargaining reflects the government's reluctant acceptance of the collective bargaining process (Wellington & Winter, 1969). *Labor–management relations* actually refers to all aspects of the interchange between labor and management, whereas *collective bargaining* refers more specifically to the process by which labor and management participate in mutual decision making regarding the work situation. In such decision making, employees organize and select a representative to work with management on their behalf. In the absence of collective bargaining, employees are on their own and must negotiate individually with their employers.

Although much of the growth in public sector collective bargaining has occurred relatively recently, some public employees have a long history of unionization. Craft workers in naval installations, for example, have been organized since the early nineteenth century, and the National Association of Letter Carriers came into existence in the late nineteenth century as an affiliate of the American Federation of Labor. Some state and local employees have also been unionized for a relatively long time. The International Association of Fire Fighters, an AFL-CIO affiliate, started in the 1880s as local social clubs and fire fighters' benefit societies. Similarly, the American Federation of State, County and Municipal Employees (AFSCME) began in 1936 under the auspices of the American Federation of Labor (AFL). The AFL and Congress of Industrial Organizations (CIO) were national umbrella organizations that provided financial, political, and technical support to individual affiliates and local organizations. Originally one organization, AFL and CIO split in 1937 over internal disagreements about approaches to collective bargaining and because of personality conflicts among some of the leaders. After years of spirited competition, they merged again in 1955 to form AFL-CIO.

Unionization, however, does not necessarily mean collective bargaining. Collective bargaining began to play an important role in public personnel administration only in the 1960s. John F. Kennedy's Executive Order 10988 in 1962 was a major force in stimulating public sector bargaining activity. It granted federal employees the right to organize and engage in collective bargaining. Executive Orders 11491 (1969) and 11616 (1971) by Richard Nixon and 11838 (1975) by Gerald Ford clarified and formalized the bargaining process for federal employees. The Civil Service Reform Act of 1978 brought about further changes, which will be discussed later in this chapter. One of the most significant features of the reform act was to spell out in statute the right to collective bargaining so that the presidents would no longer have the authority to regulate the process on their own. The process by which personnel decisions are made reflects the influence of labor organizations since the early 1960s. That influence has been curtailed since 2010, when the political environment shifted dramatically, with the election of many conservative governors and legislatures.

Government Resistance to Unions

Several factors contributed to the lack of public sector collective bargaining in the past, including an unfavorable legal environment, legal doctrines of government sovereignty and privilege, an essentiality-of-services argument, the professional status of many public employees, the pay and benefit levels of some employees, and the availability of other means by which employees could attain their objectives. In addition, the public's negative reaction to collective bargaining by government employees slowed its development.

In the current political environment, unions enjoy little public support. The 1960s and 1970s were unusual, in that public opinion tended to support public employee unions and collective bargaining. Otherwise, the public has been suspicious of the effects of bargaining activities. People are afraid that unions already have too much power and have disproportionate power when permitted to bargain with the government (Fletcher, 2012; Moe, 2011). Because unions help elect officials who are supposed to represent the public, critics feel that public employees enjoy an undue advantage if they also have unions bargaining for them (Ball. 1993; DiSalvo, 2010; Silbiger, 1975; Sowell, 2012; Summers, 1974).

However, the power of unions is often exaggerated (Fletcher, 2012). Public employee unions, especially at the federal level, are restricted from engaging in partisan political activity, and they cannot negotiate for union security agreements guaranteeing that the employees they represent will join the union or pay dues. There are also numerous restrictions on which items can be bargained over: pay and fringe benefits are excluded in federal bargaining and in some state and local jurisdictions. As some writers have pointed out, public employee unions are also at a disadvantage because they have no natural allies in the political process, so that most organized political interests find them easy targets for attack (Summers, 1974). Management often uses fear of union power to justify denying collective bargaining to public employees.

The political climate has also contributed to a legal framework in which bargaining was made difficult. Government employees were exempted from the protections of the Wagner and Taft-Hartley Acts, which spelled out the rights and responsibilities of parties in private sector bargaining. Also, before 1960, the courts consistently held that public employees did not have a constitutional right to join or organize unions, and public employers were under no obligation to bargain with employees. In 1954, by executive order, Mayor Robert Wagner granted New York City employees the right to organize; in response, the legal environment began rapidly changing. The collective bargaining apparatus was established in 1958, and the city began its bargaining process. In 1959, Wisconsin became the first state to authorize collective bargaining for public employees; however, only local government employees were affected, as state employees were exempted from the law. But with the 1962 Kennedy order mentioned above, unionization and bargaining flourished at all levels of government.

The Lloyd-LaFollette Act of 1912 granted employees the right to join labor organizations and petition Congress without fear of reprisal. However, before the Kennedy order, collective bargaining was nonexistent in the federal government service. Before the issuance of the Kennedy order, federal employees were subject to mandatory discharge and forfeiture of civil service status for union activity. Similarly, legislation in 1955 declared that a strike against the federal government was a felony and that it disqualified the participants from federal employment. The Kennedy executive order, however, signaled a turning point in labor relations. As it changed federal policy on bargaining with federal government employees, it also stimulated state and local governments to reexamine and change many of their policies.

However, state and local government relations are not governed under any common legal framework. States have their own policies or non-policies, and many other variations exist in the approximately eighty thousand local government jurisdictions across the country. Labor relations take place under policies made through a variety of sources: common law doctrine, judicial decisions, executive orders, statutes, ordinances, and the opinions of attorneys general.

Thirty-five states and the District of Columbia require collective bargaining for some or all state and local employees who wish to engage in bargaining. Eleven states permit but do not require bargaining, whereas five states ban it (National Council on Teacher Quality, 2013). The rights are extended by state statutes in most instances, but some states rely on judicial decisions or decisions by their attorneys general to provide for bargaining. Many of the policies focus on groups of employees such as teachers, police and fire, whereas others allow all employees to engage in bargaining. The right to belong to a union and to be represented by collective bargaining are not synonymous. Any employee may join a union as a constitutional right, but employees may engage in bargaining only if policy extends them that right.

Where labor relations policies exist, they range from full-fledged collective bargaining (including the right to strike) to policies of meet and confer. *Meet and confer* refers to a process in which employees have the right to sit down with management and discuss issues but do not have the right to have any ensuing agreements enforced by the political or legal system. Arizona uses the meet and confer system for local governments. In that state, some jurisdictions, especially school districts, appear to engage in full-fledged negotiations, and it is politically difficult for the jurisdiction to turn its back on an agreement, even though there is no legal requirement to honor it.

Traditionally, the *sovereignty of government doctrine* has been used to preclude public employees from engaging in collective bargaining. This doctrine holds that government is the agent of the people, and it cannot delegate authority to others, such as employee organizations, without violating the people's trust. In other words, the authority is not government's to delegate. This doctrine has waned in significance as court rulings have weakened it.

The *privilege doctrine* is another legal device used to discourage public sector collective bargaining. This doctrine holds that some of the benefits governments confer are privileges, not rights. For example, education, welfare, and the like have been adjudged to be privileges. Similarly, public employment was viewed as a privilege, and hence it does not confer the right to collective bargaining. However, as with the sovereignty doctrine, the courts have essentially abandoned the privilege doctrine, and it no longer restricts bargaining in the public sector (see Chapter 6).

Services performed by governments have been characterized as essential, and bargaining has been denied to public employees because it could potentially interfere with essential services. Particularly because collective bargaining is often thought to lead to strikes, the prohibition of bargaining has been justified as a way of preventing the interruption of services. This argument has been weakened because many of the services government provides are in fact, not viewed as essential by the public. In fact, many private sector services—the telephone or Internet, for example—would be more difficult to live without in the short run than would government service such as education and highway maintenance. Furthermore, experience with the loss of services such as sanitation, police protection, and education through strikes has demonstrated that people can cope with such situations for a limited time and has lessened the fears surrounding collective bargaining.

Public employees themselves have often been hesitant to engage in collective bargaining. Until the 1960s, unions and other labor organizations were not held in high esteem by public employees. Most jobs in the public sector are white-collar, and there has been a tendency for employees to think of labor organizations as typically blue-collar. Teachers in particular have been split over whether it is professional to belong to a union and engage in collective bargaining. However, after finding that unions could bring them gains, public employees have been changing their view, and many professional associations are becoming bargaining agents for public employees.

Whereas the pay and benefits of state and local government employees are often poor, federal employees receive great benefits. Compensation, though not excessive, also has been relatively good at the starting and middle levels of federal service. As a result, federal employees did not see as much of a need for collective bargaining as did some of their counterparts in state and local government.

Finally, public employees have sometimes been slow to organize because they have other means of gaining their objectives. The lack of centralized authority in the political system gives public employees several bodies that can grant their demands. Because the decision makers are elected politicians, they pay attention to blocs of voters, and public employees often constitute a major bloc. Public employees can also lobby legislative bodies that often retain control over their pay and benefits. Thus, if the executive does not satisfy a public employee group, that group can go to the legislative body or a competing board or agency. Public employee groups have been effective in taking advantage of these fragmented political structures, particularly at the local level.

Politics and Bargaining

A crucial difference between public sector and private sector collective bargaining is the political nature of the decision-making process in public sector bargaining (Clark, 1975; Summers, 1974, 1986). As Theodore Clark observed, collective bargaining is premised on the idea that the two parties to the bargaining process are adversaries who seek their own interests and that each party selects its representative without being influenced by the other party (Clark, 1975). In the public sector, however, political considerations violate these premises. In particular, public employee organizations participate in the selection of management through involvement in interest group politics and through the election process. In short, employee organizations have special access to management's decision-making process, thus enhancing the organizations' power vis-à-vis management. Critics of public sector bargaining decry the special position enjoyed by public employee labor organizations and suggest that unions and the like dominate the process as a result (Bennet, 1974; DiSalvo, 2010; Horton, 1973; Silbiger, 1975).

Summers, by contrast, believes that public employees need that special access because they face formidable opposition from all other interests in the political process (Summers, 1974). Because tax revenues may have to be raised, or levels of service reduced, to finance public employees' demands, the political opposition to such demands can be intense. The taxpayer revolts symbolized by California's Proposition 13 in 1978 and its stimulation of similar efforts in other jurisdictions, which endure to this day, attest to the impact that an aroused electorate can have. Similarly, public employees in San Francisco bore the brunt of taxpayer discontent with some of their gains from 1974 and 1975. In 1985, San Francisco voters rescinded an agreement establishing comparable worth. Through referenda, salaries were rolled back and limits were established regarding how to negotiate and what could be bargained for. Similarly, a 1994 referendum in Oregon wiped out the state contribution to the employee retirement system. Thus, abuses by employee unions can be cited, but active citizen participation in the political process also can dwarf the influence of public employee organizations. As noted earlier, recent elections brought to office many public officials committed to rolling back public union influence.

Governor Chris Christie of New Jersey took office in January 2010 and immediately took on public sector unions by issuing an executive order banning them from making political contributions and battled with teachers' unions over pay and benefits. Then, in 2010, Scott Walker was elected governor in Wisconsin and began a protracted effort with the legislature to weaken and even outlaw public sector unions. Similarly, Governor John Kasich of Ohio, also elected in 2010, took the same approach in that state. Debate over the role of public sector unions has waged across the country since, and unions often find themselves the object of much scorn.

The political nature of public sector bargaining is also reflected in the way management selects its representatives and decides on the policy it will bring to the bargaining table. Again, as Summers pointed out, citizens have an interest in these negotiations, whereas in the private sector, management makes such decisions without public involvement (Summers, 1974). Decisions on how public management will select a representative, and decisions on what the bargaining position will be, are matters of public concern. Accordingly, employee organizations can participate in them, again augmenting their influence. In contrast, management normally is prohibited from attempting to influence employees' selection of bargaining agents and positions.

Additionally, management representatives at the bargaining table often do not have the authority to bind the jurisdiction to the agreement they negotiate. There are many other decision makers to whom employee organizations can appeal if they do not get satisfaction in the bargaining process. Many times city councils or other legislative bodies need to ratify agreements and are hesitant to give up any authority to change elements of the agreement. Similarly, legislative bodies can retain control over many aspects of the work situation, either mandating or placing restrictions on personnel practices. For local governments, the issue is even more complicated by the fact that state legislation can mandate practices for all governmental bodies. For example, if a state minimum salary or other requirement is imposed, the local jurisdiction will have little choice but to abide by the mandate. As is often the case, the costs normally have to be borne by the local government, even though the policy comes from above.

Another political aspect of public sector collective bargaining is that personnel issues have larger policy implications. They are part of the policy-making process to the extent that political representatives make the decision in many cases that affect issues such as tax policy, budgeting, and level of services. The political representatives are influenced by what will gain them votes. Such concerns often lead to problems if a political leader does not own up to the consequences of trying to curry favor with employee organizations for the purpose of gaining elective office. Officials in some cities, such as New York City, agreed in the past to contracts whose costs had to be borne by future officials. Pension plans in particular were often subject to such political manipulation. In the short run, the politician gains, but taxpayers and succeeding officials are faced with the long-term cost. Unless the public is made fully aware of the ultimate cost, it is difficult to prevent opportunistic politicians from taking advantage of the situation. With greater public access to information since the freedom of information and open meetings laws of the 1960s and 1970s, these issues are now debated publicly somewhat mitigating the problem.

Because of these problems, the "fishbowl" approach to public sector bargaining developed. With this approach, the bargaining is done in public. In the private sector, closed-door sessions are almost universal. The public sector, however, runs into problems when it conducts closed negotiation sessions because it violates freedom of information and open meetings laws. Nonetheless, eleven states provide for closed-door bargaining (Goldwater Institute, 2011). In a democratic society, people are supposed to know what is going on so that they can retain control over the system. If bargaining is conducted in private, they cannot participate in the process and must relinquish control to those who participate in the negotiation. By contrast, when negotiation takes place in open meetings, as is required in seven states, participants may find themselves pushed into corners on issues (Goldwater Institute, 2011). Once negotiators state a position publicly, it becomes difficult to change it because they may be perceived by their constituents as backing down. Because negotiation requires compromise, it becomes difficult to bargain effectively in public sessions. There is no easy way to reconcile the need for openness in a democratic government and the need for frankness and compromise in collective bargaining.

Elements of a Labor Relations System

A public labor–management relations system is created by public policy in the form of legislation, an executive order, a court decision, or a legal opinion. The policy normally spells out who has authority for labor–management relations and the basic rules and steps in the bargaining process. Of course, the system's most basic element is the question of whether the right to bargain is to exist.

Administration of Labor–Management Relations

If the right to bargain is granted, there must be a way to administer the process; thus, most policies assign the responsibility to an existing agency or create a new one. The national government, under the Civil Service Reform act of 1978, created the Federal Labor Relations Authority (FLRA) to oversee bargaining unit determination, supervise elections, and coordinate agency labor–management activities. The FLRA consists of three bipartisan presidential appointees, with one designated as the chairperson. Also appointed is a general counsel, who investigates unfair labor practices. In case negotiations break down, the Federal Service Impasses Panel is called in to help.

At the state and local levels, the supervision of the collective bargaining process varies. Some states have created an agency whose sole purpose is to supervise public employee labor relations. These agencies usually also manage labor relations for local jurisdictions. They are often called Public Employee Relations Boards (PERB). Maine, New York, and Hawaii are examples of such states. Another approach is to assign the responsibility to personnel departments, departments of labor, or personnel boards, as is done in Alaska, Massachusetts, Montana, and Wisconsin. A combination of approaches also may be used, in which a state board may oversee collective bargaining generally, but individual departments have the specific responsibility for bargaining in their areas. Thus, departments of education and local boards of education often supervise their own bargaining.

Unit Determination

Unit determination refers to those employees who are considered a unit for bargaining purposes. The criteria for making such a decision are community of interest, desires of the employees and employer, history of experience, efficiency of management, and limiting fragmentation. *Community of interest* pertains to the similarities of the people in the proposed unit. Similarity of duties, skills, working conditions, job classifications, employee benefits, promotional ladders, and supervision are some of the factors considered. In addition, employees may be grouped together because of the amount of interchange, integration of physical operations, or centralization of administrative and managerial functions. The main concern is having a bargaining unit consisting of employees who have similar interests so they can work together. Employees often like to have many units because the narrower a group's interest are, the greater its solidarity is likely to be. Sometimes that concern is sacrificed for size, though, as an overly narrow focus may lead to very small numbers of eligible employees for the unit. Management usually prefers larger units because there are likely to be disagreements within the unit that management can exploit and also because when units are large, management has fewer employee representatives to deal with.

The two main types of units are agency and occupational units. *Agency units* are those in which a particular department or agency forms the basis for organizing the bargaining process. The Treasury Department at the national level and police and fire departments at the local level are examples of agency units. Minnesota uses agency units throughout the state service. An advantage for management is that the channels of communication are already in place in the agencies. However, as most agencies consist of employees doing a variety of jobs with differing career paths, the level of common interest may be low. Often, employees with similar skills (e.g., computer technicians) are dispersed among different agencies. Consequently, consensus is often difficult to achieve because so many types of employees are employed in the same agency.

Occupational units are based on the type of work done. Thus, all clerical staff may be in one unit, all lab technicians in another, and so on. Clearly, each group is likely to have well-defined interests, and similar work in different agencies will be covered under similar policies. Managers often have difficulty with this approach because it centralizes authority on bargained issues, thus weakening departmental control over employees.

Some jurisdictions use a combination of the two approaches. New York City, for example, bargains over some issues (overtime,

RIF policies, grievance procedures) citywide. Other issues, such as caseloads, may be negotiated at the departmental level, and still others related to items such as the salary for a particular job title may be bargained at yet another designated level. Such a system is said to have *multilevel units*.

An issue that comes up in the public sector but not in the private sector is whether supervisors should be in the same unit as the people they supervise. In the private sector, supervisors generally are not permitted to bargain, and if they are, they are in separate units. In the public sector, it is not uncommon to find supervisors in the same units with their subordinates. Police and fire departments often have everyone except the chief in the bargaining unit. Conflicts can arise because the bargaining unit's representative has to represent the employees in grievances. If the supervisor against whom a grievance is filed is also a member of the unit, there will be a conflict of interest. The steward is supposed to represent everyone in the unit and yet cannot represent both sides at the same time. Being in the bargaining unit with subordinates also compromises the supervisor's role as a member of the management team. In the public sector, these problems arise because the role of supervisors is not as clearly defined as it is in the private sector. Supervisors in the public sector often are considered lead workers in their units but are not considered part of management. Thus there is confusion over whether they should be part of the bargaining unit.

Bargaining Representatives

Management often has difficulty organizing for bargaining because of the fragmentation of political authority in government units. Nonetheless, as bargaining activity has increased, most jurisdictions involved in bargaining have hired labor relations experts to lead negotiations and administer the overall labor–management relations program. Working with the labor relations expert usually will be representatives of personnel, legal counsel, and representatives of the department or unit to which negotiations pertain.

Employees choose representatives to bargain for them. The selection process is usually specified in the labor relations policy, and it requires an election in which the employees decide whether to adopt collective bargaining and determine who will bargain for them. The winner is the exclusive representative for the bargaining unit and must represent all employees in the unit, whether they are union members or not. The election of the unit's representatives is known as the *certification election*, and like the election on whether to bargain at all, it is supervised by the agency responsible for administering the labor–management relations program. The two actions may be taken at the same election or in separate elections. Representatives of employees fall into three categories: union, employee associations, and professional associations.

Unions of course are the most readily recognized participants in collective bargaining, as they have been the traditional agents of employees in the private sector. Unions in the public sector may have only public employee members or may be mixed-membership unions, that is, have members from both the public and private sectors. As union membership in the private sector declined, unions increasingly opened up to public employee membership to maintain their strength. The largest public sector union is the American Federation of State, County, and Municipal Employees (AFSCME), with membership of approximately 1.6 million (American Federation of State, County, and Municipal Employees, 2013). However, membership tells only part of the story. Unions in the public sector must represent everyone in the bargaining unit, even though they cannot require all employees in the unit to be dues-paying members. The National Association of Government employees, with about 50,000 members, represents 150,000 workers at all levels of government (National Association of Government Employees, 2013).

Three other relatively large unions represent mostly federal government employees: The American Federation of Government Employees (AFGE) represents approximately 650,000 employees, the National Federation of Federal Employees (NFFE) represents 110,000 employees (National Federation of Federal Employees, 2013), and the National Treasury Employees Union (NTEU) represents about 150,000 employees (National Treasury Employees Union, 2013). Many public employee unions, like their private sector counterparts, are having difficulty retaining members. Fiscal stress in governments has weakened the ability of unions to do much about wages and benefits. Additionally, working conditions have improved to the point where many employees no longer see the need for unions to protect their interests even though unions have been responsible for much of the improvements workers have experienced. Taken for granted are relatively safe working conditions and programs to protect employees' security in times of illness and injury. Without a strong perceived need for their services, unions have to convince employees of their benefits, and with their current image, that is not always easy.

The uniformed services are among the most highly unionized and are represented by unions with almost exclusively public sector membership. Police officers are represented by two major organizations, the Fraternal Order of Police (FOP), with 325,000 members, and the International Brotherhood of Police Officers (IBPO), which is part of the National Association of Government Employees (International Brotherhood of Police Officers, 2013). Some other unions, such as AFSCME and the Teamsters, also represent the police in some jurisdictions. Because police protection is one of the essential services people are afraid of losing, these unions usually have been successful in obtaining their demands. Police unions usually play up the professional nature of their work and hence portray themselves to the public as professional organizations rather than as unions. Sick-ins and slowdowns are common techniques used by police employee unions. When strikes occur, the current political climate dampens the public's enthusiasm for them. Also, strikes are not always successful, as the experience of the New Orleans police in 1979 demonstrated.

The strike, timed to occur during Mardi Gras, the city's busiest tourist season, was calculated to bring pressure from business and the community to bear on public officials. The union expected that such pressure would make management settle quickly, to the benefit of the police. The actual result was that much of the Mardi Gras celebration was curtailed, and the police union lost its credibility and the support of the community. Consequently, management was able to hold out until the police were willing to settle for management's original offer. The New Orleans experience demonstrates taxpayers' growing frustration and shows that unions do not always get what they want. Similarly, President Reagan's firing of 11,500 air traffic controllers who went out on strike in 1981 was a dramatic message to public employees that strikes could be broken. This action encouraged public employers to take harder lines with their employees' representatives.

Firefighters also have a long tradition of collective bargaining in an essential service. They are almost unique among public employees, because the International Association of Fire Fighters (IAFF) exercises virtually exclusive jurisdiction over them. In contrast with the police organization, the IAFF, representing more than 300,000 firefighters, traditionally has stressed its union image in association with AFL-CIO (International Association of Fire Fighters, 2013). Although the IAFF does not officially sanction strikes, it provides assistance to striking locals.

As was noted earlier, some unions consist of membership from both the public and private sectors. During the late 1950s, private sector unions lost members and looked to the growing public sector to increase their rolls. These unions usually seek members from all levels of government rather than from just one level. The AFL-CIO now has a department devoted entirely to public sector collective bargaining. Reflecting the private sector's tradition, these unions tend to be more occupationally segregated and more likely to favor strikes. Among these mixed-membership unions are the Service Employees International Union, with a membership over 2.1 million, of whom more than one million are public employees; the International Brotherhood of Teamsters, with approximately 1.4 million members; and the Amalgamated Transit Union with approximately 190,000 employee members (International Brotherhood of Teamsters, 2013; Amalgamated Transit Union, 2013). Other unions have mixed memberships. Interests in mixed-membership unions are divided between public and private sector contingents, leading to concern about how strongly they can represent public employees' interests. However, they have the vast resources of the parent union behind them and are effective in marshaling support in the political process.

Public employee associations, such as the Vermont State Employees Association, are the second type of representative in public sector collective bargaining. Some associations on the state and local levels have existed for years. Although originally organized to improve employee opportunities and the status of public employees, many associations have redirected their activities toward collective bargaining. Because of their original purposes, they tend to be less in favor of strikes, instead relying heavily on public relations and lobbying. They are becoming increasingly militant, however, as the competition for membership grows between them and the unions. Many have merged with unions whereas others have joined together in the Assembly of Government Employees (AGE) to strengthen their clout.

Professional associations are the third type of public employee organization. Their membership is more limited than that of public employee associations in that educational or occupational criteria are imposed for membership. They generally have resisted joining the bargaining movement because they have viewed bargaining as unprofessional behavior. However, the success of unions and employee associations in recruiting and gaining benefits for their members has stimulated professional groups to organize for collective bargaining.

Among the more active professional associations in bargaining are the American Nurses Association (ANA), National Association of Social Workers (NASW), and American Association of University Professors (AAUP). The National Education Association (NEA) is the largest professional organization with a membership of over three million and is also one of the most active in the bargaining process. Its state affiliates decide how deeply involved they wish to be in bargaining (National Education Association, 2013). The NEA and its affiliates provide some of the clearest evidence of the conflict in professional organizations over the collective bargaining issue. It has been pushed further into the bargaining process by the success of the American Federation of Teachers (AFT) in recruiting members and winning benefits. To retain its membership, the NEA feels the need to become involved in collective bargaining. The rivalry between NEA and AFT led them to propose a merger, but it never occurred. Instead, they created the NEAFT Partnership to work together on common interests while allowing each organization to act separately as it sees fit. The AAUP has faced a similar conflict as a representative of college and university faculties.

Among the various types of employee organizations that become involved in the bargaining process, we see a variety of approaches to issues in labor–management relations. Unions tend to be most militant, although they vary greatly from one to another. Unions associated with both private and public sector employees are usually more likely to support the right to strike, but police and fire fighter unions also have done so in recent years. Employee and professional associations usually prefer to use public relations and lobbying to accomplish their objectives but have been pushed into more militant positions by the success of unions in their bargaining efforts. Similarly, some organizations, particularly employee associations, stress the independence of their affiliates, and the unions stress the resources their national organizations provide. All in all, approximately 37 percent of eligible public employees are union members compared with only 6.9% of eligible private sector workers (U.S. Bureau of Labor Statistics, 2012). Local government employees lead with 43.2% of workers unionized, while 31.5% of state workers and 28.1% of federal employees are unionized (U.S. Bureau of Labor Statistics, 2012).

Scope of Bargaining

For jurisdictions that have a labor relations policy, that policy usually lays out the scope of bargaining by stating what can be bargained. The policy may make bargaining on issues either mandatory or permissive. Mandatory issues are those that must be bargained, and permissive issues are those that may be bargained over if both parties wish. There are also prohibited issues, that is, issues that (according to policy) cannot be negotiated. In the federal government, for example, wages and salaries cannot be negotiated, and in many state and local governments, negotiators may be prohibited from bargaining on "management prerogatives" such as assignment of personnel and decisions about the nature of the service to be delivered. Discriminatory provisions cannot be included in agreements in any jurisdiction.

Conflict often arises over the scope of bargaining because management wishes to maintain as much management prerogative as possible in decisions and labor wishes to share in that responsibility. This conflict usually leads to a definition of the items that can and cannot be negotiated. Generally, it is assumed that management rights exist independently of the collective bargaining relationship until modified by that relationship. The PERB usually defines management prerogatives as a result of complaints brought to it by one of the parties. As with most other aspects of labor relations policy, the scope of bargaining varies greatly by jurisdiction.

A labor relations policy defines the basic rules under which labor relations take place. The policy addresses issues other than those noted above, and they will be treated separately because of their significance in the bargaining process. Those issues include impasse resolution procedures, strikes, and contract administration. They will be examined after the next section, which deals with the negotiations themselves.

The Negotiating Process

After determining what can be negotiated, and after employees have decided to use collective bargaining procedures and have selected a representative, the process may begin. Ordinarily, employees express their desire to bargain on an issue(s) by presenting proposals to the management team covering the items they wish to consider. In recent years it has been common for management to also draw up a list of demands to be considered at the negotiating table. Thus, management now sees the process as proactive rather than reactive. Once the proposals have been exchanged, the two sides meet to determine what procedures or ground rules will govern the negotiations. The proposals may be exchanged before the first meeting or at the meeting, depending on the particular case.

After each side makes and explains its proposals, they each study the other's position so that reactions and counterproposals can be made. These reactions and counterproposals become the focus of the negotiating process. However, before the actual negotiations, each side spends a lot of time in preparation. To be prepared, each side must be well versed in personnel rules and regulations and the way they are implemented, as well as in the legal limitations imposed on personnel practices. Each side will also review the previous agreement and any problems that have occurred under it. Of particular interest will be any grievances filed under the current agreement. In addition, each party normally costs out its proposals and collects data on economic indicators, productivity, budget and revenue projections, and wages and salaries in similar and surrounding jurisdictions to support their projections. Armed with these data, both sides are ready to begin negotiating.

The behavior of the parties in the negotiations is extremely important, and posturing is common. Either party may decide to take an aggressive, challenging, hard-line approach on every item, hoping to wear down the other side. Alternatively, the strategy may be to focus on a few issues that are of particular importance and to make concessions on other less important issues. Yet another approach is to appear conciliatory in order to establish goodwill. Often participants attempt to impress their own constituents as much as their adversaries in the negotiations. The strategy chosen normally depends on how far apart the parties are and how important the issues are. Relative political power is also a factor in the public sector, as was illustrated by some of the examples cited earlier, particularly in New York City, where employee organizations can bring other political forces into play. However, political tactics can sometimes backfire. For example in 1981, the Professional Air Traffic Controllers Organization (PATCO) miscalculated its power to influence the Reagan administration through appeals to citizens and the business community.

Most collective bargaining ends in an agreement at the negotiating table. Then each side has to take the agreement back to its constituency for approval. The members of the employee organization vote on the ratification of the agreement. If they vote no, more negotiation will be necessary. If they vote yes, management must usually go to the relevant legislative body for approval and funding. Occasionally a city council or school board rejects an agreement, in which case the negotiations must be restarted, but ordinarily the agreement wins approval. At the state and federal levels, specific legislative approval is usually not required, but in states in which salary and benefits are negotiated, funding for the provisions requires legislative appropriations and thus indirect approval.

Impasse Resolution Procedures

If the parties do not reach an agreement at the negotiating table, there are several alternatives available to help them resolve the impasse. These alternatives are called impasse procedures and include mediation, fact finding, arbitration, and a referendum. All use outside parties, usually called third parties. There are many types of third parties. At the national level, the Federal Mediation and Conciliation Service (FMCS), an independent agency, provides mediation services and is also available to the private sector and state and local governments. The Federal Service Impasses Panel (FSIP), which is part of the Federal Labor Relations Authority, also provides mediation and other impasse resolution services to federal agencies. State and local governments sometimes have their own services for impasse resolution, but more commonly they seek federal help or the services of consultants who specialize in such work. The American Arbitration Association also has trained people to provide impasse resolution services under contract. In smaller jurisdictions, respected members of the community may be asked to perform this function as a public service.

Mediation

Mediation is used by most jurisdictions that permit bargaining. In mediation, a neutral individual—usually trained in labor relations—tries to get the two parties to resolve their differences through compromise. Though they cannot impose decisions on the parties, the mediators meet with each party and discuss points of disagreements and how they might be reconciled. Then they recommend solutions to the parties in hopes that the parties will work out the differences themselves.

Fact Finding

Fact finding is a variation of the mediation process. In fact finding, a neutral third party works with both parties to the dispute and conducts a formal investigation of the issues separating them. The fact finder then issues a formal report stating the "facts" of the situation. The idea here is that by formally pinpointing the differences, the report will put pressure on the parties to resolve their differences. The reports usually must be made public in the hope that public opinion and pressure will cause the parties to settle.

Arbitration

If fact finding fails, the next step is more controversial. Because public jurisdictions generally prohibit strikes, some form of final, binding decision becomes attractive. The alternative normally available is arbitration. In arbitration, a neutral third party has the authority to impose a settlement or, in the case of advisory arbitration, is asked to recommend a solution. Conventional arbitration is binding in the sense that if parties go to arbitration, they are bound to accept the arbitrator's decision. The arbitrator does much the same work a mediator or fact finder does—evaluate the situation and then decide on an equitable solution. The difference is that the decision is binding.

In some instances, final-offer arbitration is used. Each party presents the arbitrator with its final offer for settlement, and the arbitrator then selects the better of the two. The logic behind this approach is that the parties can be expected to offer the most reasonable solution out of fear that the arbitrator may choose a worse settlement proposed by the other party. Connecticut and Indiana use forms of final-offer arbitration.

Arbitration is also often differentiated as either voluntary or compulsory. Voluntary arbitration means that the parties voluntarily choose to go to arbitration. In compulsory arbitration, they have no choice but to go to arbitration at some specified point. Thus, the law may require arbitration if mediation and/or fact finding has failed or after a certain period of impasse. The difference between these types of arbitration lies only in how the parties arrive at arbitration; once the process starts, it is the same.

A combination form of impasse resolution is the med-arb approach used in Wisconsin municipalities and school districts. In the med-arb, a mediator attempts to resolve the impasse. If this is unsuccessful, the mediator then becomes an arbitrator. This system is supposed to be more efficient in that the mediator already knows the situation, and thus, as an arbitrator, does not have to spend time becoming familiar with it. Knowing that the same person is going to arbitrate if mediation is unsuccessful also may encourage the two parties to work out their differences along the lines of the mediator's suggestions. It has not been used much in the United States.

Referendum

The fourth impasse procedure is the voter referendum, in which the contested issues may be taken to the public for a vote (Hansen & Allen, 1985; Hogler & Thompson, 1985). Colorado permits municipalities to use this method. As with final-offer arbitration, the referendum approach can bring pressure to get the decision made through the negotiating process to avoid potentially harsher agreements from the outside. However, complex bargaining issues do not lend themselves very well to an election campaign that requires gaining support of voters with notoriously short attention spans.

The impasse procedures outlined here progress from the least to the most coercive in terms of the ability of outside parties to impose settlement. However, there is interaction among the processes. The person serving as mediator sometimes becomes the fact finder or arbitrator if the process moves to those stages. The developments in mediation and fact finding provide part of the basis for the arbitration process if it progresses that far. Variations in each of the procedures also may combine elements from one or more of the "pure" impasse procedures described above. Jurisdictions vary in whether any or all of the procedures are available. Where more than one is available, the mildest form is usually used first, and then the process moves through the more coercive choices.

Strikes

If impasse procedures are not available or do not resolve the impasse, employees may decide that they have no alternative but to strike. Although most jurisdictions prohibit strikes by public employees, there have been plenty of strikes in the public sector. During the 1960s and 1970s, public sector strikes were frequent. However, since 1980, the number of public sector strikes has dropped. The PATCO experience, high unemployment, and the public's disaffection with labor unions all probably contributed to decreased militance by employee organizations. Nonetheless, occasional public employees do strike such as public school teachers in Chicago in September 2012 and New York City school bus drivers in January 2013. Opposition to strikes is evident to the extent that all but ten states prohibit strikes, and where they are permitted, they generally are limited to certain types of employees. Police, fire, hospital, and corrections personnel are usually excluded, though they do engage in illegal strikes on occasion.

States such as Alaska, California, Hawaii, Idaho, Illinois, Michigan, Minnesota, Montana, Oregon, Pennsylvania, and Vermont give public employees limited rights to strike through legislation or court decisions, but in most states, strikes by public employees are strictly forbidden. However implementing legislation banning strikes is difficult. Officials, including judges, are reluctant to enforce no-strike legislation by jailing strikers because of the possible martyr effect. The people jailed become heroes to other employees for being willing to go to such lengths for their cause. As noted earlier, however, some jurisdictions have been effective in handling strikes. The firing of the PATCO strikers broke the strike, and it has been used as a symbol of management's tougher stance. However, even though successful in the short run, such tactics damage the morale of other employees and the credibility of management with its workforce.

Contract Administration

Once an agreement is reached, it must be implemented; the process for doing this is contract administration. This process gives meaning to the agreement and thus is an important part of collective bargaining. Implementation is generally management's responsibility, but the employees will react to what they perceive to be management's misinterpretations of the agreement. Many provisions in a contract may be vague, causing problems in interpretation, or the parties may disagree on what is meant by terms such as reasonable time, just cause, and normal practices. Similarly, unanticipated situations may develop and must be dealt with under the contract's terms.

Although the labor relations office may have the overall responsibility for implementing the agreement, the first-line supervisor is the key person for management in contract administration. He or she has continuous contact with the employees and thus effectively carries out the agreement's provisions. To make sure supervisors understand the contract and implement it consistently, they are given training in regard to the contract. The contract's provisions are interpreted for the supervisors, who also are instructed carefully about the contents of the contract.

Employees may complain about the way part of the agreement is or is not implemented, and normally one individual is chosen as the shop steward or union representative whose job is to represent the employees and resolve their complaints. The steward also monitors the contract's implementation to ensure compliance with the agreement and raises objections as appropriate. Most of management's contact with the employees concerning the contract's administration is through the steward.

Despite efforts to implement the agreement correctly, problems often develop, and the parties may not be able to resolve disagreements over specific provisions. In most bargaining agreements, this eventuality is provided for by grievance arbitration. The process normally calls for an employee with a complaint to file a written grievance with his or her immediate supervisor. The complaint may be settled at that level, but usually the issue can be appealed for resolution up through top management and eventually to the public employee relations board or its equivalent. If the parties are still unable to resolve the issue, arbitration will be invoked. The process is essentially the same as the arbitration procedure for resolving negotiation impasses. If the collective bargaining agreement contains no grievance arbitration clause, personnel or civil service rules will provide a mechanism for dealing with complaints involving the agreement's implementation.

Unfair Labor Practices

Both management and labor are prohibited from engaging in unfair labor practices, which usually are defined by statute. At the national level, the 1978 Civil Service Reform Act spells out unfair labor practices, and most state statutes do the same by drawing on the national legislation or guidelines developed by the National Labor Relations Board for the private sector. Unfair labor practices include the following:

By Management:

1. Failing to bargain in good faith
2. Interfering with the right to organize
3. Attempting to influence the outcome of a bargaining election or the selection of a representative
4. Retaliating against individuals who exercise their right to organize

By Labor:

1. Coercion of employees in their exercise of the choice to bargain or in selecting a representative
2. Unfair work stoppages
3. Failure to bargain in good faith
4. Collusion with management in discriminating against nonunion workers.

Statutes, rules, and regulations define many more unfair labor practices, and the agencies that implement labor relations policies specify still more in response to complaints brought by management or labor. Statutory provisions are often vague; thus, it is up to the responsible agencies to give specificity to issues such as bargaining in good faith.

Charges of unfair labor practices are adjudicated by the Federal Labor Relations Authority at the federal level. States provide for the resolution of such charges in their own way, with most giving the PERB or a comparable authority the responsibility for resolving complaints. They normally have the authority to order the offending party to cease its actions.

Impact of Public Sector Bargaining

The effects of collective bargaining are felt in all areas of management and service delivery. There are clear implications for financial management, budgeting, personnel and planning, and the roles of employees and managers in the system.

In the area of financial management and budgeting, collective bargaining agreements often lock a jurisdiction into positions from which it cannot easily extricate itself. As the effects of taxpayers' demands clearly illustrate, voters believe that collective bargaining adds to the cost of government. However, the empirical evidence continues to be confusing. Recent studies suggest that collective bargaining increases the cost to government but that overall increases have been relatively small (Ashraf, 1997; Lewis, 1986; Munell, Aubry, Hurwitz, & Quinby, 2011). The advantage varies by occupation and jurisdiction. Because personnel costs typically make up as much as 80 percent of a jurisdiction's budget, it is inevitable that increased personnel costs will affect the cost of government unless there is a reduction in personnel and services. As a result, jurisdictions try to offset personnel costs by increasing productivity or reducing the number of people employed. The sustained fiscal stress governments have faced since the 1980s cause them to make trade offs. Clearly, the bargaining process puts costs under constant scrutiny, providing the potential for containment and the elimination of questionable spending.

Budgeting processes are also affected by bargaining. Negotiation and agreement typically take place before the budget is drawn up; thus, flexibility in budgeting may be diminished. If management or the legislative body refuse to appropriate funds to cover the agreement's costs, including salaries and wages, problems with the employee organization are certain to arise. Though legislative bodies have the power to adopt governmental budgets, the bargaining process actually affects that authority, as the decision makers need to consider what will happen in negotiations. Budgeting and planning thus become more difficult.

Because many states permit bargaining on all aspects of the employment situation, all elements of the personnel system can be negotiated. It seems clear that merit system principles and personnel rules and regulations will increasingly become the subject of negotiation and will change in the process, although in many states two separate systems seem to be emerging: the civil service and collective bargaining systems. Employees in bargaining units are governed according to the agreements that are negotiated between their representatives and management so that some personnel actions are different from those for all other employees, who are managed according to the civil service or the general personnel policy of the jurisdiction. For example, employees in a bargaining unit may bargain for more leave time than is typically granted to employees.

Collective bargaining has many effects on management. Traditionally, management has taken the position that bargaining is detrimental to its ability to manage. With collective bargaining, management must share its power to govern, and thus it has much less discretion. However, management can and does reap benefits from participating in collective bargaining if it is willing to embrace the process. Lanning S. Mosher pointed out that management can be improved through the bargaining process because it forces management to become better skilled at cooperation, persuasion and compromise. By identifying management's weaknesses and negotiating training needs, the bargaining process provides leverage for obtaining the resources necessary to prepare for negotiating and working with labor organizations (Mosher, 1978). Management also is under pressure to do a better job when it knows its activities will be under scrutiny in the bargaining process.

Collective bargaining has the potential to create a variety of working conditions, as each group of employees bargains with management. However, with a standard general policy under which agreements are bargained, the process can produce decisions that reflect a general perspective rather than the particular concerns of the moment or situation. In other words, it helps establish a general policy within which decisions can be made.

For employees, bargaining also has many effects, not the least of which is the ability to help determine what the working conditions are to be. Workers often find that unionization and bargaining help them develop a consciousness of the importance of their work; this has been particularly true of employees in jobs such as sanitation and garbage collection. During the 1960s, racial minorities who dominated these positions found unionization to be both a way of gaining dignity as human beings and a force for racial and social justice. Generally, employees feel that collective bargaining protects them against arbitrariness in personnel and managerial decisions. Also because employees participate in the decision-making processes, they are likely to be more committed to the organization, and hence more productive, than when management unilaterally dictates policy. In fact, management often has an ally in the employee representative in getting its policies across. Employees are much more receptive to decisions that are explained by one of their own; otherwise they may oppose change and refuse to accommodate management's desires. Some studies also indicate that unionized organizations are more productive (Eberts & Stone,1987; Freeman & Medoff, 1984; Sojourner, Town, Grabowski, & Chen, 2012; Sulzner, 2002).

The Evolving Bargaining System

The politics of the 1990s and 2000s, with continuous pressure for cutting government and privatizing many government functions, place the labor movement in a difficult situation. The election of politicians who promise downsizing of government hits labor hard, as downsizing usually means cutting employees. Decreasing revenues ensure that cuts will be necessary. Management relations and labor leaders understand that a new approach to their relationship is necessary. In many places, labor relations has evolved into a more cooperative approach. This new style of labor relations is seen at all levels of government (Kirkner & Sharfstein, 2001–2002; Masters, Albright, & Eplion 2006; Sulzner, 2002).

This cooperative approach has labor and management working together rather than as adversaries. Both sides recognize
that the ultimate aim is the same—public service. Thus, labor sits
down with management to determine ways to get the work done.
In places where labor and management are not cooperating, the
old acrimony in the relationship hurts everyone, including the
public. In the federal service, the Clinton administration encouraged Joint Labor Partnership Councils to foster cooperative approaches. For example, the Internal Revenue Service Center in
Ogden, Utah, developed a labor–management partnership. The
partnership council created initiatives such as the attendance
of union representatives at budget meetings of agency directors
and division staff, joint instructorship at training sessions for all
employees, and a conflict resolution council to attempt to resolve
complaints about unfair labor practices in an informal process.
The IRS developed a successful reengineering of the whole service following the Ogden Office's success using the cooperative
approach. George W. Bush eliminated the approach upon taking
office, though subsequently Barack Obama reinstated the authority for them. Transportation Security Administration (TSA)
agents lost their collective bargaining rights under Bush as well,
which Obama reinstated upon his election. At the state and local
level, systems vary greatly. The strong anti-union sentiment of
the 2010 and 2012 elections emboldened legislators and public
managers against labor, which diminished cooperative efforts.
Still, cooperative approaches, such as the longstanding Phoenix
Fire Department cooperative process, are cited as models for successful labor–management relations. Thus, the environment for
public labor management relations at all levels of government
continues to change.

Summary

Public sector collective bargaining was one of the most visible elements of public personnel management in the 1960s and 1970s.
During the 1980s, the growth in the movement leveled off considerably as the political and economic environments became
less supportive. Facing financial and political constraints, public
employee unions were forced to reconsider their strategies. They
became less militant and more conciliatory toward management.
Management in the public sector, however, became more strident

as it saw the opportunity to use its new clout to regain some of the things it gave up in the earlier days. Since 2010, labor–management relations has again become a divisive issue in the public sector. Despite the reduced popularity of collective bargaining and unions, public managers still must deal with the process. Thus, public policy provides for a variety of ways of recognizing and bargaining with unions. There are also many alternatives for dealing with impasses. Although it is illegal in most places, public employees strike frequently.

Clearly, management will have to continue to bargain with employees, but the nature of the bargaining relationship is constantly evolving. New issues arise that provide the basis for continued efforts by unions. Unions have encroached on management flexibility, but they have also been effective in improving policies and practices. Thus, their impact on personnel administration has been both positive and negative.

Exercises

1. Interview an officer of a public employee union or employee association. Find out what the mission of the organization is and how it goes about attempting to accomplish its mission. Ask about the kind of relationship the union or association has with the public employer.

> Write a report on your findings. In your report, discuss the effect you think the political environment has on this union or association.

2. Contact a Public Employee Relations Board or comparable organization that has open hearings. Find out when it will be having a hearing on a case brought before it, and attend the hearing.

> Describe the nature of the issues raised in the hearing. What is your impression of the hearing process? Is it what you expected? Why or why not?

3. Form into an even number of groups of four or five, each representing either management or labor. Then have each management group meet with a labor group. Assume that the groups are going to negotiate a labor agreement.

> During this meeting, negotiate the bargaining rules that will be used in the negotiations.

4. The city has a policy that prohibits strikes by public employees. Over the past two years, the city budget has been cut, and jobs were eliminated. The Public Works Department lost twenty positions—10 percent of what it originally had. Because of the age of the city's infrastructure, the work load actually increased. Employee morale dropped to the point that people lost their sense of commitment. For the last two weeks, about 20 percent of the employees were calling in sick each day.

Management believes that the union is staging a job action or sick out which it considers an illegal strike. It filed an unfair labor practice complaint. You are the hearing officer hearing the complaint.

What information do you need? What do you lean toward recommending? What is the reasoning behind your recommendation?

Selected Websites

Bloomberg BNA. A publisher of information on legal and regulatory policy and actions on management and labor. Publishes extensively on labor relations as well as other employment issues.

www.bna.com

Labor and Employment Research Association (LERA). Membership organization of people interested in human resources and labor relations. Holds conferences and publishes research on labor topics.

leraweb.org.

National Council on Teacher Quality (NCTQ). Nonprofit research and policy group focusing on quality in schools. Publishes reports on teacher collective bargaining.

www.nctq.org/p/

National Public Employee Relations Association (NPELRA). A membership organization of employees and others interested in labor-management relations. Conducts research and publishes on all aspects of labor relations. Also conducts conferences on the issue.

www.npelra.org

Section on Personnel and Labor Relations (SPALR), Section of the American Society for Public Administration (ASPA) which sponsors panels and workshops promoting a wider recognition of the role of human resources in government and nonprofits, including labor relations.

http://www.aspanet.org/public/ASPA/Membership/ASPA_Chapters_and_Sections/ASPA/MemberTools/ChapterSectionListIPart.aspx?hkey=0d92dd21-5340-47a2-a9e4-4d6d1e25fc1a#

U.S. Department of Labor Bureau of Labor Statistics (BLS), Collects and publishes data on all aspects of employment and labor relations.

www.bls.gov

elaws Advisors (elaws). Provides interactive tools with information on federal employment laws.

www.dol.gov/elaws

Working for America Institute (WAI). An AFL-CIO organization that provides technical assistance and support to improve work organizations through research, information dissemination, and technical assistance to labor leaders, community activists, and public officials.

www.workingforamerica.org

Each union and employee association has its own web site that provides information about it as well as on labor topics.

References

Amalgamated Transit Union. (2013). Retrieved from www.atu.org/union.

American Federation of State, County and Municipal Employees. (2013). *About AFSCME*. Retrieved from www.afscme.org/union/about.

Ashraf, J. (1997). The effects of unions on professors' salaries: The evidence over twenty years. *Journal of Labor Research, 23*, 339–449.

Ball, C. (1993). Union donations to congressional candidates. *Review of Public Personnel Administration, 13*, 8–18.

Bennett, G. (1974). The elusive public interest in labor disputes. *Labor Law Journal, 25*, 678–681.

Clark, R. T., Jr. (1975). Politics and public employee unionism: Some recommendations for an emerging problem. *Cincinnati Law Review, 44*, 680–689

DiSalvo, D. (2010). The trouble with public sector unions. *National Affairs, 5*(Fall). Retrieved from www.nationalaffairs.com/publications/detail/the-trouble-with-public-unions.

Fletcher, B., Jr. (2012). *They're bankrupting us and 20 other myths about unions.* Boston: Beacon Press.

Fraternal Order of Police. (2013). Retrieved from www.grandlodgefop.org.

Eberts, R. W., & Stone, J. A. (1987). Teacher unions and the productivity of public schools. *Industrial and Labor Relations Review, 40*, 354–363.

Freeman, R. B., & Medoff, J. L. (1984). *What do unions do?* New York: Basic Books.

Goldwater Institute. (2011). *Airing out the smoke-filled rooms: Bringing transparency to public union collective bargaining.* Phoenis, AZ: Goldwater Institute.

Hansen, R. L., & Allen, J. B. (1985). Public referendum: Is it an effective mechanism for resolving collective bargaining impasses? A union perspective. *Journal of Law & Education, 14,* 471.

Hogler, R. L., & Thompson, M. J. (1985). Collective negotiations in education and the public interest: A proposed method of impasse resolution. *Journal of Law & Education, 14,* 443.

Horton, R. D. (1973). *Municipal labor relations in New York City.* New York: Praeger.

International Association of Fire Fighters. (2013). Retrieved from www.iaff.org/about/default.asp

Inernational Brogherhood of Teamsters. (2013). Retrieved from www.teamsters.org.

International Brotherhood of Police Officers. (2013). Retrieved from www.ibpo.org/about_us.shtml.

Kearney, R. C. (2008). *Labor relations in the public sector* (4th ed.). Boca Raton, FL: CRC Press.

Kirkner, R., & Sharfstein, S. (2001-02). Aligning traditional collective bargaining with nontraditional labor relations. *The Public Manager, 30*(4), 27–30, 35.

Lewis, H. G. (1986). *Union relative wage effects: A survey.* Chicago: University of Chicago Press.

Masters, M. F., Albright, R. R., & Eplion, D. (2006). What did partnerships do? Evidence from the federal sector. *Industrial and Labor Relations Review, 59*(3), 367-385.

Moe, T. M., (2011). *Special interest: Teachers unions and America's public schools.* Washington, DC: Brookings Institution Press.

Mosher, L. S. (1978). Facing the realities of public employee bargaining. *Public Personnel Management, 7,* 243–248.

Munnell, A., Aubry, J. P., Hurwitz, J. & Quinby, L. (2011). *Unions and public pension benefits.* Chestnut Hill, MA: Center for Retirement Research at Boston College.

National Association of Government Employees. (2013). About NAGE. www.nage.org/about_us.shtml

National Council on Teacher Quality. (2013). *State bargaining rules.* Retrieved from www.nctq.org/tr3/scope.

National Education Association. (2013). Retrieved from www.nea.org.

National Federation of Federal Employees. (2013). Retrieved from www.nffe.org.

National Treasury Employees Union. 2002. Retrieved from www.nteu.org/

Silbiger, S. (1975). The missing public: Collective bargaining and employment. *Public Personnel Management, 4,* 290–299.

Sojourner, A.J., Town, R.J., Grabowski, D.C., & Chen, M.M. (2012). Impacts of unionization on employment, product quality and productivity: Regression discontinuity evidence from nursing homes. *National Bureau of Economic Research Working Paper,* Retrieved from www.nber.org/papers/w17733.

Sowell, T., (2012). The power of public-employee unions. *Education News,* Retrieved from educationviews.org/the-power-of-public-employee-unions/.

Sulzner, G. T. (2002). Revisiting the reinvented union. In C. Ban and N. M.Riccucci (Eds.), *Public personnel management: Current concerns, future challenges* (3rd ed.). (pp. 113–133). New York: Longman.

Summers, C. (1986). Bargaining in the government's business: Principles and politics. *Toledo Law Review, 18,* 265.

Summers, C. W. (1974). Public bargaining: A political perspective. *Yale Law Journal, 83,* 1156–2000.

U.S. Bureau of Labor Statistics. (2012). *Union members summary.* Retrieved from www.bls.gov/news.release/union2.nr0.htm.

Welington, H. H., & Winter, R. K., Jr. (1969). The limits of collective bargaining in public employment. *The Yale Law Journal, 78,* 1107–1127.

9

Social Equity and Diversity in the Workplace

The demographics of the United States are vastly more diverse than ever before, and so is the landscape of public organizations in the twenty-first century. In 1900, the U.S. population was 76.1 million, of which 66.8 million (88%) were White, 8.8 million (11.6%) Black, and 500,000 (0.1%) Hispanic.[1] In 2010, the U.S. population was 308.7 million, of which 196.8 million (63.7%) were White,[2] 38.9 million Black (12.6%), 14.6 million Asian (4.8%), 50.4 million Hispanic (16.3%), 9 million (2.9%) multiracial, and 540,013 (0.2%) American Indian and Alaskan Native. In the past decade the Hispanic population grew by 43% from 35.3 million in 2000 to 50.4 million in 2010 (Humes, Jones, & Ramirez, 2011). In 2010, females outnumbered males comprising 50.8% of the US population (Howden & Meyer, 2011).

Changes in the demographic landscape of the United States have resulted in a change in the composition of the public workforce. More public employees are women, people of color, people

---

1. The U.S. Office of Personnel Management defines Hispanic or Latino as "a person of Mexican, Puerto Rican, Cuban, South or Central American, or other Spanish culture origin, regardless of race."

2. "White" refers to "a person having origins in any of the original peoples of Europe, the Middle East, or North Africa. It includes people who indicated their race(s) as "White" or reported entries such as Irish, German, Italian, Lebanese, Arab, Moroccan, or Caucasian" (U.S. Census Bureau, 2011, p. 3).

with disabilities, foreign-born, and/or part-timers. Reflecting the aging of the American population, they are also older. Public policy enhances opportunities for people previously discriminated against, even though many programs directed at increasing opportunity have faced serious challenges.

Public workforce diversity creates challenges for public personnel systems as well as for managers, supervisors, and employees in the line departments. Personnel managers are tasked with implementing and monitoring diversity programs; providing training and assistance on diversity to managers, supervisors, and employees; and assessing the success of their efforts. This chapter deals with the challenges faced by public managers attempting to create, train, and manage a diverse and inclusive workforce in a time of rapid social change.

Creation of a Diverse Workplace

Traditionally, diversity was discussed in regard to gender and race. However, increasingly, diversity policies are broadening their criteria to include religion, ethnicity, language, region, sexual orientation, age, differences in ability, and socioeconomic and educational backgrounds (Broadnax, 2010; Choi & Rainey, 2010; Gazley, Chang, & Bingham, 2010; Naff, 2001; Pitts, 2005; Pitts & Wise, 2010; Ronquillo, 2010; Wise and Tschirhart, 2000). Diversity in public employment has been increased through nondiscrimination, equal employment, affirmative action programs, and other policies that remedy employment discrimination. One objective of these policies is to make the public service representative of society as a whole. The policies also require that non-job-related factors not be considered in personnel decisions.

Representative Bureaucracy

Representative bureaucracy is a concept that has been important in public personnel management since the beginning of our government. As was noted earlier, George Washington and his successors made sure to include influential political groups in their administrations, and the Jeffersonians and Jacksonians made clear that government offices should be held by people supportive of the president. Political leaders at all levels have used appointments to public office as a means of rewarding supporters or consolidating the support of others. Thus, a form of representativeness has always been a major part of personnel decisions. Since the 1960s, the concept has been redefined and now includes a concern that all elements of society be represented whether or not they have political power. Of course, if people have political clout, their concerns are likely to be considered more quickly. Representative bureaucracy is thus seen as a way to ensure that the preferences and interests of various groups are considered (Bradbury & Kellough, 2011; Meier & Capers, 2012).

According to Mosher (1982) and Rosenbloom and Featherstonhough (1977), representative bureaucracy can be characterized as active or passive representation. In active representation, employees are expected to act in the interest of all sectors of society, regardless of the group to which they belong. In *passive representation,* a person is assumed to represent the interests of the group from which he or she comes. Thus, in passive representation, the representatives' personal characteristics and social background are expected to have an impact on job performance and outcomes. Advocates of such representation believe the bureaucracy should reflect the composition of society as a whole. Passive representation is exemplified by the goals and timetables that affirmative action plans use to make the public service reflect the population accurately. There are major differences, though, in the ways people perceive the linkage between active and passive representation. The assumption underlying equal employment opportunity and affirmative action programs is that passive representation eventually will lead to the active representation of everyone as all groups become members of the bureaucracy and thus have a say in what is done (Bradbury & Kellough, 2008; Krislov & Rosenbloom 1981; Lim, 2006; Meier, 1993; Meier & Stewart, 1992; Selden, 1997; Thompson, 1976). That assumption is the subject of much study and disagreement (Rosenbloom & Featherstonhough, 1978; Sigelman & Carter, 1978). Despite these differences of opinion, government has acted on the premise that all groups in society should be represented and will influence the public service in its actions. Another important consideration is that individuals are more likely to feel comfortable in dealing with bureaucrats from their own groups. Thus, one of their intended effects of these policies is making bureaucracies and their programs more accessible to groups previously denied such access.

The relationship between representative bureaucracy and performance was first tested by Meier, Wrinkle, and Polinard (1999) using Texas education data. The authors found that the presence of minority teachers had a significant and positive impact on the educational outcomes of minority students; they concluded that representative bureaucracy is more effective than unrepresentative bureaucracy. Thus, as Rosenbloom and Kinnard (1977) observed, representative bureaucracy is advocated in order to (1) provide distributive justice and equal opportunity and (2) allow for input from all socioeconomic groups. Research also suggests that a representative bureaucracy is a more responsive bureaucracy (Meier, 1993; Meier & Stewart, 1992; Selden, 1997; Selden, Brudney, & Kellough, 1998).

Development of an Unrepresentative Bureaucracy

Although the Jeffersonians and Jacksonians democratized the public service in many ways, the U.S. public service has never been really representative of society as a whole. Among the reasons for this are political considerations and traditions. Some also argue that the bureaucracy, by its nature, requires skills that are not distributed equally throughout the population (Gardner, 1961; Glazer, 1975; Krislov & Rosenbloom, 1981). As a result, when hiring staff, bureaucracies often discriminate in favor of middle-class people who have the necessary skills. However, for social and political reasons, many people do not acquire the necessary skills for working in government agencies.

Jacksonian Democracy opened the public service to the common man, but the new participants were still exclusively white men. The reign of the spoils system simply entrenched a broader constituency of white men in the public service who were the friends and relatives of those already holding political power. Consequently, newly emerging groups had few opportunities to enter the system. With the blanketing-in procedures allowing the executive to extend civil service protection (see Chapter 2), white men were more or less ensured of control over the bureaucracy and over the selection of new members. By the time minority group members and women achieved political influence, the spoils system had been fairly-well destroyed as a means of staffing the federal bureaucracy and was on the way out in many state and local jurisdictions as well.

Although the Civil War emancipated the slaves, African Americans had little political power until after the mid-twentieth century. Though the Fourteenth Amendment, ratified in 1868, granted all citizens rights that could not be impinged upon by state laws, the amendment required implementation, and many barriers developed to restrict its effect. A gradual process of judicial and legislative extension of rights to minority groups and women took place during the late nineteenth and early twentieth centuries. The Nineteenth Amendment, which was ratified in 1920 and granted women the right to vote, was supposed to open the doors to political power and influence to women, but they, like African Americans, found that constitutionally guaranteed rights do not automatically translate into rights in practice. Instead, much effort is required to realize such rights. However, a concern for the rights of minorities and individuals alike began developing in the mid-twentieth century. The Warren Supreme Court and its libertarian and civil rights orientation jolted the conscience of citizens and political leaders, resulting in court decisions and legislation prohibiting discrimination against minorities and (eventually) women.

Reflecting the changing legal environment, women and minorities have come a long way since the passage of Title VII of the Civil Rights Act of 1964 and Equal Employment Opportunity Act of 1972, which prohibit employment discrimination on the basis of race, color, religion, sex, or national origin. Gender was included with Lyndon B. Johnson's Executive Order 11246 in 1967. The same year the Age Discrimination in Employment Act (ADEA) was passed to provide similar protections to workers over the age of 40. Despite the steady progress women and minorities have made in the last 50 years, challenges remain. In 2012, only 23.7 percent of legislators were women (Center for American Women and Politics, 2012) and only 9 percent of mayors in the 100 largest cities were women. Women continue to face challenges (e.g., the "glass ceiling") while climbing the ladder to reach leadership positions (Alkadry & Tower, 2006; Guy, 2010; Guy & Killingsworth, 2007; Kelly & Newman, 2001; Pynes, 2000; Sabharwal, 2010; Stivers, 1993; Tower & Alkadry, 2008). However, women are well represented in the overall federal workforce. In 2009, women held 44 %percent of the positions in both professional and administrative occupations and 30% of the SES positions (MSPB, 2011). However, challenges, including "glass walls" (segregation of women in certain types of jobs or occupations), remain (Kelly & Newman, 2001; Kerr, Miller, & Reid, 2002; Miller, Kerr, & Reid, 1999; Naff, 2001; Reid, Kerr, & Miller, 2003; Riccucci, 2009; Riccucci & Saidel, 1997; Sneed, 2007). Riccucci (2009) reported higher percentages of women in agencies such as the Departments of Education, Health and Human Services, Housing and Urban Development, whereas men were concentrated in the Departments of Transportation, Defense, and Homeland Security.

Minorities, especially Hispanics, are underrepresented at all GS levels in the federal government. In 2010, Hispanics constituted 6.1% of the total federal civilian workforce, which is below their participation rates in the U.S. workforce (15%) (Department of Labor, 2012). Only 3.1% of Senior Executive Service (SES) level federal employees are Hispanic. Overall, minorities constitute 18.1% of the SES, which is approximately half of their representation in the overall workforce (33.5%) (Office of Personnel Management, 2010). Research suggests that the change from the longstanding tenure system to employment-at-will has negatively impacted the job satisfaction, organizational commitment, and loyalty of minority groups, especially African Americans (Bowman, Gertz, Gertz, & Williams, 2003; Wilson, 2006).

Toward the latter part of the twentieth century, the rights of two other groups began to be recognized and began receiving protection under the law. One group, people with disabilities, gained legislative protections, including employment protection, through the Americans with Disabilities Act of 1990 (ADA). As indicated in Chapter 5, the Americans with Disabilities Amendments Act of 2008 (ADAAA), signed into law by President George W. Bush expanded the rights and protections afforded to persons with disabilities. Disability is defined as a physical or mental impairment that substantially limits one or more major life activities. A record of such an impairment, or being regarded as having such an impairment, would be used to identify a disabled individual.

The ADAAA expanded the definition of major life activities to include (but not to be limited to) caring for oneself, performing manual tasks, seeing, hearing, eating, sleeping, walking, standing, lifting, bending, speaking, breathing, learning, reading, concentrating, thinking, communicating, and working. Major bodily functions include, but are not limited to, funtions of the immune system, cell growth, digestive, bowel, bladder, neurological, brain, respiratory, circulatory, endocrine, and reproductive functions (EEOC, 2008). Under ADAAA, an employee can be classified as disabled if impaired in any major life activities. For example, hypertension, asthma, bipolar disorder, schizophrenia, diabetes, lupus, and epilepsy are considered disabilities under ADAAA, which requires employers to provide for "reasonable accommodations."

The LGBT (lesbian, gay, bisexual, and transgender community)[3] is the other minority group that began to have success in obtaining the same rights as other citizens through court victories and policies adopted by the federal government executive branch as well as some state legislatures and local governing bodies. These nondiscrimination policies fell far short of providing equal opportunities in all employment-related issues, particularly when competing for high-level positions. The passage of ENDA (Employment Non-Discrimination Act), a bill pending in the Congress, will signal a major victory for LGBT groups. As of 2012, twenty-one states and the District of Columbia have laws that prohibit employment discrimination based on sexual orientation.

From Nondiscrimination to Affirmative Action.

Because nondiscrimination laws and regulations failed to achieve the expected results, government leaders instituted new approaches. President John F. Kennedy, a recipient of strong minority group support, emphasized positive action to promote the well-being of those who had been discriminated against. African Americans in particular were appointed to prominent positions in the public service. President Lyndon Johnson pushed through the Civil Rights Act of 1964, which helped open doors to

---

3. The American Psychological Association defines transgender as "persons whose gender identity, gender expression, or behavior does not conform to that typically associated with the sex to which they were assigned at birth. Gender identity refers to a person's internal sense of being male, female, or something else; gender expression refers to the way a person communicates gender identity to others through behavior, clothing, hairstyles, voice, or body characteristics." For more detail, refer to http://www.apa.org/topics/sexuality/transgender.aspx

employ minorities, especially African Americans. He also signed Executive Order 11246, which prohibited discrimination by U.S. Government contractors. Subsequent presidents have also been concerned with minority group support. Richard Nixon took a special interest in Hispanics, as did Ronald Reagan in his 1984 reelection campaign.

As women developed greater political consciousness in the late 1960s and 1970s, both parties, at all levels of government, began to demonstrate concern for women's rights (and votes) by trying to increase the public employment of women. In the 1984 presidential election, the Democratic Party nominated a female vice presidential candidate in an attempt to exploit the perception that the Reagan administration lacked concern for women's issues. The Reagan administration responded that it did not talk about women's issues but did employ them in prominent positions. However, one of the complaints of minorities and women was that the Reagan administration did not emphasize equal employment and affirmative action issues and weakened agencies such as the Civil Rights Commission and the Equal Employment Opportunity Commission. The 1992 election featured a sharp distinction, with President George Bush's campaign appealing to white middle-class men and the Clinton campaign promising to include all segments of society in government. The 1994 midterm elections, however, resulted in a congressional majority seemingly bent on dismantling affirmative action requirements. The administration of George W. Bush, elected in 2000, pointed to its appointment of women in its cabinet and other high-level positions as evidence of its support for women in employment.

Equal employment opportunity and affirmative action have been the two main approaches to expanding employment opportunities for women and minority group members. Equal employment opportunity does not necessarily result in increased employment; it merely requires that all groups have the same chance to compete for positions and are treated equally once employed. Of particular concern is that personnel decisions be made on the basis of criteria that are pertinent to the work. Equal opportunity requires neutrality on issues other than merit and ability in the personnel process. The Civil Rights Act of 1964 provides the basic requirements for equality of opportunity. Because that act applies only to private sector employees, the 1972

Equal Employment Opportunity Act was passed to extend the policy to state and local governments. The Americans with Disabilities Act of 1990 and the Civil Rights Act of 1991 reaffirmed nondiscrimination as federal policy and provided strong enforcement tools, as will be explained later.

Implementating legislation requires enforcement agencies. Therefore, monitoring mechanisms have been created to ensure that the acts are implemented. The Equal Employment Opportunity Commission and the Civil Rights Commission are the principal agencies at the national level that have enforcement responsibilities. Each federal department or agency that distributes grants or services or has contracts with other employers, including state and local governments, has some type of compliance office to ensure that equal employment opportunity exists. Monitoring agencies have difficulty gaining compliance because they are usually inadequately staffed and are often on functional agencies' periphery. Standards for what constitutes equal opportunity also tend to be vague and difficult to enforce. As a result of these problems, the concept of affirmative action developed.

Affirmative action requires employers to make a conscious effort to eliminate from their personnel systems, intended and unintended discrimination, as well as to remedy the effects of past discrimination. Thus, it calls for an examination of all personnel functions to identify possible barriers to equal employment opportunity so that they can be removed. The key to determining whether discrimination exists is to be found not in the policy's intent but in what occurs as a result of that policy. In *Griggs v. Duke Power Co.* (1971), the Supreme Court established the doctrine that prohibited discrimination can be unintentional, occurring as a result of personnel practices. Once a plaintiff establishes "disparate impact," meaning that the practice had a disproportional impact on protected groups, the burden shifts to the employer to demonstrate "business necessity" to avoid liability for the discrimination. In *Wards Cove Packing Co. v. Antonio* (1989), the Supreme Court reversed itself and shifted the burden back to the plaintiff to prove that the discrimination was intentional, making it much more difficult for complainants to win their cases.

In the 1980s, affirmative action became a major public issue and was challenged in the courts and through electoral politics. Critics of affirmative action equate it with quotas and reverse discrimination. By 1989, Supreme Court decisions limited or undermined affirmative action efforts. Congress decided to counter with a new Civil Rights Act in 1990, but President George Bush vetoed it. Many viewed the conflict as political posturing. Congress passed the Civil Rights Act of 1991, and President Bush signed it, presumably with an eye on the 1992 election. Bill Clinton supported affirmative action.

In the 1990s, the Supreme Court did not rule directly on affirmative action but allowed numerous lower court decisions on it to stand. At the appellate court level, cases have varied in outcome, thus making a Supreme Court test almost inevitable. The Court did take the position that racial classifications in federal set-aside programs require strict scrutiny analysis, meaning that the policy must satisfy a compelling governmental interest and must be construed narrowly to meet its specific goals (*Aderand v. Pena,* 1995). It also let stand an Eleventh Circuit Court decision invalidating a promotion plan favoring African American firefighters (*In re Birmingham Reverse Discrimination Employment Litigation,* 1996). Similarly, it declined to review an award of $425,000 to a white engineer who claimed he was passed over so that an African American could be promoted (*Claus v. Duquesne Light Company,* 1994). In *Ricci v. DeStefano* (2009), the landmark case of reverse discrimination, out of 118 firefighters who took the test for management positions, 21 passed, 19 of whom were white and 2 Hispanic. Fearing lawsuits, the city invalidated the test because none of the African American firefighters passed the examination. The firefighters who passed the test sued the city including Mayor DeStefano, under Title VII of the Civil Rights Act of 1964 and the Equal Protection Clause of the Fourteenth Amendment. The city's position was struck down by the Supreme Court, which ruled that the City of New Haven's action in discarding the tests was a violation of Title VII.

In *Hopwood v. State of Texas* (1996), the Supreme Court let stand a Fifth Circuit decision striking down an affirmative action admissions program at the University of Texas Law School. Without ruling on the substance of affirmative action, it ruled in 1999 in *Lesage v. Texas* (1999) that the appellate court erred in not considering whether the University of Texas doctoral program in education would have reached the same admission decision if there had been no affirmative action. The opposite ruling of the two Michigan cases in 2003–*Gratz v. Bollinger* and *Grutter v. Bollinger* have further sparked the controversy surrounding affirmative action (for further details, see Chapter 5).

The politicization of affirmative action has led to efforts at the state and local levels to prohibit affirmative action programs. In 1996, California voters approved Proposition 209, which forbids the use of affirmative action in public employment, education, and contracting. A similar initiative passed in the state of Washington in 1998. Georgia, Florida, Nebraska, Arizona, New Hampshire, and Oklahoma followed suit, banning government-sponsored affirmative action programs. Such efforts have been successful in some jurisdictions but unsuccessful in others. Michigan's six-year ban on affirmative action in college admissions was struck down as unconstitutional by a federal appeals court in November 2012. Texas will reconsider the issue of affirmative action in college admissions as it awaits the Supreme Court ruling on *Fisher v. University of Texas at Austin* (2012). In some states, governors have addressed the issue through executive order. The result is that public employers have no clear guidance on what to do.

As Riccucci notes, public employers tend to hold on to affirmative action as a way to increase diversity in their workforces and to avoid costly litigation (Riccucci, 2002a). Most research suggests that affirmative action benefits minority college student admissions (Card & Krueger, 2005; Espenshade & Chung, 2005; Long, 2007). States that eliminated affirmative action in college admissions instituted percentage plans. Examples include a top-4% plan in California, which guarantees entry to the students who rank in the top 4 percent of their high school to any University of California campus. Texas has a similar plan for the top 10 percent and Florida for the top 20 percent. Long (2007) argues that "the success of top X percent programs hinges on there being sufficient numbers of minorities in the top X percent of their high school classes. Unfortunately, blacks and Hispanics are highly underrepresented at the top of their high school classes" (p. 323).

Critics of affirmative action argue that merit and competence are sacrificed to meet diversity hiring goals and timetables. Their opposition is based on the belief that the quality of public service suffers from affirmative action hiring practices. In fact, research indicates that these arguments are flawed. In reviewing 200 studies of affirmative action, economists Holzer and Neumark (2000) found little evidence that affirmative action affected overall performance. They also found that supervisors rank the job performance of affirmative action hires the same as they rank other employees.

Some critics have an interest in maintaining the status quo and preventing the opening of the workplace to hitherto unrepresented or underrepresented groups. Many employees and employee groups have been in the forefront of battles to protect their turf from intrusion by minorities and women. However, as employee associations and unions have seen their memberships level off or decline, their stance has changed, and now they are often among the strongest advocates of minority and women's causes. They see support for minorities and women as an issue of workplace justice and a way to attract new members.

The record so far indicates that the fear of critics that affirmative action would lead to women and minorities squeezing out white men from the workplace were not well founded. Although minorities and women are increasingly evident in government employment, they are not represented at all levels of employment in proportion to their numbers. Although change is occurring, higher levels of management are still essentially the preserve of white men (Guy, 2003; Naff, 2001; Riccucci, 2009). This phenomenon is referred to as a *glass ceiling* because it presents a barrier to the advancement of women and minority group members. Because of the disproportionate representation of women and minorities at the lowest levels of public bureaucracies, there is now more emphasis on upward mobility programs and eliminating discrimination in promotion policies (Guy & Newman, 2004; Hsieh & Winslow, 2006; Kim, 2004; Miller, Kerr, & Reid, 1999; Riccucci, 2009; Riccucci & Saidel, 1997; Selden, 2006). Riccucci (2009) observes:

> Affirmative action policies, civil rights laws, and litigation have no doubt helped to create some equity in terms of entry into government jobs and, in some cases, pay. But affirmative action policies, legislation, and even litigation also must be aimed at the upper, higher-paying levels of government jobs. As noted, social equity in the upper reaches of government is critical for effective democratic governance. (p. 379)

The ultimate goal of affirmative action is to make sure that factors irrelevant to the performance of duties are not considered in the employment process. However, in the short run, it could be necessary to consider gender and race in order to equalize the balance and redress past discrimination. The concept of affirmative action has developed a negative connotation. As Riccucci (1991) notes, it often is viewed as leading to "preferential treatment," "quotas," and "reverse discrimination." Because of this negative image, employers increasingly focus on diversity in the workplace to avoid using the term *affirmative action*. In many cases, employers simply rename old practices (Selden, 2006).

Besides discrimination based on race, ethnicity, and gender, the issue of age discrimination is now also being addressed. For example, the Age Discrimination in Employment Act of 1967 (ADEA) prohibits age discrimination. In 1974, it was amended to include state and local governments within its purview. However, the Supreme Court ruled that Congress did not have the power to give individuals the right to sue states to enforce federal law (*Kimel v. Florida Board of Regents,* 2000). Consistent with the Court's other decisions strengthening states' rights under the Constitution since the mid-1990s, the decision raises serious questions about Congress legislating social justice in the workplace and suggests that people will have to turn to state legislatures and courts in combating age discrimination. With people living longer, there is a greater age range among employees in organizations today (Chambers & Riccucci, 1997). The aging of the workforce and the differences in attitudes toward work of younger employees present a challenging environment for personnel managers. However, perhaps the greatest challenge faced by personnel managers is how to deal with ever-increasing health care costs of an aging population and workforce.

The percentage of the population that is 65 and older is expected to increase from 13 percent in 2010 to 16 percent in 2020. The aging population combined with increased life expectancy puts additional pressure on government-run programs like Social Security, Medicare, and Medicaid. With changing demographics, rising health care costs and dwindling resources, public managers have to seek alternative-community-based care and forge public–private partnerships to deliver services to the elderly (Wolf & Amirkhanyan, 2010). Organizations are also providing wellness programs to lower health care costs and improve overall well-being and productivity. Overwhelming evidence suggests that employer-based wellness initiatives lower health care costs and improve the health of employees. A meta-analysis conducted by researchers at the Harvard Medical center found that for every dollar spent on wellness programs, the cost of medical care fell by about $3.27, absenteeism cost fell about $2.73 for every dollar spent (Baicker, Cutler, & Song, 2010). Wellness programs also produce benefits in worker productivity and personal well-being. For example, research has shown that 80 percent of all workers' compensation claims result from stress or trauma in employees' work lives or personal lives (Atkinson, 2000, p. 46). Stress affects the emotional state of employees, resulting in increased absenteeism that can cause lost work time, costing organizations up to 25% loss in productivity. Wellness programs thus have the potential to both reduce health care costs and improve productivity and job satisfaction.

Accommodating employees of varying ages with various life challenges and requirements can be a daunting task for personnel managers. Younger workers often require flexibility to deal with their children's needs. Single-parent families can also present special challenges. Other employees have elder care issues, as they become responsible for aging relatives. Many people, called the "sandwich generation," have both child care and elder care responsibilities. Nontraditional families such as same-sex couples, sometimes with children and possibly differing family needs, might require understanding by supervisors and colleagues. Policies against sexual orientation discrimination can have an impact on the workplace environment. Having openly lesbians and gays in the workforce can produce tensions because the efforts to ensure their acceptance run counter to the strongly held beliefs of some employees.

The Americans with Disabilities Act of 1990 seeks to help employees with disabilities gain acceptance and fair treatment in the workplace. Besides accommodating people with disabilities, organizations need to deal with the attitude of managers, supervisors, and other employees toward people with disabilities. ADA has generated a great deal of litigation about what constitutes disability and what accommodations are reasonable. There is much debate about whether obesity constitutes a disability. Under rare circumstances, the courts have ruled morbid obesity to be a disability (*Connor v. McDonald's Restaurant,* 2003; *Nedder v. Rivier College,* 1996).

Religion is another element of diversity that impacts the workplace. The religious landscape of the United States is also very diverse with 78.4% of the adult population reporting affiliation to various forms of Christianity (Protestant, Catholic, Mormon, Jehovah's Witness, and Orthodox among others). Approximately 5% of the U.S. population belongs to other faiths, such as Judaism (1.7%), Buddhism (0.7%), Islam (0.6%), Hindu (0.4%), and other world faiths (1.5%). The remaining 16% of the population is not affiliated with any particular religion (Lugo et al., 2008). In the wake of the September 11, 2001, terrorist attacks, employers have had to deal with prejudices against people of Middle East origin and of the Islamic faith. Dealing with religious diversity has been a challenge for employers, but 9/11 raised the level of tension, and hostility against Muslims. Another religious sect that has faced post-9/11 backlash is the Sikh community—estimated at 500,000– 700,000 in the United States (Groves, 2012). The Sikh religion requires that men wear a turban and grow a beard; thus they are often mistaken as Muslims. Since 9/11, the Sikh Coalition has reported more than 700 hate crimes against Sikhs. The 2012 mass shootings in the Sikh temple in Oak Creek, Wisconsin, that killed six and wounded several others is rated among the worst hate crimes toward Sikhs in the United States.

All of the tensions surrounding diversity call for attention to managing the diverse workforce. A challenge for public managers is to capitalize on the opportunities that diversity presents. Research has demonstrated that diversity programs have multiple positive effects for public organizations. Employers have found that service delivery is enhanced when the public service looks more like the public it serves. People feel more comfortable in interacting with their public servants if they are similar to them. Additionally, some jurisdictions have experienced fewer complaints from citizens based on discrimination in treatment by public employees and organizations after they diversified their workforce (Chambers & Riccucci, 1997).

Management of Diversity

If organizations are to be productive, are to provide high-quality service, and are to relate well to their client base, they must manage a diverse workforce. Ignoring the tensions that inevitably develop in a diverse workplace will lead to resources wasted on recurring and unresolved problems. If potential tensions are not addressed in a positive fashion, they are also likely to lead to low morale and a hostile work environment. These conditions, in turn, can lead to disgruntled employees, turnover, and litigation. To avoid such problems, management can use numerous strategies to ensure that diversity is valued throughout the organization (Choi & Rainey, 2010; Cox, 2001; Naff, 2001; Riccucci, 2002b).

Roosevelt Thomas introduced the concept of *managing diversity* in 1990. He defined it as a way of thinking with the objective of creating an environment that will "enable every member of the workforce to perform to his or her potential" (p. 112). Similarly, Gilbert and Ivancevich (2000, p. 75) define it as "the systematic and planned commitment by organizations to recruit, retain, reward, and promote a heterogeneous mix of employees." Pitts (2006) argues that "diversity management is a multifaceted concept" and should include recruitment programs, programs aimed to increase cultural awareness, and pragmatic management policies. Kellough and Naff (2004) surveyed a selection of federal agencies to understand what is commonly included in diversity management programs. They identified seven core steps of effective diversity management: ensure management accountability; examine organizational structure, culture, and management systems; pay attention to representation; provide training; develop mentoring programs; promote internal advocacy groups; and emphasize shared values among stakeholders. Managing diversity is thus a proactive approach adopted by top management to create an environment in which each employee's full potential is realized.

Leadership by top management is essential to establishing and maintaining an effective diverse workforce. Thus, top managers must become personally involved and must commit the resources to ensure that diversity exists and is valued. Nothing works better than management modeling the desired behavior in its own activities. Other successful strategies might include mentoring programs, monitors, advocates, and managers and supervisors willing to be flexible enough to accommodate the various needs of employees (Kellough & Naff, 2004; Pitts, 2006, 2009).

Management needs to commit the resources to provide regular diversity training for all employees. The training should address the meaning of diversity and the reasons that valuing it is important for the organization and all of its employees. Employees need to be trained on how to work in a diverse environment and how to understand and work with people of different cultures and backgrounds. Teaching strategies for creating an inclusive work environment is important.

Diversity programs do not work if accountability for success is ignored. Thus, managers, supervisors, and all employees need to be held accountable. It starts with involving all of them in the development of diversity programs and policies so that everyone is committed to the program's success. Performance evaluation must include a diversity component to ensure that everyone recognizes it as being a serious commitment. Of course, accountability has different dimensions and becomes much more focused for supervisors and managers who do the hiring and training.

Impacts of Diversity

The development of diverse workplaces has impacted organizations far beyond making them more representative of society. Having a diverse workforce leads to improvements in decision-making processes, increased flexibility and creativity, innovation and learning, high retention rates, better performance, and higher job satisfaction (Choi, 2009; Cox, 1991; Naff & Kellough, 2003; Riccucci, 1997; Pitts, 2009; Thomas & Ely, 1996). Thus, diversity programs may improve communication among groups and individuals in the organization and lead to better cooperation. They may also lead to more creative solutions to problems by the fact that a diverse workforce may see issues from a range of perspectives and may offer different approaches to dealing with a problem.

As discussed in Chapter 7, diversity programs have caused organizations to be more sensitive to issues such as harassment and to enact policy changes needed to better accommodate the differing needs of a diverse workforce. The effect of diversity programs has been most pronounced in benefit programs. With dual-career couples, the sandwich generation, unmarried couples, single parents, and all the other variations of employee circumstances being a reality of the workforce, traditional benefit programs no longer meet the needs of employees. Thus, employee benefit packages have been adapted to meet the changing demographics of the workplace (Cayer, 2003, 2010). Called family-friendly or work-life benefits, they include such things as flexible work hours, dependent care, telecommuting, domestic partner benefits, professional development, employee assistance, and financial planning. Many organizations roll their traditional benefits into their work-life benefits programs. An important feature of the plans is giving employees flexibility to choose the benefits important to them rather than having the same benefits for everyone. Such plans are known as cafeteria-style benefit plans.

Another issue of equity involves relatives working in the same organization. Employers often have nepotism policies ranging from prohibiting family members from being employed in the same agency to policies to ensure that family members do not supervise one another. However, what constitutes a family member or relative is less than clear in today's society. Do same-sex couples fall under nepotism policies? What about people who are romantically involved? Should they be covered under nepotism policies? The answers to these questions have implications for employees' perceptions of fairness and equity.

Summary

Public employees in a democracy are usually considered to be the servants of the general public, and as such, they should be responsive to that public. In recent years, efforts to make the public service responsive have included making the members of the public service representative of society. Thus, equal employment opportunity and affirmative action programs try to ensure that all segments of society have the opportunity to compete for public jobs and, once employed, are treated fairly in the personnel processes. Through affirmative action and equal employment opportunity, the public service can become more sensitive to the interests of all and thus accomplish the goal of being democratically responsive. As controversy surrounds the concept of "affirmative action," employers increasingly label their efforts "diversity programs." As the workplace becomes more diverse, numerous challenges emerge that require new management techniques and expertise.

Exercises

1. Interview the director of the office responsible for equal employment opportunity or diversity programs for a public agency or jurisdiction (a public college or university might be a good choice).

> Find out what the office does. What are its biggest challenges? Its biggest successes? Write a report on what you have found. What sense do you have of how successful the office has been?

2. Access the Internet to find historical information about the employment of women or minorities in government.

> From the information you retrieve, write an assessment of how much progress has been made. How do you account for the current situation regarding public employment of minorities or women?

3. Conduct a barrier survey of any two of the following local public organizations/facilities:

1) public library   2) driver's license agency
3) city hall   4) local public school/university
5) state capitol   6) public transit
7) fire station   8) other local public agency

> Identify physical obstacles or architectural barriers that limit the accessibility to the facility, or to activities within the facility, for someone with a disability covered under the Americans with Disabilities Act. Consider access for someone with disabilities in hearing, vision, mobility, or another physical disability. Then describe in detail the nature of the barriers and what needs to be done to make the facilities accessible. (The barriers could apply to customers or employees.)

For more details on what constitutes disability, visit the EEOC Website: http://www.eeoc.gov/laws/statutes/ada.cfm

4. Carrie Southern supervises the clerical division of the public works department. The department is made up of several divisions, some that focus on management support and others that provide direct public works services such as street maintenance and repair. Southern found that she makes approximately 30 percent less than three male supervisors in the department. In examining the situation with four other female supervisors, she noticed that each receives 20 to 30 percent less than the male supervisors.

Southern talked with her female colleagues, and they all agreed that the pay structure seemed discriminatory. They asked for a meeting with the director of public works and asked him to rectify the situation. He denied the request saying that the pay structure was within his discretion to establish and that he believed it was fair. Southern and her colleagues appealed to the next level, the assistant city manager. Normally, the assistant city manager would ask the personnel department to investigate, but the personnel director is married to the director of public works. You are called in as a consultant to investigate the situation and prepare a report and recommendations for the assistant city manager.

> Prepare a request for information on which you will base your report and recommendations. Indicate what you will need to examine and why you need the particular information you are requesting.

5. The water district has a nepotism policy stating that spouses cannot be employed at the same time in the district. The policy also says that if unmarried employees subsequently marry, one must resign. Candace Wilson and Enrique Partune have both worked for the water district for six years. They met on the job; a romance bloomed, and they decided to marry. Upon learning of the impending marriage, the district manager reminded them of the policy and requested that one of them resign. Both declined to resign. After they were married, they were told again that one would have to resign. They again declined. Each was suspended for fifteen days without pay and was informed that if one had not resigned by the end of suspensions, they both would be terminated.

They appealed their suspensions, claiming that the policy was discriminatory. They noted that at least one same-sex couple and two heterosexual couples had lived together without marriage and continued employment with the district.

You are the hearing officer hearing the appeal. How would you rule?

6. In an MPA class discussion on issues of race and gender, the students are discussing a paper in which the researcher provides the narrative of a young Hispanic girl who is sexually abused by a relative. One white student says "it is very important that the issue of rape and sexual abuse be brought to the forefront and that stricter laws be enforced against such violence because we know that such heinous crimes are common in minority communities." A few students look uncomfortable and there is silence in the classroom. One African American student speaks up, she says "I don't agree with your assessment, at first I liked what you were saying, but you made it all about race and not women's rights. This is outrageous!"

How should a student react in such a situation? Should the teacher say something to diffuse the situation? Discuss stereotypes you hold about other groups.

7. In *Webb v. City of Philadelphia* (2009), Kimberlie Webb, a police officer with the City of Philadelphia since 1995, requested in 2003 to wear a head scarf (khimar) with her uniform, owing to her religious beliefs that require women to cover their hair at all times. Her request was denied by the police department; the policy did not authorize the wearing of any religious symbols or clothing as part of the uniform. Webb filed a complaint with the Equal Employment Opportunity Commission under Title VII of the Civil Rights Act as incorporated under the Equal Employment Opportunity Act of 1972. While her complaint was pending, she wore the khimar to work. She was suspended for 3 days and was later charged with insubordination of her commanding officer's orders. The Court of Appeals in 2009 upheld the police departments' refusal to accommodate Webb's request. The court

ruled that providing any accommodation would create an undue burden on the department and would intrude on the cohesiveness, cooperation, and esprit de corps.

Discuss the case and its outcome in light of the First amendment to the U.S. Constitution that guarantees freedom of speech and religious expression.

Selected Websites

Center for Women in Politics and Public Policy (CWPPP) at the University of Massachusetts in Boston. The Center is committed to advancing women's participation in public life.

http://www.umb.edu/cwppp/

Conference of Minority Public Administrators (COMPA). Section of the American Society for Public Administration that is an advocacy group for minorities in public administration. Recognizes the contributions of minorities through publications, conferences, and awards.

http://www.compaonline.org/contents/

Human Rights Campaign (HRC). Advocacy group for the interests of the lesbian, gay, bisexual, and transgender community (LGBT). Tracks policies dealing with LGBT issues and publishes reports on progress, including in employment.

www.hrc.org

Job Accommodation Network (JAN). A free consulting service that provides information relating to the Americans with Disabilities Act (ADA) and job accommodations.

http://janweb.icdi.wvu.edu

Institute for Research on Race and Public Policy (IRRPP) at the University of Illinois at Chicago. A campus wide research center that focuses on promoting and coordinating engaged research on racial justice and related issues of poverty.

http://www.uic.edu/cuppa/irrpp/

National Center for Transgender Equality (NCTGE). Founded in 2003, NCTGE is a social justice organization dedicated to advancing the equality of transgender people through advocacy, collaboration, and empowerment.

http://transequality.org/

National Organization for Women (NOW). Advocacy organization for women. Collects and publishes information on the status of women in the workforce.

www.now.org

Section on Women in Public Administration (SWPA). A section of the American Society for Public Administration that provides networking for and information on women in public administration. Recognizes contributions of women through awards and conference panels and is an advocacy group.

http://www.aspaonline.org/swpa/

U.S. Department of Labor. Publishes information on all aspects of the labor force. Publishes *Monthly Labor Review*, which updates statistics monthly.

www.dol.gov

U.S. Department of Labor, Bureau of Labor Statistics (BLS). Collects and disseminates statistics on labor-related issues including employment patterns.

www.bls.gov

U.S. Equal Employment Opportunity Commission (EEOC). Has responsibility for enforcing nondiscrimination and equal employment laws and policies. Also publishes data on employment of minorities and women.

www.eeoc.gov

References

Aderand v. Pena, 115 S. Ct. 2097 (1995).

Alkadry, M. G., & Tower, L. E. (2006). Unequal pay: The role of gender. *Public Administration Review, 66*(6), 888–898.

Atkinson, W. (2000). Wellness, employee assistance programs: Investments, not costs. *Bobbin, 41*(9), 42–49.

Baicker, K., Cutler, D., & Song, Z. (2010). Workplace wellness programs can generate savings. *Health Affairs, 29*(2), 304–311.

Bowman, J. S., Gertz, M. G., Gertz, S. C., & Williams, R. L. (2003). Civil service reform in Florida state government, employee attitudes 1 year later. *Review of Public Personnel Administration, 23*(4), 286–304.

Bradbury, M., & Kellough, J. E. (2011). Representative bureaucracy: Assessing the evidence on active representation. *The American Review of Public Administration, 41*(2), 157–167.

Bradbury, M. D., & Kellough, J. E. (2008). Representative bureaucracy: Exploring the potential for active representation in local government. *Journal of Public Administration Research and Theory, 18*(4), 697–714.

Broadnax, W. D. (2010). Diversity in public organizations: A work in progress. *Public Administration Review, 70,* s177–s179.

Card , D., & Krueger, A. B. (2005). Would the elimination of affirmative action affect highly qualified minority applicants? Evidence from California and Texas. *Industrial and Labor Relations Review 58*(3), 416–434.

Cayer, N. J. (2010). Employee benefits: From health care to pensions. In S. E. Condrey (Ed.), *Handbook of human resource management in government* (pp. 817–834). San Francisco: Jossey-Bass.

Cayer, N. J. (2003). Public employee benefits and the changing nature of the workforce. In S. W. Hays & R. C. Kearney (Eds.), Public personnel administration: Problems and prospects (4th ed.) (pp. 167–179). Upper Saddle River, NJ: Prentice-Hall.

Center for American Women and Politics (2012). Women in state legislatures: 2012. Rutgers, The State University of New Jersey. Retrieved from: http://www.cawp.rutgers.edu/fast_facts/levels_of_office/documents/stleg.pdf

Chambers, T., & Riccucci, N. M. (1997). Models of excellence in workplace diversity. In C. Ban & N. M. Riccucci (Eds.), *Public personnel management: Current concerns, future challenges* (2nd ed.) (pp. 73–90). New York: Longman.

Choi, S. (2009). Diversity in the US federal government: Diversity management and employee turnover in federal agencies. *Journal of Public Administration Research and Theory, 19*(3), 603–630.

Choi, S., & Rainey, H. G. (2010). Managing diversity in US federal agencies: Effects of diversity and diversity management on employee perceptions of organizational performance. *Public Administration Review, 70*(1), 109–121.

Claus v. Duquesne Light Company, 46 F.3d 1115 (3rd Cir. 1994), cert. denied, 1155 S. Ct. 1700 (1994).

Connor v. McDonald's Restaurant, U.S. Dist. LEXIS 4108, (D. Ct. March 17, 2003).

Cox Jr., T. (2001). *Creating the multi-cultural organization: A strategy for capturing the power of diversity.* San Francisco: Jossey-Bass.

Cox, Jr., T. (1991). The multicultural organization. *The Executive, 5*(2), 34–47.

Department of Labor (2012). The Latino labor force at a glance. Report Retrieved from: http://www.dol.gov/_sec/media/reports/HispanicLaborForce/HispanicLaborForce.pdf

Espenshade, T. J., & Chung, C. Y. (2005). The opportunity cost of admission preferences at elite universities. *Social Science Quarterly, 86*(2), 293–305.

Equal Employment Opportunity Commission (2008). ADA Amendments Act of 2008. Retrieved from: http://www.eeoc.gov/laws/statutes/adaaa.cfm

Fisher v. University of Texas at Austin. U.S. Supreme Court, Docket 11–345, Accepted for review February 12, 2012.

Gardner, J. (1961). *Excellence: Can we be equal and excellent too?* New York: Harper & Row.

Gazley, B., Chang, W. K., & Bingham, L. B. (2010). Board diversity, stakeholder representation, and collaborative performance in community mediation centers. *Public Administration Review, 70*(4), 610–620.

Gilbert, J. A., & Ivancevich, J. M. (2000). Valuing diversity: A tale of two organizations. *The Academy of Management Executive, 14*(1), 93–105.

Glazer, N. (1975). *Affirmative discrimination: Ethnic inequity and public policy.* New York: Basic Books.

Gratz v. Bollinger, 539 U.S. 244 (2003).

Griggs v. Duke Power Co., 401 U.S. 424 (1971).

Groves, R. (2012, August 13). Rising above deadly ignorance of religious diversity. *Winston-Salem Journal.* Retrieved from:http://www.journalnow.com/opinion/columnists/article_9b1c51b0-964a-5f80-97d2-00c6b0af5985.html

Grutter v. Bollinger, 539 U.S. 306 (2003).

Guy, M. E. (2010). In search of middle ground: Preachy, screechy, and angry versus soft, sweet, and compliant. In Maria J. D'Agostino & Helisse Levine (Eds.), *Women in Public Administration: Theory and Practice* (pp. 299–308). Sudbury, MA: Jones & Bartlett Learning.

Guy, M. E. (2003). The difference that gender makes. In S. K Hays & R. C. Kearney (Eds.), *Public personnel administration: Problems and prospects* (4th ed.) (pp. 256–270). Upper Saddle River, NJ: Prentice-Hall.

Guy, M. E., & Killingsworth, J. A. (2007). Framing gender, framing work: The disparate impact of traditional HRM practices. In A. Farazmand (Ed.), *Strategic public personnel administration: Building and managing human capital for the 21st Century, 2* (pp. 399–418). Westport, CT.: Praeger.

Guy, M. E., & Newman, M. A. (2004). Women's jobs, men's jobs: Sex segregation and emotional labor. *Public Administration Review, 64*(3), 289–298.

Holzer, H., & Neumark, D. (2000). Assessing affirmative action. *Journal of Economic Literature, 38*, 483–568.

Hopwood v State of Texas, 78 F.3d 932 cert. denied (1996).

Howden, L. M., & Meyer, J. A. (2011). Age and sex composition: 2010. United States Census Bureau Briefs.

Hsieh, C., & Winslow, E. (2006). Gender representation in the federal workforce: A comparison among groups. *Review of Public Personnel Administration, 26*(3), 276–295.

Humes, K. R., Jones, N. A., & Ramirez, R. R. (2011). Overview of race and Hispanic origin: 2010. United States Census Bureau Briefs.In Re Birmingham Reverse Discrimination Employment Litigation (BRDEL), 20 F.3d 1525 (11th Cir.1996); cert. denied.

Kellough, J. E., & Naff, K. C. (2004). Responding to a wake-up call, an examination of federal agency diversity management programs. *Administration & Society, 36*(1), 62–90.

Kelly, R. M., & Newman, M. (2001). The gendered bureaucracy: Agency mission, equality of opportunity, and representative bureaucracies. *Women & Politics, 22*(3), 1–33.

Kerr, B., Miller, W., & Reid, M. (2002). Sex-Based occupational segregation in US state bureaucracies, 1987–97. *Public Administration Review, 62*(4), 412–423.

Kim, C. K. (2004).Women and minorities in state government agencies. *Public Personnel Management, 33*(2), 165–180.

Kimel v Florida Board of Regents, 528 U.S. 62 (2000).

Krislov, S., & Rosenbloom, D. H. (1981). *Representative bureaucracy and the American political system*. New York: Praeger.

Lesage v Texas, 120 S. Ct. 467 (1999).

Lim, H. H. (2006). Representative bureaucracy: Rethinking substantive effects and active representation. *Public Administration Review, 66*(2), 193–204.

Long, M. C. (2007). Affirmative action and its alternatives in public universities: What do we know? *Public Administration Review, 67*(2), 315–330.

Lugo, L., Stencel, S., Green, J., Smith, G., Cox, D., Pond, A., Miller, T., Podrebarac, E., & Ralston, M. (2008). *US religious landscape survey*. Washington, DC: Pew Research Center.

Meier, K. J. (1993). Representative bureaucracy: A theoretical and empirical exposition. *Research in Public Administration, 2*(1), 1–35.

Meier, K. J., & Capers, K. J. (2012). Representative bureaucracy: Four questions. In G.B. Peters & J. Pierre (Eds.), *The Sage handbook of public administration* (pp. 420–430). Sage Publications.

Meier, K. J., & Stewart, J. (1992). The impact of representative bureaucracies: Educational systems and public policies. *The American Review of Public Administration, 22*(3), 157–171.

Meier, K. J., Wrinkle, R. J., & Polinard, J. L. (1999). Representative bureaucracy and distributional equity: Addressing the hard question. *Journal of Politics 61*, 1025–39.

Merit Systems Protection Board (2011). *Women in the federal government: Ambitions and achievements. A Report to the President and the Congress of the United States by the U.S. Merit Systems Protection Board.* Retrieved from: http://www.mspb.gov/netsearch/viewdocs.aspx?docnumber=606214&version=608056&application=ACROBAT

Miller, W., Kerr, B., & Reid, M. (1999). A national study of gender-based occupational segregation in municipal bureaucracies: Persistence of glass walls? *Public Administration Review, 59*(3): 218–230.

Mosher, F. C. (1982). *Democracy and the Public Service* (2d ed.) New York: Oxford University Press.

Naff, K. C. (2001). *To look like America: Dismantling barriers for women and minorities in government.* Boulder, CO: Westview.

Naff, K. C., & Kellough, J. E. (2003). Ensuring employment equity: Are federal diversity programs making a difference? *International Journal of Public Administration, 26*(12), 1307–1336.

Nedder v. Rivier College, 944 F. Supp. 111 (1996).

Office of Personnel Management (2010). SES Facts & Figures. Retrieved from: http://www.opm.gov/ses/facts_and_figures/demographics.asp

Pitts, D. (2009). Diversity management, job satisfaction, and performance: Evidence from US federal agencies. *Public Administration Review, 69*(2), 328–338.

Pitts, D. W. (2006). Modeling the impact of diversity management. *Review of Public Personnel Administration, 26*(3), 245–268.

Pitts, D. W. (2005). Diversity, representation, and performance: Evidence about race and ethnicity in public organizations. *Journal of Public Administration Research and Theory, 15*(4), 615–631.

Pitts, D. W., & Recascino Wise, L. (2010). Workforce diversity in the new millennium: Prospects for research. *Review of Public Personnel Administration, 30*(1), 44–69.

Pynes, J. E. (2000). Are women underrepresented as leaders of nonprofit organizations? *Review of Public Personnel Administration, 20*, 35–49.

Reid, M. F., Kerr, B., & Miller, W. (2003). *Glass walls and glass ceilings: Women's representation in state and municipal bureaucracies.* New York: Praeger Publishers.

Ricci v. DeStefano, 129 S. Ct. 2658, 2671, 174 L. Ed. 2d 490 (2009).

Riccucci, N. M. (2009). The pursuit of social equity in the federal government: A road less traveled? *Public Administration Review, 69*(3), 373–382.

Riccucci, N. M. (2002a). The immortality of affirmative action. In C. Ban & N. M.Riccucci, (Eds.), *Public personnel management: Current concerns, future challenges* (3rd ed.) (pp. 72–84). New York: Longman.

Riccucci, N. M. (2002b). *Managing diversity in public sector workforces.* Boulder, CO: Westview.

Riccucci, N. M. (1991). Affirmative action in the twenty-first century: New approaches and developments," in C. Ban & N. M. Riccucci (Eds.), *Public personnel management: Current concerns, future challenges* (2nd ed.) (pp. 88–99). New York: Longman.

Riccucci, N. M., & Saidel, J. R. (1997). The representativeness of state-level bureaucratic leaders: A missing piece of the representative bureaucracy puzzle. *Public Administration Review, 57*(5), 423–430.

Ronquillo, J. C. (2010). Diversity at work: Building an agenda for future research. *Public Administration Review, 70*(1), 170–173.

Rosenbloom, D. H., & Featherstonhough, J. G. (1977). Passive and active representation in the federal service: A comparison of blacks and whites. *Social Science Quarterly, 57*, 873–882.

Rosenbloom, D. H., & Featherstonhough, J. G. (1978). Response to Sigelman and Carter. *Social Science Quarterly, 58*, 726–728.

Rosenbloom, D. H., & Kinnard, D. (1977). Bureaucratic representation and bureaucratic behavior: An exploratory analysis. *Midwest Review of Public Administration, 11*, 35–42.

Sabharwal, M. (2010). Research productivity and career trajectories of women in public administration. In M. J. D'Agostino & H. Levine (Eds.), *Women in public administration: Theory and practice* (pp. 67–80). Sudbury, MA: Jones & Bartlett Learning.

Selden, S. C. (2006). A solution in search of a problem? discrimination, affirmative action, and the new public service. *Public Administration Review, 66*(6), 911–923.

Selden, S. C. (1997). *The promise of representative bureaucracy: Diversity and responsiveness in a government agency.* Armonk, NY: M. E. Sharpe.

Selden, S. C., Brudney, J. L., & Kellough, J. E. (1998). Bureaucracy as a representative institution: Toward a reconciliation of bureaucratic government and democratic theory. *American Journal of Political Science, 42*(3), 717–744.

Sigelman, L., & Carter, R. L. (1978). Passive and active representation in the federal service: A reanalysis. *Social Science Quarterly, 58,* 724–726.

Sneed, B. G. (2007). Glass walls in state bureaucracies: Examining the difference departmental function can make. *Public Administration Review, 67*(5), 880–891.

Stivers, C. (1993). *Gender images and public administration: Legitimacy and the administrative state.* Newbury Park, CA: Sage.

Thomas, Jr, R. R. (1990). From affirmative action to affirming diversity. *Harvard Business Review, 68*(2), 107–117.

Thomas, D. A., & Ely, R. J. (1996). Making differences matter. *Harvard Business Review, 74*(5), 79–90.

Thompson, F. J. (1976). Minority groups in public bureaucracies, are passive and active representation linked? *Administration & Society, 8*(2), 201–226.

Tower, L. E., & Alkadry, M. G. (2008). The social costs of career success for women. *Review of Public Personnel Administration, 28*(2), 144–165.

Wards Cove v. Antonio, 109 U.S. 2115 (1989).

Wilson, G. (2006). The rise of at-will employment and racial inequality in the public sector. *Review of Public Personnel Administration, 26*(2), 178–187.

Wise, L. R., & Tschirhart, M. (2000). Examining empirical evidence on diversity effects: How useful is diversity research for Public-Sector managers? *Public Administration Review, 60*(5), 386–394.

Wolf, D. A., & Amirkhanyan, A. A. (2010). Demographic change and its public sector consequences. *Public Administration Review, 70*, s12–s23.

10

Continuing Challenges for Public Personnel

Public administration has been characterized as being like life in the swamp, where the ground is unstable, the path is unclear, and mean and hungry alligators are ready to strike (Cayer, Baker, & Weschler, 2010). For the personnel administrator in the public sector, the challenges of the administrative swamp are legion. This book has examined the role of public personnel administration in the context of continuing challenges in the public sector's efforts to deliver high-quality, efficient, and responsive service. As we look to the future, new challenges and opportunities arise. The major challenges for public sector personnel management are (1) competitiveness in hiring, (2) resource limitations, (3) new and evolving technology, (4) threat of law suits, (5) privatization and outsourcing, (6) violence in the workplace, (7) changing workplace demographics, and (8) continuous reform.

Competitiveness in Hiring

In the immediate future, public personnel administrators face a competitive environment for recruiting employees in an ever-changing job market. The economic downturn and high rates of unemployment since the global recession hit in 2008 have strengthened the job pool. As the economy improves, however, the situation will change. In addition, close to one million federal employees are forecasted to retire by 2016. Similar challenges are experienced by state and local governments as they compete for talent to attract, recruit, and retain a productive future workforce. Thus, all employers will face strong competition for qualified candidates.

To be attractive to good applicants, the public sector will have to develop recruitment strategies to address the concerns of the "new age employee" (Mir, Mir, & Mosca, 2002), who tends to be committed to a career but not necessarily to an organization. On average, people are likely to work in six or seven organizations over their careers rather than have a long career in a single organization, as in the past. Thus, employees will be more interested in professional growth and responsibility than in loyalty to the organization. Personnel systems and managers need to adapt to this reality by providing opportunities for growth and independence. However, government agencies are often hindered by the slow pace of hiring and cumbersome procedures. This often discourages qualified applicants from applying for government jobs. However, as addressed in Chapter 5, the federal government has undertaken several hiring reforms since 2008. In the future, it will be important to monitor the progress of these initiatives and track any demonstrable impact on federal hiring.

Personnel policies need to be flexible in order to meet employee needs while still providing the public with a high standard of service. Studies show that university students preparing to enter the job market rate the balance between work and personal life needs as important in their consideration of jobs (O'Bannon, 2001; Schramm, 2006). Work–life-balance is of increasing importance to Generation X and Generation Y workers (Downing 2006; Ng, Schweitzer, & Lyons, 2010; Tang et al., 2012; Twenge et al., 2010). Employees need flexibility in leave (time off). Increasingly, people want time off when they want it, not when it is convenient to the organization. If the organization wants to attract and retain employees, it needs to scrap rigid rules on advance requests and timing of leave. As the economy and job market improve, more employees will be confident that they can find another job and consequently more likely to quit if they do not get what they want. The U.S. Bureau of Labor Statistics projects that by 2016, 2 million jobs will be created in the state and local government workforce, of which the largest increase is expected in the following occupations (Dohm & Shniper, 2007):

Accountants

Computer Specialists

Urban/Regional Planners

Lawyers

Library Technicians and Assistants

Correctional and Police Officers

Firefighters

Gaming Service Workers

Education Administrators

Teachers and Instructors (of all types)

Child Care Workers

Bus Drivers

Recreational Protective Service Workers

Police, Fire, and Ambulance Dispatchers

Construction Equipment Operators

Water and Liquid Waste Treatment Plant and
System Operators

All Health Care Occupations (except Dentists,
Secretaries, and Psychiatric Technicians).

Being competitive in recruiting employees requires being able to offer competitive compensation as well. Budget constraints in the public sector have left many public employers at a disadvantage, relative to private-sector employers, in the pay they offer. Increasing benefit costs, especially in health care, also constrain state and local public sector employers. Thus, public personnel administrators face serious challenges in providing comprehensive benefits packages and are forced to come up with innovative new benefits programs.

Resource Limitations

Doing more with less has been a theme of government reform for the past several decades. Reducing government spending and cutting taxes have been popular and constant political issues since the late 1970s. Economic downturns that occurred in 2001 and 2002 and more recently in 2008 and 2009 exacerbate the situation as tax revenues decline. At the same time, demands for services are rising, as more people are out of work and need help. Public managers have to deliver those needed services with fewer resources.

Fewer resources mean agencies need to find ways to reduce costs. The easiest target is personnel because this area is by far the largest expense of governments. As jobs are cut, tensions develop in the organization. What criteria should be used for deciding who is cut? How is the work to be done with fewer employees? When cuts are made, expectations do not diminish. People who retain their jobs often feel guilty about the fate of those laid off and feel stressed as their workload increases. Personnel managers must deal with employee stress, burnout, and emotional problems. Consequently, morale declines, and productivity suffers.

Fewer resources make it difficult, if not impossible to keep benefits competitive. As benefit costs increase, costs are shifted to employees. Public employees have gone from having benefits that cover the entire medical insurance cost to having to share responsibility for such costs. Cafeteria-style benefits are becoming increasingly popular as a way of offering an array of services to fit individual needs. For example, individuals who have dental or eye care covered under their spouse's plan can usually elect other benefits, such as short- and long-term disability and life insurance. Increasingly, the burden of choosing benefits and investing in retirement is shifting from employer to employee.

Thus, most public employers now require employees to pay part of their health care premiums and to contribute to their retirement programs. At the same time, the level of benefits is being reduced. For example, employees who once had full coverage for many health care services now pay co-pays, which seem to increase every year. Deductibles are also increasing regularly.

New and Evolving Technology

It is impossible to predict what technological advances will occur, but it is certain that public personnel management will be affected by them. New technology brings new expertise and ways of solving old problems. The introduction of the computer after World War II, accentuated in the 1970s by the advent of the minicomputer and the personal computer, is among the most significant changes in technology. Because of computers, personnel offices have been able to operate more efficiently while personnel functions have changed. Technology allows employees to do their work much more quickly and with increasing accuracy and efficiency. Technology has made possible the delivery of government information and services to citizens through the Internet (e-government). The Government Paperwork Elimination Act (GPEA) was passed in 2003, which requires federal public websites to comply with GPEA and use electronic forms, filing and signatures for conducting official business.

The challenge for personnel management is to manage the integration of technology into the organization. Employees resist change because they fear learning new things and fear the impact change might have on their status within the organization or even on their job security. Computers are now found throughout public organizations, but there are still challenges in dealing with them. On the technical side, various parts of an organization do not always have compatible systems. In these cases, introduction of computers can actually increase work and lead to inefficiency. Turf battles can erupt over what system or software to use. Technology also impacts the human relations factor in public management (Getha-Taylor, 2010). The author argues that the explosion of social networking sites have reduced face-to-face interactions, which is key in building trust and effective communication among employees and management. The challenge is "to balance the virtual and personal networks that together benefit their organizations" (p. 170).

Access to information is a benefit of computer use to organizations. Employees can access information relevant to their jobs from around the world almost instantaneously. They can communicate quickly and with many people at once. This communication capacity can also create problems. The explosive growth of social media sites (e.g. Facebook, Twitter, MySpace, Pinterest) adds to the challenge of balancing virtual and professional networks that can add value to the organization (Getha-Taylor, 2010). Unfortunately, social media has made it increasingly difficult for employees to keep separate their personal and professional lives. Managers have had to create policies on the appropriate use of technology and social media, as well as discipline policies for inappropriate use. Email access is an important tool for managers and employees, but it also can lead to problems. People need to think twice about the content of their message before sending emails to a wide audience. Whether intentional or inadvertent, mailings can result in embarrassment, hurt feelings, and conflict within the organization. Further, computer viruses and cyber security are problems in public organizations deploying services to citizens through e-government (Chen, Chong, & Zhang, 2004).

Innovations in technology also enhance opportunities for telework. Employees can work from home and from dispersed locations, thus reducing dependence on centralized facilities. Telework presents general advantages to a community by easing the burden on its transportation infrastructure and reducing automobile pollution. For people with dependent care responsibilities or other constraints, telework allows them to remain at home, where they can be available for caretaker responsibilities. The challenge for managers is how to monitor and assess employee productivity when they are not present at the workplace. Because telework leads to a decrease in interpersonal contact, it can diminish the sense of cohesiveness of the organization. The National Space and Aeronautic Administration (NASA), which consistently ranks among the best places to work in the government, offers flexible schedules and working hours to reduce the stress of balancing work and family needs.

Technology also affects personnel organizations and functions and holds out the possibility of moving to a virtual human resources management system (West & Berman, 2001). Although the development of such a system has been gradual, public employers now recruit online, accept online applications, use computer-based testing, and even conduct preliminary interviews online or via Skype or other forms of telecommunication. Moreover, using third-party private vendors for e-recruitment is becoming popular among government agencies. The most commonly used third-party for-profit vendors are Govloop.com, Jobaps.com, and Monster.com. Other nonprofit agencies providing similar services are Partnership for Public Service and Publicservicecareers.org (Llorens, 2011). Once hired, employees can even be trained through a computer-assisted learning system. E-learning is an increasingly common method of training employees. Technology can also assist employees in learning about and managing their benefits package. Payroll and benefits management lend themselves to computerization. Consequently, employees can select and process benefits without seeing or talking to a benefits specialist. Almost any personnel function can be conducted, at least in part, online or through computer software.

Technology also impacts the speed at which services are delivered to the citizens. For example, in December 2012, the New York Metropolitan Transportation Authority's Subway launched a time app for passengers with iPhones and iPod Touch devices to monitor the minutes-to-arrival times for trains on several lines. Other cities have similar applications (apps) to pay bills and receive information on services. Such apps will become commonplace in the future and will change the way government interacts with citizens.

Cooperative programs among jurisdictions are also likely to continue to expand as a way to limit costs (Zeemering, 2008). Such agreements for recruiting, examining, and certifying are certain to attract more attention in the future. These programs can improve the ability of small jurisdictions to perform personnel functions without adding greatly to their costs. Although the initial benefit to large jurisdictions will not always be apparent, the large jurisdictions will be able to save resources by sharing the costs of such operations with other units of government that use the services.

Privatization and Outsourcing

Privatization and outsourcing of services and functions have become popular as advocates of reducing the size of government have succeeded in elections across the country (Battaglio & Condrey, 2006; Kettl, 2000; Shafritz, Russell, & Borick, 2007). Privatization, sometimes called "outsourcing," involves the delivery of governmental services or functions by nongovernmental entities. The entities may be private for-profit enterprises or nonprofits. A variation is contracting with other governmental jurisdictions.

Advocates of privatization believe that contracting for services is more efficient and less costly. Mundane personnel tasks such as benefits and payroll are often outsourced by the government (Coggburn, 2007; Kellough & Nigro, 2006). Texas and Florida have outsourced several functions of benefits, payroll, and staffing to Convergys, a private vendor (Battaglio & Condrey,

2006; Coggburn, 2007). In Texas, the company was awarded an $85 million five-year contract with the state Health and Human Services Commission to provide personnel functions such as recruitment and selection, payroll, benefits, performance management, and position classification (Coggburn, 2007). However, several problems were reported in the process due to technical, procedural, and methodological issues. Initial glitches resulted in a few employees receiving warrants instead of direct deposits (Coggburn, 2007).

Because certain services require a large capital investment, small jurisdictions find that it is more cost efficient to contract out those services. Some cities, for example, have found that they can contract with private water companies or fire protection services more economically than they can provide the services on their own. Local governments often contract with other jurisdictions for water, health, and computer services. Not the least of the savings are employee benefit costs. By contracting out, governmental jurisdictions avoid having to pay for expensive health care and retirement programs.

Privatization requires personnel administration to adapt and change (Brudney et al., 2005; Fernandez & Smith, 2006). It requires (1) a careful assessment of the service being contracted, (2) expertise in advertising, obtaining and assessing proposals (bids), and (3) expertise in drawing up agreements. Then the contract or agreement must be monitored, enforced, and evaluated. For the personnel function, these activities require recruitment and/or training of employees with requisite expertise.

Once privatization occurs, employers must address the needs of public employees who are displaced. Employers also need to deal with the remaining employees, who might feel their job security to be at risk. Privatization inevitably affects relationships with employee unions or associations as well, resulting in the need to be attentive to them.

Outsourcing personnel functions is a form of privatization used by several state and local agencies. It began in the early 2000s and is widely used by several state and local agencies (Battaglio & Ledvinka, 2009; Coggburn, 2007; Siegel, 2000). A governmental jurisdiction may contract out any or all personnel functions. Many human resources services have traditionally used private vendors. Thus, health care benefits are typically provided under contract with private insurance vendors. Head hunters are often used for recruitment. What is relatively new is the employment of outside vendors to operate recruitment, testing, evaluation, and other day-to-day human resource functions. Continued use of privatization in government services, public–private partnerships, and similar arrangements are becoming common practice. To meet the changing needs of human resources, curricula in public administration programs should include topics such as staffing, developing, and managing contract employees (Llorens & Battaglio, 2010).

Litigation

Personnel managers are the objects of constant litigation. Discrimination and equal employment opportunity issues have spawned considerable litigation (Bradbury, 2007; Jaegel & Cayer, 1991). The Americans with Disabilities Act of 1990 and the more recent ADA Amendment Act of 2008 resulted in a large amount of litigation challenging every aspect of personnel management. The increasing prevalence of lawsuits necessitates new expertise in the personnel field. In the past, personnel offices were not thought to need experts in the law. However today, legal staffs well trained in the public personnel field are common. Personnel offices need people to represent them in all aspects of employee relations. They also have to keep abreast of changing laws and policies. Human resource professionals also realize that the best protection against litigation is to educate managers and supervisors throughout the organization on how to avoid awkward and damaging situations that could lead to legal problems. Also thorough reference and background checks can prevent potential hiring of ill-considered applicants who perform poorly and then sue the department when they are fired (Woska, 2007). Managers and supervisors need regular training in constantly changing laws, regulations, and judicial interpretations of policy that affect personnel management and to take steps to ensure that violations of these complex policies do not occur.

Violence in the Workplace

The Occupational Safety and Health Administration (OSHA) agency defines workplace violence as "any act or threat of physical violence, harassment, intimidation, or other threatening disruptive behavior that occurs at the work site. It ranges from threats and verbal abuse to physical assaults and even homicide (OSHA's website)."[1] Workplace violence now claims more than two million victims and costs employers in the United States several billion dollars in lost productivity (OSHA's website). A report by the National Crime Victimization Survey indicated that in 2009, over 500,000 nonfatal violent crimes (rape/sexual assault, robbery, and aggravated and simple assault) occurred in the workplace involving employees 16 or older (Harrell, 2011). Reports of homicides in the workplace have become common on the evening news.

The causes of such violence are many, including the stressful economic situation in which people find themselves, domestic problems, drug abuse, and other personal problems. With the proliferation of technology and social media, cyberbullying and stalking have emerged as newer threats in the workplace. Battling these threats requires adaptability and responsiveness from the personnel department. For employers and personnel systems, a number of actions and steps need to be taken to address workplace violence. Employers can develop programs and policies to help avoid violent acts by employees, former employees, spouses of employees, and clientele. (Bowman & Zigmond, 1997; Romano et al., 2011). Personnel decisions such as termination often provide the immediate spark for violent action. OSHA classifies workplace violence into the following four categories:

Type 1— Criminal Intent: Violent acts by people who enter the workplace to commit a robbery or other crime or current or former employees who enter the workplace with the intent to commit a crime.

Type 2 — Customer/Client/Patients: Violence directed at employees by customers, clients, patients, students, inmates or any others to whom the employer provides a service.

Type 3 — Co-worker: Violence against co-workers, supervisors, or managers by a current or former employee, supervisor, or manager.

Type 4 — Personal: Violence in the workplace by someone who does not work there, but who is known to, or has a personal relationship with, an employee (OSHA, 2011).

1 OSHA Website: http://www.osha.gov/SLTC/workplaceviolence/

Employers need to be able to assess the social climate in their organization to determine if any employees are potentially violent and what steps could be taken to prevent violence. Employers should educate employees, supervisors, and managers to understand the signs of potential violent behavior and ways to deal with people who are exhibiting signs of uncontrolled anger or emotional instability. Policies addressing violence are needed in all aspects of the workplace, including ways of dealing with the aftermath of violence.

Violence in the workplace has caused many employers to conduct more thorough background checks, but former employers often are reluctant to disclose information pertinent to assessing a former employee's potential for violence (Kondrasuk, Moore, & Wang, 2001), out of fear of lawsuits. The irony is that they can be sued for negligence if they fail to disclose pertinent information and the individual commits violence at a new place of employment. Because of these concerns, most states now have reference immunity laws that protect them from providing information as long as the information is complete and accurate and is without malice. Courts have adopted the same principles. Once employed, individuals need to be observed during the probationary period for any signs of trouble. Social workers and health care professionals are most vulnerable to workplace violence. LGBT employees in particular have faced the threat of violence and harassment (Colvin, 2007). Having policies that foster an inclusive and supportive environment for LGBT employees, as well as other groups who have faced discrimination is becoming increasingly important as the workforce diversifies.

The Employee Assistance Plan (EAP) mentioned earlier is important in dealing with troubled employees. Having access to counseling and other services of the EAP allows an employee to release built-up tension and anger. It also can refer employees to other resources to help resolve whatever other problems they have. The EAP also typically provides training for supervisors to help them identify and deal with stressed and potentially irrational and dangerous employees. When violence occurs in the workplace, counseling for employees is also an important EAP service. Workplace violence, especially those that result in fatality leave employees in need of help in grieving and healing from the trauma. The EAP or other counseling intervention is important in helping employees cope with traumatic events.

Of course, providing a secure and safe work environment in the first place is of paramount concern to employers. Without becoming fortresses, organizations cannot completely prevent incidents of violence, but precautions can be taken, especially by offices that deal with disgruntled employees. Employers need a plan to deal with unforeseen violent situations. Managers and supervisors need to be able to recognize the warning signs of violent behavior among troubled employees, such as "depression, threats, menacing or erratic behavior, aggressive outbursts, references to weaponry, verbal abuse, inability to handle criticism, hypersensitivity to perceived slights, and offensive commentary or jokes referring to violence" (Romano et al., 2011, p. 3). Thus, crisis management and intervention plans are part of the human resources management agenda of the 2000s.

Changing Workplace Demographics

As noted throughout this book, the demographic composition of the workforce is changing. Consequently, the workplace environment is also changing. The challenge of managing diverse organizations has already been addressed. However, other challenges remain. Because of revenue limitations and efforts to avoid future costs, many public employers use part-time and temporary employees and volunteers. These categories of employees with nonstandard work arrangements (NSWAs) present their own challenges (Mastracci & Thompson, 2005). Employers are understandably reluctant to invest the time and resources to train temporary and part-time employees. However, it is difficult to imagine how such employees can be as productive and dependable as the full-time and fully-trained employees they are replacing.

Equity and fairness for part-time and temporary employees are also issues. Frequently, these employees cannot participate in benefits programs or are ineligible for pay increases. Some employers use temps or part-timers precisely to avoid paying for benefits. The practice raises concerns about social equity. Temps and part-timers can also feel less connection and commitment to the organization, especially if their employment is short-term, which raises issues of motivation and compliance with organization policy and norms. Unmotivated workers lead to low morale and low productivity.

As highlighted in Chapter 9, personnel administrators will have to deal with the impending retirement of baby boomers and the influx of a large number of millennial generation people entering the workplace. Succession planning for preparing future leaders will continue to play an integral role in workforce planning. Also, with the wars in Iraq and Afghanistan coming to a close, integrating veterans into the workforce will be a challenge. In 2010, only 48% of male and 57.2% of female veterans were employed (Department of Labor, 2011). Meeting the employment and training needs of veterans will be paramount.

Continuous Reform

Because government reform is on the agenda of virtually all politicians, public personnel management systems are under constant scrutiny. Each president has a unique strategy for changing the public bureaucracy. President George W. Bush's "Strategic Management of Human Capital" agenda focused on the strategic alignment of organizational goals, talent management, leadership and knowledge management that includes succession planning, creating a results-oriented culture and improving accountability. The human capital initiative of the Bush administration focused on recruiting high-quality employees and developing strategies for motivation and performance. Another agenda under George W. Bush was privatization of government activities.

These changes are consistent with continuing efforts at the state and local levels for the reform of personnel systems. There is a strong effort to eliminate civil service protections, as has been done in Georgia and Florida. In 2006, 28 states had employment-at-will arrangements (Condrey & Battaglio, 2007). A spirited debate about returning to a spoils system in the public sector also is taking place. Although no one suggests going back to the prereform spoils system of government administration as was practiced in the nineteenth century, many argue that managers should have greater control over personnel decisions and that incompetent employees should not be protected by personnel department rules and regulations (Condrey & Maranto, 2001; Hays, 2004).

Although a few of Bush's management agendas continued under Obama, these presidents generally took different approaches to improve performance. For example, Obama replaced the Bush administration's Program Assessment Rating Tool (PART), which rated federal agencies on a 0–100 scale to evidence-based performance. The focus shifted from rating agencies as successful or unsuccessful to requiring agency heads to define goals and explain performance trends. Another goal under Obama's management agenda was to transform the federal workforce and make it attractive to future generations of workers by focusing on work–life balance issues and performance-based pay, as discussed in Chapter 5.

Summary

As noted at the beginning of this book, broader changes in the social and political environment lead to pressure for changes in what personnel administration does and how it does it. The same changes that affect the rest of society will be important to managers of public personnel. The increasing diversity of the American demographic landscape is already changing the composition of the public workforce. Public personnel management will continue to be a product of the political environment in which it operates, and that environment is ever changing.

Selected Websites

Bureau of Justice Statistics. Mission is to collect, analyze, publish, and disseminate information on crime, criminal offenders, victims of crime, and the operation of justice systems at all levels of government.

bjs.ojp.usdoj.gov/index.cfm

Center for Digital Government: National research and advisory institute on information technology policies and best practices in state and local government.

www.centerdigitalgov.com/

Center for State and Local Government Excellence. A non-partisan, non-profit organization, does research to shed light on issues of retirement and benefits and to put them into perspective for policy leaders and the public.

slge.org/

E-governance Institute. Institute within Rutgers University's National Center for Public Productivity; collects and shares information to enhance understanding and use of the Internet and information technologies and their relationship to the performance of government.

spaa.newark.rutgers.edu/home/ncpp/institutes/e-governance-institute.html

Futures Without Violence. Nonprofit institution that works to prevent domestic violence. Publishes data and sponsors educational efforts. Includes material on the relationship between domestic and workplace violence.

www.futureswithoutviolence.org/

International Public Management Association for Human Resources (IPMA-HR). Membership organization that disseminates information and holds conferences on all aspects of human resources including trends and innovations.

www.ipma-hr.org/

National Association of State Personnel Executives (NASPE). Organization of state personnel directors that publishes a newsletter and reports on innovations in state personnel practices.

www.naspe.net

National Center for Injury Prevention and Control. Agency that provides research and assistance on workplace injuries and how to prevent them.

http://www.cdc.gov/injury/index.html

U.S. Department of Labor, Occupational Safety and Health Administration (OSHA). Agency with responsibility to ensure safety in the workplace, including workplace violence. Collects and publishes information on the issue,

www.osha.gov

The Government Innovators Network. A marketplace of ideas and examples of government innovation for policy makers, policy advisors, and practitioners at the John F. Kennedy School of Government at Harvard University. Also known as the ASH Center,

www.innovations.harvard.edu/

References

Battaglio, R. P., Jr., & Condrey, S. E. (2006). Civil service reform: Examining state and local cases. *Review of Public Personnel Administration, 26*(2), 118–138.

Battaglio, R. P., Jr., & Ledvinka, C. B. (2009). Privatizing human resources in the public sector legal challenges to outsourcing the human resource function. *Review of Public Personnel Administration, 29*(3), 293–307.

Bowman, J. S., & Zigmond, C. J. (1997). State government response to violence. *Public Personnel Management, 26*(2), 289–300.

Bradbury, M. (2007). The legal and managerial challenge of obesity as a disability: Evidence from the federal courts. *Review of Public Personnel Administration, 27*(1), 79–90.

Brudney, J. L., Fernandez, S., Ryu, J. E., & Wright, D. S. (2005). Exploring and explaining contracting out: Patterns among the American states. *Journal of Public Administration Research and Theory, 15*(3), 393–419.

Cayer, N. J., Baker, D. L., & Weschler, L. F. (2010). *Public administration: Social change and adaptive management* (3rd ed.). San Diego: Birkdale Publishers.

Chen, Y-S., Chong, P.P., & Zhang, B. (2004). Cyber security management and e-government. *Electronic Government: An International Journal, 1*(3), 316–327.

Coggburn, J. D. (2007). Outsourcing human resources: The case of Texas health and human services commission. *Review of Public Personnel Administration, 27*(4), 315–335.

Colvin, R. A. (2007). The rise of transgender-inclusive laws how well are municipalities implementing supportive nondiscrimination public employment policies? *Review of Public Personnel Administration, 27*(4), 336–360.

Condrey, S. E., & Battaglio, R. P. (2007). A return to spoils? Revisiting radical civil service reform in the United States. *Public Administration Review, 67*(3), 425–436.

Condrey, S. E., & Maranto, R. (Eds.). (2001). *Radical reform of the civil service.* New York: Lexington Books.

Department of Labor (2011). *The veteran labor force in the recovery.* Retrieved from http://www.dol.gov/_sec/media/reports/VeteransLaborForce/VeteransLaborForce.pdf

Dohm, A., & Shniper, L. (2007). Employment outlook: 2006-16. Occupational employment projections to 2016. *Monthly Labor Review, 130*(11), 86–125.

Downing, K. (2006). Next generation: What leaders need to know about the millennials. *Leadership in Action. 26,* 3–6.

Fernandez, S., & Smith, C. R. (2006). Looking for evidence of public employee opposition to privatization an empirical study with implications for practice. *Review of Public Personnel Administration, 26*(4), 356–381.

Getha-Taylor, H. (2010). Human relations 2.0. *Public Administration Review, 70*(s1), s170–s172.

Harrell, E. (2011). *Workplace violence, 1993-2009: National crime victimization survey and the census of fatal occupational injuries.* Report by U.S. Department of Justice, Bureau of Justice Statistics.

Hays, S. W. (2004). Trends and best practices in state and local human resource management lessons to be learned? *Review of Public Personnel Administration, 24*(3), 256–275.

Jaegal, D., & Cayer, N. J. (1991). Public personnel administration by lawsuit: The impact of Supreme Court decisions on public employee litigiousness. *Public Administration Review, 51*(3), 211–221.

Kellough, J. E., & Nigro, L. G. (Eds.). (2006). Civil service reform in the states: Personnel policy and politics at the subnational level. Albany, NY: SUNY Press.

Kettl, D. F. (2000). *The global management revolution: A report on the transformation of governance.* Washington, DC: Brookings Institution.

Kondrasuk, J. N., Moore, H. L., & Wang, H. (2001). Negligent hiring: The emerging contributor to workplace violence in the public sector. *Public Personnel Management, 30*(2), 185–196.

Llorens, J. L. (2011). A model of public sector e-recruitment adoption in a time of hyper technological change. *Review of Public Personnel Administration, 31*(4), 410–423.

Llorens, J. L., & Battaglio, R. P., Jr (2010). Human resources management in a changing world: Reassessing public human resources management education. *Review of Public Personnel Administration, 30*(1), 112–132.

Mastracci, S. H., & Thompson, J. R. (2005). Nonstandard work arrangements in the public sector trends and issues. *Review of Public Personnel Administration, 25*(4), 299–324.

Mir, A., Mir, R., & Mosca, J. B. (2002). The new age employee: An exploration of changing employee-organization relations. *Public Personnel Management, 31,* 187–200.

Ng., E. S., Schweitzer, W. L., & Lyons, S. T. (2010). New generation, great expectations: A field study of the millennial generation, *Journal of Business Psychology, 25,* 281–292.

O'Bannon, G. (2001, July 18–20). Managing our future. *IPMA News.*

OSHA (2011). *Enforcement Procedures for investigating or inspecting workplace violence incidents.* Report Retrieved: http://www.osha.gov/OshDoc/Directive_pdf/CPL_02-01-052.pdf

Romano, S. J., Levi-Minzi, M. E., Eugene, A., & Bulzomi, M. J. (2011). Workplace violence prevention. *FBI Law Enforcement Bulletin, 80*(1), 1–31.

Schramm, J. (2006). *SHRM workplace forecast.* Society of Human Resource Management Report.

Shafritz, J. M., Russell, E. W., & Borick, C. P. (2007). *Introducing public administration* (5th ed.). New York: Pearson Longman.

Siegel, G. (2000). Outsourcing personnel functions. *Public Personnel Management, 29*(2), 225–236.

Tang, T. L. P., Cunningham, P. H., Frauman, E., Ivy, M., & Perry, T. L. (2012). Attitudes and occupational commitment among public personnel: Differences between Baby Boomers and Gen-Xers. *Public Personnel Management, 41*(2): 327–360.

Twenge, J. M., Campbell, S. M., Hoffman, B. R., & Lance, C. E. (2010). Generational differences in work values: Leisure and extrinsic values increasing, social and intrinsic values decreasing. *Journal of Management, 36*(5), 1117–1124.

West, J. P., & Berman, E. M. (2001). From traditional to virtual HR. *Review of Public Personnel Administration, 21*(1), 38–64.

Woska, W. J. (2007). Legal issues for HR professionals: reference checking/background investigations. *Public Personnel Management, 36*(1), 79–89.

Zeemering, E. S. (2008). Governing interlocal cooperation: City council interests and the implications for public management. *Public Administration Review, 68*(4), 731–741.

Appendix

The following list includes journals that publish materials on public personnel administration on a regular basis. Because other journals also publish on the topic, readers should not regard this list as exhaustive.

Administration and Society

Administrative Science Quarterly

Advances in Developing Human Resources

The American Review of Public Administration

Compensation and Benefits Review

Disability and Society

Disability, Handicap and Society

Disability Studies Quarterly

Disability Compliance Bulletin

Employee Assistance Quarterly

Employee Benefit Plan Review

Employee Benefits Journal

Employee Relations Law Journal

Governing

Government Executive

Government Union Review

Harvard Business Review

Human Relations

Human Resources Abstracts

Human Resources Development Review

Human Resources Management Review

Industrial Relations

Industrial and Labor Relations Review

IPMA News

Journal of ASTD

Journal of Collective Negotiations in the Public Sector

Journal of Human Resources

Journal of Labor Research

Journal of Public Administration Research and Theory

Labor Law Journal

Management

Mental and Physical Law Reporter

Monthly Labor Review

National Disability Law Reporter

Personnel

Personnel Psychology

Public Administration Quarterly

Public Administration Review

Public Integrity

Public Management

The Public Manager

Public Personnel Management

Public Productivity and Management Review

Review of Public Personnel Administration

State and Local Government Review

Work and Occupations

Index